Rural Tour' op

PEFC™
PEFC/16-33-111
CATG-PEFC-052
www.pefc.org

D0418519

LC048271

TOURISM AND CULTURAL CHANGE
Series Editors: Professor Mike Robinson, *Centre for Tourism and Cultural Change,*
Leeds Metropolitan University, Leeds, UK and Dr Alison Phipps, *University of Glasgow,*
Scotland, UK

Understanding tourism's relationships with culture(s) and vice versa, is of ever-
increasing significance in a globalising world. This series will critically examine the
dynamic inter-relationships between tourism and culture(s). Theoretical explorations,
research-informed analyses, and detailed historical reviews from a variety of
disciplinary perspectives are invited to consider such relationships.

**Full details of all the books in this series and of all our other publications can be
found on http://www.channelviewpublications.com, or by writing to Channel View
Publications, St Nicholas House, 31–34 High Street, Bristol BS1 2AW, UK.**

TOURISM AND CULTURAL CHANGE
Series Editors: Professor Mike Robinson, *Centre for Tourism and Cultural Change, Leeds Metropolitan University, Leeds, UK* and Dr Alison Phipps, *University of Glasgow, Scotland, UK*

Rural Tourism Development
Localism and Cultural Change

E. Wanda George, Heather Mair and Donald G. Reid

CHANNEL VIEW PUBLICATIONS
Bristol • Buffalo • Toronto

Library of Congress Cataloging in Publication Data
A catalog record for this book is available from the Library of Congress.
George, E. Wanda
Rural Tourism Development: Localism and Cultural Change/E. Wanda George,
Heather Mair, and Donald G. Reid.
Tourism and Cultural Change: 17
Includes bibliographical references and index.
1. Tourism–Social aspects–Canada–Case studies. 2. Tourism–Economic aspects–Canada–Case studies.3. Rural development–Canada–Case studies. 4. Sustainable development–Canada–Case studies.
I. Mair, Heather. II. Reid, Donald G. III. Title. IV. Series.
G155.C2G46 2009
306.4'8190971–dc22 2009001599

British Library Cataloguing in Publication Data
A catalogue entry for this book is available from the British Library.

ISBN-13: 978-1-84541-100-8 (hbk)
ISBN-13: 978-1-84541-099-5 (pbk)

Channel View Publications
UK: St Nicholas House, 31-34 High Street, Bristol BS1 2AW, UK.
USA: UTP, 2250 Military Road, Tonawanda, NY 14150, USA.
Canada: UTP, 5201 Dufferin Street, North York, Ontario M3H 5T8, Canada.

The policy of Multilingual Matters/Channel View Publications is to use papers that are natural, renewable and recyclable products, made from wood grown in sustainable forests. In the manufacturing process of our books, and to further support our policy, preference is given to printers that have FSC and PEFC Chain of Custody certification. The FSC and/or PEFC logos will appear on those books where full certification has been granted to the printer concerned.

Typeset by Datapage International Ltd.
Printed and bound in Great Britain by MPG Books Ltd.

Contents

List of Figures and Tables

Figures

Tables

Chapter 1

Introduction to Rural Tourism Development

Introduction

Rural tourism represents a merging of perhaps two of the most influential yet contradictory features of modern life. Not only are the forces of economic, social, cultural, environmental and political change working to redefine rural spaces the world over, but broad global transformations in consumption and transportation patterns are reshaping leisure behavior and travel. For those concerned with both the nature of change in rural areas and tourism development, the dynamics and impacts of integrating these two dramatic shifts are not well known but are becoming increasingly provocative discourses for study.

While many students of tourism have assessed its qualities and developments, both positive and negative, at the local and global level (see for instance, Smith, 1989; Inskeep, 1991; Haywood, 1993; Hunter & Green, 1995; Hunter, 1997; Murphy, 1998; Mowford & Munt, 1998; Hall & Jenkins, 1998; Fuller & Reid, 1998; Var & Ap, 1998; Robinson, 1999; Yu & Chung, 2001; Barthel-Bouchier, 2001; McIntosh *et al.*, 2002; Urry, 1990, 1995) and many students of rural change have done the same (see for instance, Mormont, 1987; Halfacree, 1993; Bryden, 1994; Shucksmith, 1991; Ray, 2001) the purpose of this book is to bring these two discourses together. We aim to link changes at the local, rural community level to broader, more structural considerations of globalization in order to allow for a deeper, more theoretically sophisticated consideration of the various forces and features of rural tourism development.

While several authors (Murphy, 1985; Gunn, 1985; Blank, 1989; Pearce *et al.*, 1996; Reid *et al.*, 2001) highlight the importance of community involvement in planning tourism and rural community development, our collective experience as instructors, practitioners, students and authors of tourism and rural community development, tells us that there has been both a lack of grounded research in this area as well as any larger overarching theoretical interpretations. Those concerned with community development, rural restructuring and economic growth, in

1

addition to the implications of tourism, are in need of new and relevant resource materials to address the demands of currently changing times. With this book, we aspire to contribute to these investigations in a different way. While most works generally highlight *tourism* as the subject of development, often positioning the community as merely its vehicle, we reverse this stance and make the *local community* the subject, thereby situating tourism as just one in a collection of potential options for rural development and sustainability.

The Role of Social Theory: The Benefits of a Political Economy Approach

Perhaps one of the primary contributions of the book is our deliberate effort to cast each of the case studies within an overarching social theory framework. While authors such as Britton (1991) light the way for critical theoretical investigations of tourism developments by linking them to larger social, political and economic structural changes, a book of case studies can help lend some grounded understandings to what is often high level and seemingly unrelated theory. In the same way, many collections of case studies of tourism development, in both rural and urban areas, while providing unique insights about the particularities of tourism development, do not advance enough in what must be on-going efforts to build theoretical and conceptual tools to make sense of these developments at a broader level.

Political economy perspectives seek to highlight the inter-relationships between politics and economics. Simply put, in this view, the actions of the economy are not a predestined outcome of the workings of the market's 'invisible hand', but are the product of politics and power relationships and social struggle. Thus, a project that investigates tourism development from a political economy perspective throws into light (and question) the political underpinnings of its predominantly economic rationalizations. The economic imperative of tourism development, then, becomes problematized. Clement and Vosko (2003: xv) make the case for the Canadian political economy more generally:

> We wish to critique economic essentialism in two ways: by arguing that the "economic" itself is a social, political, cultural and ideological construct … and by arguing that there is no "essentialism", or sameness in the economy, because time and space are ever-present variables for political economy.

Thus, the particular ways in which tourism is developed in rural areas cannot be simplified, as areas change over time and across space. A political economy approach creates room for such a nuanced under-standing because it challenges underlying assumptions. Moreover, it also allows room to consider other theoretical explanations for why tourism developments are being created in rural areas. As rural communities struggle with the growing gap between resources and responsibilities (i.e. economic and political restructuring), tourism becomes increasingly popular and appealing as a mechanism for stimulating rural growth in troubled times. As the case studies in this text make clear, although the broader, more structural power relationships shaping the attractiveness of tourism in rural areas are similar, the ways in which these changes manifest themselves are unique to each place.

While the case studies collected here are all Canadian, much can be taken from the lessons learned in this book and extended internationally. There are few places where the effects of the neoliberal forces of economic and political restructuring are not being felt and the diversity of cases presented here can be used to capture and appreciate some of this diversity. That is not to say that every case in the world is like a Canadian case, but those selected here are diverse enough to offer useful fodder for building a conceptual framework to help explain and understand these developments in other places. The Canadian political economy, with its relatively poor and rich areas, its conundrum of rural development and its trajectory of political economic restructuring since the 1970s, contains a number of distinct cases, each teeming with opportunity for learning about the particularities and generalities of tourism development in rural areas anywhere.

Thus, cases used in this book were carefully chosen and can be grouped in the following way. First, two cases from the Eastern Atlantic region of Canada illustrate attempts at rural tourism development along Canada's periphery, and reveal the particular ways that tourism has been crafted as a mechanism to stimulate development in coastal, fishing-dominated and relatively less developed areas. Second, a case from Southern Ontario, Canada's heartland and economic core, shows how tourism can be used as part of a strategy addressing the downturn in long-standing manufacturing opportunities. Third, a case from the Western region of Canada exemplifies a novel approach that one rural Alberta community has undertaken towards developing its tourism potential. Put together, these cases demonstrate the different ways that tourism is positioned as a local response to political and economic shifts in a nation that is itself undergoing rapid change, both continentally and globally. Before outlining the structure of the book, it is first useful to highlight some of the more prominent themes underscoring our approach.

Dominant Themes Underpinning this Text

Four dominant themes underlie the development of contemporary tourism in rural areas and these permeate throughout this text. These themes include: (1) tourism in a globalizing world; (2) cultural change and processes of rural community commodification; (3) the importance of resistance and (4) the rural appeal. These four themes provide the underpinning for this book.

Tourism in a globalizing world

Thomas Friedman (2000) interprets globalization as an internationalizing system, a process that is working worldwide. Globalization is interpreted as both a system and a process – a system of interlinking and dynamic components where any change in one affects the whole system, and a process of global activity and interaction that takes place within the system.

The difference between earlier forms of globalization and today's system lies in the degree and intensity with which the world is being tied together into a single global marketplace and the number of people and countries that comprise this system (Friedman, 2000). While earlier eras of globalization were built around transportation and access to cheap resources, today it is constructed on technology – new innovations in science, medicine, mechanical devices, but most particularly, new information technologies. Modern globalization, according to Rees (2000), is a social construct, featuring particular characteristics: the international integration of economic entities, the rising prominence of trans-national corporations, the transportation of resources and manufactured goods all over the world and instantaneous opportunistic movement of finance capital across national boundaries.[1] As a dominant mechanism in globalizing the world, tourism needs to be understood as both a 'cause and effect' variable, affecting all life in modern society. The growth and invasion of tourism to newer regions, particularly lesser developed areas, carries with it major consequences and impacts, both positive and negative (Ayad, 1999; Jafari, 1996; Patin, 1999; Schackley, 1999; Robinson, 1999; Russo, 1999; UNESCO, 1996). Tourism, with its complex inward and outward functions and structure, is a socioculturally embedded phenomenon with diverse dimensions and untold influences of which economics is only one (Jafari, 1996). However, the economic forces of this mega-industry and the study of its potential have been instrumental in bringing tourism to the national and international forefront, as an attractive economic opportunity for many (Jafari, 1996).

The tourism phenomenon is an extraordinary occurrence, which developed historically from an activity of the privileged few to a mass cultural lifestyle and became accepted as a basic need of the modern world (Hudman & Hawkins, 1989). Mobility represents the crux of tourism activity. Parrinello (2001) argues that without the tourist's mobile experience, there would be no tourism. Tourism, as we know it today, can be considered globalization of mobility.

'Tourism is about selling dreams' (Schouten, 1996: 53) and related to an 'eternal search for the meaning of life'. It is about experiencing beyond the ordinary (Schouten, 1996); it is as if there is a search for the 'roots of our existence'. Ironically, as we see global expansion and increased mobility, these 'dreams' and 'searches' for experience and meaning are increasingly being sought by tourists in rural countryside where they can *experience* the perceived idyllic settings, but often, in doing so, cause disruption to local life and communities.

In their quest for experiencing beyond the ordinary, contemporary tourists are demanding new niche types of tourism, specific to their interests, needs and quirks. As a consequence of globalization, the tourism offerings that cannot be obtained in one country can be realized in another. Contemporary tourism products (experiences) have emerged that transcend notions of reality. In a globalizing world, we are seeing cultures encounter, confront, clash, challenge and mesh with each other. Tourism in a globalizing world means not only new demands but also new opportunities – new destinations to travel to, new cultures to explore, and new tourism products and experiences to consume, along with a whole new set of dynamics surrounding the phenomenon as it unfolds. As rural areas confront globalization, many are turning to tourism as one local response in hopes of sustaining their economies. This theme permeates throughout the cases presented here.

Cultural change and the processes of rural community commodification

Culture, and its many dimensions, is a deeply embedded aspect of tourism. Culture manifests in continually evolving societies; hence, cultural change is not a new and novel concept. It has indeed been the foundation to advanced civilizations throughout history. Currently, however, among a myriad of impacts resulting from globalization and advanced technologies, we can see an acceleration of cultural change in societies around the world. What might also be considered a new impact today is the intense commodification of culture for tourism that occurs through processes by which cultural dimensions and aspects, originally conceived as social constructs in community evolution and way of life, are transformed into commodities for exchange with consuming tourists. Paralleling the momentum of globalization, a concept discussed earlier, there appears to be increased interest in the rural domain and smaller local communities; this interest has generated a new and growing niche market of tourists who are attracted by the unique features of rural ways of life. From previous research, which will be illustrated later in this text, evidence suggests that when a local rural community's culture becomes its dominant tourism product, various dynamics are set in motion which not only initiate major changes to the community's structure and economy, but also to its cultural fabric – the essence of its being. In such instances, one can argue a metamorphosis of local culture takes place, that is, a community's culture loses its original context and evolves into something totally different through a process, metaphorically speaking, of 'cannibalization' or 'consumption of self'. Another factor, which, arguably, can be attributed directly to globalization, tourism and cultural change, is gentrification, a concept that has historically been applied to urban slum areas, but which now appears to be manifesting in many rural communities. Such profound changes raise questions and concerns about the ability to achieve any notion of rural community sustainability.

The importance of resistance

It should be noted that our efforts to present the material in such a way as to shed light on the larger, structural political economic forces shaping tourism in each case, are not meant to crowd out the fact that in each case, this process has not been completely one-sided. Indeed, as the case presentations will make clear, each of these communities has struggled to make tourism its own. Each has had its own particular set of forces, and stakeholders, driving its tourism development. For example, if not resisting tourism outright, some communities have attempted to create a community-based process for controlling the nature and kind of tourism it pursues. As we, as professionals and researchers, have often been involved in fostering these attempts, our perspectives may be especially valuable here.

The rural appeal

While not a primary theme of this book, attention must also be given to the demand side of rural tourism development. Indeed, the intensification of travel to rural areas, in Canada and elsewhere, is the product of a number of important changes, including the growth of disposable income and leisure time, changes to transportation networks and technologies, as well as such forces as 'nostalgia' and 'escapism' that engender a powerful attraction to rural experiences, especially for urban dwellers. As populations converge upon urban and metropolitan zones, as is the case in Canada (Statistics Canada, 2002), and join globalizing systems where work styles are fast paced, highly mechanized and technological, and lifestyles are generally more individualistically absent of cultural attachments, many experience fragmented or lost identities. Some authors suggest this leads to increased desires for 'escapism' and 'search for meaning' in one's life; people seek experiences to satisfy these desires (Urry, 1995; Schouten, 1996). Many seek the rural experience to reconnect with a past, perceived simpler life or their 'roots'. Nostalgia is a strong motive for tourists choosing destinations. In one Canadian province, the government has capitalized on the lure of nostalgia by introducing its own 'Come Back Home' campaign targeted at those who earlier relocated to urban and metropolitan regions of the country. Dann (1994) expressed four types of nostalgia: longing for paradise; the simple life; past times; and the return to childhood. Schouten (1996), however, argues that these types of nostalgia all mean basically the same thing: an escape from the stress or tedium of ordinary daily life. Thus, we suggest that intensified travel to rural areas may be a form of 'escapism' from globalization.

Defining Rural and the Rural Landscape

The rural landscape and local rural communities, with their distinct ways of life and culture, are increasingly the targets for new tourism destinations and markets. Is there a difference between a rural landscape and other communities? Traditionally, rural areas have always been associated with agriculture, and one may argue, primary resource industries generally, including fishing. Even with a steady decline in agriculture (Statistics Canada, 2002) rural areas comprise the bulk of land space in the world. Rural areas are difficult to define and the criteria used by various nations differ greatly (Organization for Economic Cooperation and Development (OECD), 1994).

Like the term *community,* the term *rural* has been a major challenge to theorists and scholars who continue to search for its meaning (Bryden, 1994; Halfacree, 1994; Mormont, 1987). In Bryden (1994), Shucksmith discusses notions of rural. He talks about various theorists' attempts to define rural, using different and contestable approaches: descriptive; spatial determinism; locality; primary production domination; social representation; and others (Shucksmith, 1994). Generally, however, we understand notions of *rural* as a polar opposite to notions of *urban,* for example rural community versus urban community, and recognize that, with the advances of globalization and technology, they are both in a complex process of change.

In its 1994 document, the OECD purported that *rurality,* in the wider debate, focuses on three dominant discussion points: population density and size of settlements; land use and its dominance by agriculture and forestry; and traditional social structures and issues of community identity and heritage. OECD (1994) assessed varying definitions used by different countries, including Canada; it concluded that rural settlements may vary in size, but they are small and always with a population of fewer than 10,000 inhabitants (OECD, 1994). Using this definition, the Canadian case sites that will be discussed in this text – Canso, Lunenburg, Port Stanley and Vulcan – can all be defined as rural communities. According to the OECD (1994), characteristics of rural society were difficult to determine because of variations between countries and continents. Moreover, Flinn (1982, in OECD Document, 1994: 11) notes three very different types of traditional lifestyles within rural United States:

- Small town society, close-knit, strongly believing in democracy but often not in close contact with nature.
- Agrarian society, based on family farming, farm life and the calendar of the season.
- Ruralists, living outside towns but not farming; independents who value open space, nature and 'a natural order'.

In similar efforts to explain rural, other commentators have introduced the concept of a rural-urban continuum as a way of coping with the complexity of the situation, and the problems of comparing areas, which are perceived to be rural, but possess many different character-istics (OECD, 1994) (see Table 1.1). With industrialization and rapid urbanization, new social structures were produced that were different from the traditional societies of the rural areas. Using the concept of a continuum, rural communities at a local level can be assessed on a

Table 1.1 Rural versus urban typology

Rural	*Urban*
Community	Association
Social fields involving few but multiple role relationships	Social fields involving many overlapping role relationships
Different social roles played by same person	Different social roles played by different people
Simple economies	Diverse economies
Little division of labor	Great specialization in labor force
Ascribed status	Achieved status
Education according to status	Status derived from education
Role embracement	Role commitment
Close-knit networks	Loose-knit networks
Locals	Cosmopolitans
Economic class in one of several divisions	Economic class in the major division
Conjunction	Segregation
Integration with work environment	Separation of work environment

Source: Frankenberg, 1966, in OECD (1994: 11).

sliding scale from extremely remote to highly urban or somewhere in between, depending on a community's situation. An example may be the several small towns in rural areas often referred to as urban design areas but which fall within the rural regional framework, for example, towns in Atlantic Canada (Truro, Lunenburg, Wolfville – communities in Nova Scotia).

Generally, the notion of *rural* is constructed, perceptually at least, as a contrast to the *urban*. Arguably, tourists and others perceive that rural communities, with their peculiar social structures and culture, are in contrast to those of urban communities, and moreover, as having been resistant to the throes of modernization and globalization. However false these assumptions may or may not be, in tourism development, this perception is a key factor. 'The retention of older ways of life and thinking is important in retaining rural character. It is this residual character which, combined with the scenic values and recreation opportunities of the countryside, that attracts tourists from urban areas' (OECD, 1994: 11).

Various commonly accepted definitions of rural are used depending on how they relate to a particular political situation or need. However, the rural dimension is, by and large, understood as the opposite to that of urban as suggested above. Similarly, there are commonly accepted perceptions of differences between rural and urban communities. Generally, though, 'community' is understood as connected with notions of: membership; shared spaces of place and identity; shared interests, customs and modes of thought or expressions; collectivism, human association and social networks.

Tourism Development in Rural Areas

The concept of rural tourism, and local culture, was the subject of the 1994 document, *Tourism Strategies and Rural Development* (OECD, 2001). The document's aim was to examine and present the case for rural tourism as a potential strategy to pull rural regions out of decline. With increasing shifts in tourism demands from conventional tourism destinations – resorts, beaches and large cultural centers – to rural areas, it became necessary to examine the concept more closely and its potential to benefit rural regions. Rural tourism is not new, but like tourism generally, was mainly the privilege of the rich and affluent until the mid-20th century, as a way to escape the mundane and stresses of the industrialized domain. Since then, there have been larger numbers of visitors to rural countryside areas, as tourism 'has broken free of large and specialized resorts into small towns and villages to become truly rural' (OECD, 1994: 8).

Further, 'rurality is almost always seen as an important condition, possessing very valuable characteristics worthy of preservation ... while the global condition has become steadily more urban, most commentators have stressed the importance of retaining key differences between urbanization and the rural realm' (OECD, 1994: 13). This notion is important to rural regions contemplating tourism because it connotes differentiation and competitive advantage.

The OECD document (1994: 14) states rural tourism should be:

- Located in rural areas.
- Functionally rural, built upon the rural world's special features; small scale enterprise, open space, contact with nature and the natural world, heritage, traditional societies and traditional practices.

- Rural in scale – both in terms of buildings and settlements – and therefore, small scale.
- Traditional in character, growing slowly and organically, and connected with local families. It will often be very largely controlled locally and developed for the long-term good of the area.
- Sustainable – in the sense that its development should help sustain the special rural character of an area, and in the sense that its development should be sustainable in its use of resources. Rural tourism should be seen as a potential tool for conservation and sustainability, rather than as an urbanizing and development tool.
- Of many different kinds, representing the complex pattern of rural environment, economy and history.

The majority of Canada's 33 million people are concentrated in four metropolitan centers – Toronto, Montreal, Calgary and Vancouver. When we speak of tourism in most other areas of Canada, particularly in Atlantic Canada, the Prairies and other regions with sparse populations, we are generally referring to *rural tourism*. According to the above discussion, all four case sites that will be described and discussed in the following chapters, can be considered rural tourism destinations. In the evolution of rural tourism, two common myths, according to OECD (1994), have grown up about its role. The first is that rural tourism is farm-based tourism (and, undeniably, a distinct form of commodified culture). Another is that diversification into tourism will universally save the farming industry. Agri-tourism is but one aspect of rural tourism. Other rural areas, such as the cases that will be discussed later in this book, are not agriculture-based, yet have substantial or well-developed tourism. In fact, the Economic Planning Group of Canada (EPG) (2000) in a consulting report state, 'In many coastal communities [*as in the cases of Lunenburg and Canso, Nova Scotia, for example*] suffering from the decline of the fishery, tourism is providing a vital new economic activity, one that builds on the community's assets – its people, its heritage and its unique character' (p. 17), in other words, through commodification of the local culture. The Report continues, 'For many small communities and rural areas, tourism is not only important as an employer, it is one of the few sectors in rural areas that is growing and adding new jobs' (EPG, 2000: 17).

Outline of the Book

Although grounded in the case studies presented here, each of the chapters and sections builds upon our principal argument that any understanding of tourism and rural development must address the inherent power relationships. In this book, we connect prominent, relatively well-researched understandings of tourism with a more critical look into a perhaps less critically understood notion: globalization. By positioning tourism as a mechanism for globalization and then moving on to consider the inherently political processes by which this takes place in rural areas, we create the political economic scaffolding upon which the book rests.

In this book, we extend the global discussion 'down' to the local level and present a focus on tourism as a 'mechanism' for development. We consider the challenges and opportunities of rural development, not just in Canada but also more widely. Drawing on recent works about the appeal of localism in the face of what are often considered to be the homogenizing and delocalizing tendencies of globalization, we offer an analysis of where and how tourism fits in these developments and the opportunities it does and does not present for meaningful and community-controlled development.

As a core principle, *tourism as a rural response to globalization* sets the context for presenting four case studies in this book. Each case, indeed, exemplifies a distinct rural response. As noted above, these carefully selected cases are undoubtedly Canadian, but can be used to reflect upon the situation in other rural places and similar 'spaces' around the world. We make linkages between the 'on-the-ground' details of a particular case, the overarching themes noted earlier and a particular theoretical concept(s) discussed at the beginning of each case. Further, we discuss three important issues that have emerged from a cross-case analysis: (1) changes to the physicality of the rural landscape, (2) community/ citizen engagement and (3) need for planning.

The book comprises 14 chapters, the first of which provides an introduction to the text and sets the context for the book. Chapter 2 outlines the political economy of rural tourism development in Canada over the past 30 years. In Chapters 3–6, we present our four case studies. In Chapter 7, we provide a synopsis of the four cases, outlining key emergent issues and premises that arise from analysis of the case studies presented in preceding chapters. In Chapter 8, we delve into discussion about the complex role of tourism in rural tourism. In Chapter 9, we discuss tourism-related changes to the physical rural landscape, including gentrification and rebranding of the rural areas. In Chapter 10, we look at the role of tourism policy and how it shapes tourism development. In Chapter 11, we discuss the importance of community engagement and citizen involvement in tourism planning and development. In Chapter 12, we bring into focus the concept of sustainability and its application to rural communities and tourism. In Chapter 13, we take a holistic approach to discuss theoretical concepts that speak to and reflect on the cases as a whole and discuss the imperative of appropriate planning. Our experiences in crafting and implementing participatory, community-based attempts at tourism planning are highlighted, and opportunities for alternative approaches as well as future research are examined and discussed. In our concluding chapter, Chapter 14, we seek to address the outcomes of our efforts to critique the cases that are presented by identifying opportunities for new ways of posturing tourism in rural areas and suggesting new approaches for policy aimed at moving tourism and the rural agenda forward.

Methodological Approach

To compile this book, we have pulled together and drawn upon our previous works as three academic researchers who, over the past decade, have conducted tourism-related investigations in rural communities across various regions of Canada. Some of these works are the result of doctoral research projects undertaken by two of the authors between 2000 and 2004. Others are the results of efforts undertaken by the third author in an on-going research program at the University of Guelph, Ontario. Our scholarly research activities, collectively, reflect enlightening and important new insights and provocative viewpoints about tourism development in rural areas, particularly as manifested in local responses to the wide-reaching impacts of globalization. Subsequently, these insights and viewpoints have provided the fuel for this book, which takes shape, essentially, as a compilation of the collective reflections of the authors' long-standing experiences on the ground and in rural communities. These reflections are presented and illustrated here in a series of research case studies.

The case studies presented in this volume are based on research done in communities that had been carefully selected as having a 'rural' condition. Contextually, this condition is generally understood in terms of geographical and cultural dimensions as previously discussed.

Case study approach: A method, a format

As noted, this book is a composition of case studies based on the authors' researches. The case study construct comes from an interpretive paradigm, 'an inquiry process of understanding a social or human problem, based on building a complex, holistic picture, formed with words, reporting detailed views of informants, and conducted in a natural setting' (Creswell, 1994: 1–2). 'A case study is an empirical inquiry that: a) investigates a contemporary phenomenon within its real-life context; when b) the boundaries between phenomenon and context are not clearly evident; and in which c) multiple sources of evidence are used' (Yin, 1989: 23). Further, Yin contends the case study is applicable where 'the situation exists when an investigation has an opportunity to observe and analyze a phenomenon previously inaccessible to scientific investigation' (p. 48). As all our research 'cases' discussed in this text can be positioned within this methodological paradigm, we conceptualize and present them within this context. Pedagogically, the case study format provides a sound framework to present individuals' reflections about specific situations (communities). Each 'case' is a standalone and illustrative study that highlights specific theoretical concepts. The following narrative provides a short sketch of each of the four Canadian 'cases' that are illustrated in this book:

(1) The case of Canso, Nova Scotia
      Canso is a remote rural community on the North-east tip of Nova Scotia. In the early 1990s, the community boasted a population of about 1000, the majority of who were employed at the local government-subsidized fish plant or on local fishing vessels for most of their working lives. When the Atlantic fishery collapsed in the region in the early 1990s, this small community was immediately and seriously impacted by the subsequent closure and loss of its mainstay industry. Responding to the demise of Atlantic Canada's prime economic resource, which also impacted hundreds of other small rural fishing communities along the seacoast, the provincial government intervened with a flurry of activities to develop a myriad of programs and incentives aimed at promoting tourism as a possible economic alternative. During an intense period of grieving, the community, reacting out of desperation and, in spite of not having the necessary infrastructure, adequate resources or know-how, set about to develop tourism as its 'economic savior'. Motivated by a desperate need to address serious economic problems in the community, Canso, in a novel approach, deliberately contrived a tourist attraction based on a cultural icon. The event has since bolstered the local economy by drawing large numbers of visitors, both locally and internationally, to the region. Theoretical concepts that are presented in this case are: tourism

destination development, community (place) identity and cultural tourism (creative cultural industries).

(2) The case of Vulcan, Alberta

With a population of 1940 (Statistics Canada, 2006), Vulcan is located about an hour's drive south of Alberta's biggest (and booming) oil and gas city of Calgary. While the fortunes of Vulcan may not, at least currently, appear to rest with tourism development, community downturn in the mid-1980s pushed a group of community members to take the opportunities presented by tourism development very seriously indeed. This chapter presents the story of the development of *Star Trek*-related tourism in Vulcan Alberta insofar as it represents a predominantly problem-based and supply-driven response to economic downturn. Further, research in Vulcan indicates that what is left in the community is a rather contrived, if negotiated, tourism development. Theoretical concepts that are illustrated in this case are: contrived tourism and the contested meanings of place.

(3) The case of Lunenburg, Nova Scotia

Lunenburg, a rural community on the Eastern coast of Canada, about 120 km from the province's capital city, Halifax, has a population of approximately 2600. This small community has had a longstanding and prosperous fishing-based economy and was a laggard in receiving the widespread impacts associated with the collapse of the Atlantic Canada fishing industry in the early 1990s. The tentacles of globalization are considered by many to be contributing factors to the fishery collapse in the region. When the impacts finally hit this community, however, a fortuitous and timely event occurred that would catapult tourism development and new opportunities in the community. In 1995, Lunenburg was awarded UNESCO World Heritage Site designation; this quickly triggered new tourism demand to the area. The community, in response, repositioned itself as an international cultural tourism destination, a dramatic shift from its former status as fishing community. Spearheaded by the UNESCO designation and increased tourism demand, this new opportunity promised to help alleviate some of the problems that began to emerge in the community due to the collapse of the fishing industry. The new designation led to a restructuring of community and economy, which initiated a set of dynamics that would dramatically change the community forever. The theoretical concepts discussed in this chapter are: commodification of culture and gentrification.

(4)   The case of Port Stanley, Ontario
      Port Stanley is a rural community that engages tourism extensively
      in its economic diversification structure. Tourism was not new to the
      area, as this location has had a long and interesting history as a
      tourism destination. Whether by good luck or good management,
      the community, however, has also taken care to include other
      economic industries in its economic structure. Port Stanley is
      situated on the north shore of Lake Erie, approximately half way
      between Toronto, Ontario, Canada and Detroit, MI, USA. It lies
      within a populous section of South-western Ontario and has been
      subjected to changing fortunes over the years because of technolo-
      gical alterations that have affected travel patterns and the changing
      fads and fancies of travelers. Port Stanley enjoys a strategic
      geographic position on the North American continent and is blessed
      with natural amenities that have and will continue to make it a
      tourism destination area. Over time, tourism has unfolded through
      an evolutionary and dynamic process, which has been dominantly
      demand-driven. The theoretical concepts that are the focus of this
      chapter are: rejuvenation and integration.

Research methods

   Both qualitative and quantitative methods were used to collect data
for these four case studies, including: document analysis; newspaper
analysis, Internet searches; participant-observation; field observation; in-
depth and informal interviews, survey (Lunenburg case) and photo-
graphic and audio analysis. Research approach and methods, as applied
to each individual case study, are detailed in each of the four relevant
chapters.

Contribution to Research

   Although globalization, arguably, is a relatively new phenomenon
reshaping our current world, a parallel phenomenon is quickly emerging
– associated local responses of rural regions throughout the world. In
this book, we examine and discuss responses of four different rural
communities across Canada, much like other nations, that are considered
largely rural. This book is important because it illustrates the complexity
of globalization and its wide-reaching impacts on rural societies in the
struggle to respond, particularly when they adopt tourism as the answer.
By offering new understandings, new perspectives and new theories
about the local-global nexus, we assert that this text of case studies on

tourism, localism and cultural change in rural areas will make a significant contribution to existing scholarly research on this subject. This book will provide a new 'lens' with which researchers and policy-makers can view local-global interactions and dynamics, and in particular, the rural dilemma instigated by forces of globalization.

Analytical Framework

Along with the four central themes outlined earlier in this chapter that permeate our collective research and the case studies presented here, we will expand our analyses by examining each case's particular approach to tourism development. We consider what has been the motivating factor behind tourism development in each circumstance – economic problems in the community or a new economic opportunity that emerged – and what force – supply or demand – has been the main driver of development processes at each site. Within this context, we have constructed a four-quadrant analytical framework, suggesting four classifications of approaches to tourism development: (1) contrived; (2) deliberate; (3) responsive and (4) integrated/evolutionary, which will be applied to each case's situation. This four-quadrant framework, or matrix, is shown in Figure 1.1. These classifications are not intended to frame one approach as better or worse than another, but rather, to help us understand the nature of tourism development in the four case communities presented in this book.

In Figure 1.1, we show two intersecting axes. The horizontal axis refers to what has motivated tourism development (motivation factor) in a particular community. Why does it need tourism? Has tourism development been initiated to address a community problem or has it unfolded as a potential opportunity? The vertical axis relates to whether tourism development processes or approaches are predominantly driven by supply or demand forces, similar to what is often referred to in marketing theory as 'push-pull' factors. These factors relate to how the development is planned and implemented, and appear directly related to the motivation behind development, that is, whether or not motivation has been problem-based or opportunity-based. For example, if tourism development has been undertaken to address an economic problem, it is highly likely that it is supply-driven, as least initially. This will be illustrated in Chapter 6, in the case of Canso, Nova Scotia. Four quadrants are also shown in Figure 1.1 to illustrate four types or classifications of approaches to tourism development, which may have

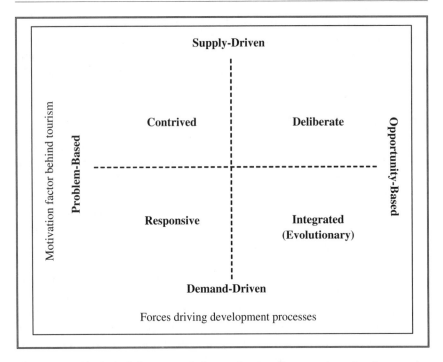

Figure 1.1 Analytical framework for understanding tourism development

been influenced by the motivation factor and/or dominant forces driving the development processes.

The two quadrants labeled 'contrived' and 'responsive', are shown on the left side of the horizontal axis, indicating two different approaches to development that have been initiated primarily to address economic problems (motivating factor) in a community, for example, collapse of a traditional industry. Our collective research shows that such approaches to tourism development often stem from economic crises in communities or in situations where sudden change has taken place that threatens the economic and social future of a community. External factors associated with globalization often cause these situations. In many instances, tourism is perceived as the 'economic savior' and quickly considered as a potential response, often initiated with neither planning nor foresight about what impacts tourism may have on a host community. Some communities may not have necessary or adequate resources that will attract and accommodate tourists. In certain cases, attractors may need to be created and constructed. In other cases, a catalyst or opportunity appears and a community responds to take advantage, as is shown in the case of Lunenburg and somewhat, in the case of Vulcan. These types of development are often undertaken, haphazardly, without serious planning, to address an immediate problem or perceived opportunity, and might be considered reactive by nature.

In other communities, however, more systematic and proactive approaches to tourism development have been implemented. Tourism is frequently viewed as an opportunity to diversify and to improve the local economy. Two different types of approaches, identified and labeled as 'deliberate' and 'integrated/evolutionary', are shown on the right-hand side of the quadrant to represent development that has been initiated primarily as a potential opportunity (motivation factor). Research shows that the impacts of these types of tourism development are less severe and intrusive in a community. Developments are deliberately and, hopefully, more carefully planned or they may be more subtle and evolutionary in nature. Also, a more spontaneous type of tourism development may occur over long periods of time without any deliberate planning and without any outstanding impacts on a community. This type of development has been integrated into the community's overall economic structure, that is, tourism is only one of several economic generators within a community's economy. This will be illustrated in the case of Port Stanley.

While certain cases may rest mostly in one quadrant, the different approaches taken to tourism development are not clear-cut and cannot easily be placed in any one specific quadrant. In some cases, it may straddle more than one type of approach. As mentioned above, the framework, as used here, is merely an analytical tool for helping us to understand why and how tourism was developed in each of the four case communities; it is not intended to argue the merits of one approach over another.

In Chapter 2, we outline and discuss the political economy of rural tourism development within Canada that has taken place over the last **30** years.

Note

1. Rees argues, however, that contrary to corporate apologists, globalization is not the inevitable product of rapid advances in electronic, communications and transportation technologies. He states that these things make contemporary globalization possible but human beings foster the process and determine the form it takes.

Chapter 2

Political Economy of Rural Tourism Development in Canada

Introduction

Questions of rural development and change, in Canada and elsewhere, are undeniably complex. Nonetheless, introducing some of the major issues affecting development in rural Canada helps to lay the groundwork for a more in-depth understanding of the social, economic, political, cultural and spatial relationships influencing the nature and kind of tourism development we see today. The purpose of this second chapter is to lay this groundwork by using a political economy framework to briefly outline the evolution of rural tourism development in Canada. First, we set out our understanding of key terms, including neoliberalism and the notion of restructuring. Then we move to look at the general trends in rural development, as they have been influenced by restructuring and neoliberalism and end that section with a particular emphasis upon the most recent period. Third, we discuss the broader aspects of rural development policy over this time period with a view to emphasizing some of the underlying assumptions about rural growth as they underscore particular policies and have influenced the turn towards tourism-led growth in rural areas. Last, we highlight briefly some of the challenges and opportunities presented by the growing attention to, and encouragement of, tourism development in rural areas. All of this helps set the stage for the rest of the book as we investigate a few particular cases within the Canadian context.

Key Terms: Neoliberalism and Restructuring

The notion of restructuring invokes considerations of profound changes in the way relations of production, consumption and exchange are organized. While a predominantly economic term, it has been used to describe fundamental changes in the organization of many aspects of social and economic arrangements, from entire political-economic systems (e.g. *perestroika* in the former Soviet Union) to changes in the vertical operations of single corporations, internationalized production systems (e.g. Dicken, 1998), welfare state policy arrangements (e.g. McKeen & Porter, 2003) and municipal government structures (e.g. Andrews, 2003).

However, understanding restructuring as it pertains to our particular consideration of rural tourism requires a focus on development policy. Further, it is important to understand that when we speak of restructuring in this way, we must remember that it is a very particular form, influenced as it was by theories of growth framed within the broader neoliberal ideology. Neoliberalism, simply put, is a political and economic ideology based upon some tenets of neoclassical economics and libertarianism where government involvement in the workings of the market is deemed inefficient and the responsibility of the individual for self-reliance are paramount.

By the late 1970s and early 1980s, questions of how to respond to the uncertainties of economic change brought on by recession and a newly emerging form of globalization, were increasingly answered with words such as 'privatization', 'deregulation', 'downsizing', 'free trade' and 'free enterprise'. The power of this ideology can hardly be overstated. As Marchak (1991) argues, these words became evermore meaningful and powerful influences on development policy. Indeed, the 1980s was a period when many policymakers in many parts of the world were working within a neoliberal mindset and making assumptions about notions such as growth and economic success based upon the neoliberal agenda. As Allen *et al.* (1998) write, it was a 're-making of social relations along neoliberal lines, according to a particular blueprint of "success"' (p. 9), where success meant individual self-reliance, entrepreneurialism, 'hard work', and managing in the face of state withdrawal of support.

These broad ideological changes at the national and international level led to shifts in policies that had a dramatic effect on local government and everyday life in rural communities around the world. The next section offers a brief, generalized look at the trajectory of development and change in rural Canada.

The Context of Canadian Development and Rural Policy: A Brief Historical Overview

Political economists have long drawn attention to the fact that Canada's economic growth and trade relations were based upon the provision of natural resources or staples (generally semimanufactured or raw), to both the central parts of Canada as well as other countries (Clarke-Jones, 1987; Drache & Gertler, 1991; Innis, 1954, 1956; Teeple,

2000; Williams, 1994). Settlement of Canada stretched from East to West, following the path of natural resource exploitation and agricultural development; first of fish and fur, then timber, minerals and wheat. This exploitation was enhanced by the development of rail across the country and was encouraged by economic trading relationships with its colonial rulers and, increasingly, the growing American nation to the south. The dependence of Canada's small communities upon natural resources (agriculture, forestry, fisheries, mining) has left them vulnerable to change on both the supply and the demand side of the economic relationship. For instance, as natural resources are extracted, environmental degradation follows which, as in the case of the Atlantic ground fishery, leads to the exhaustion of supply. In addition to this, technological developments, including labour and land-saving technologies and cheaper, human-made substitutes, serve to encourage the reduction of demand for natural resources. Thus, even today, the natural resources with which Canada enters into international trade relationships (particularly with the United States and Pacific Rim economies) places rural communities (generally bound to these natural resources for economic survival) in a position where their existence is dependent upon external and often uncontrollable economic forces.

Under the National Policy of 1879, manufacturing, processing and other industrial developments were encouraged and protected from external competition in the Central parts of the Canadian nation, as the so-called industrial heartland of Southern Ontario and Quebec was formed. While most of these industrial/manufacturing developments were centred in or near the growing urban areas of Central Canada, some small communities built around small-scale industrial development, (e.g. food processing and textiles), also sprung up in the early settlement period. Not surprisingly, patterns of settlement mirrored these developments. Small populations settled on the periphery of the single-industry towns where they worked to process the natural resources, while larger urban areas attracted increasingly concentrated settlements. Supports such as equalisation payments were built into the development arrangements to ensure that those regions without strong industrial bases would enjoy equal access to infrastructure and services as they supplied the raw materials to keep the system running. Until the latter half of the 20th century, this exchange relationship of natural resources based development on the periphery and industrial development and production in the centre, while somewhat uneven, fashioned a period of prosperity for most of the country.

What is rural development in regards to policy? As Blake (2003: 190) argues, it can mean many things:

> While rural development is often taken to mean the various government policies designed to improve the employment opportunities, income levels and the general standard of living in rural communities, it can also mean the various transportation initiatives and other public services which are provided for the development of all of Canada. It might also include the various social programs which were designed, in some instances, to raise income levels and the standard of living of all Canadians.

After the Second World War, Canadian policy concerning rural development followed a 'redistributive state' approach, dominated by Keynesianism and encouraged by a quickly growing economy. Government attention to the needs of the population through the transfer of funds was evident through programs such as Old Age Pension funds, Unemployment Insurance programs and Family Allowances (Blake, 2003). As Blake notes, policies at this time did not reflect an overt effort to foster growth in particular regions, or even to engage very directly with concerns about rural development, but government did tend to 'step in' from time to time:

> ... the early federal attempts to deal with specific problems in particular sectors might be considered an early form of rural and regional development. Because much of the economic distress in agriculture and the fishery seemed to revolve around fluctuations in commodity prices, Ottawa believed that its initiatives such as the Agricultural Marketing Act of 1949, for instance, could fix the problem. It was assumed by policy makers that by stabilizing markets and prices, rural incomes could be increased and farming communities sustained and regional disparity reduced. Together with other government initiatives to improve productivity and increase production of farmers and fishermen, the belief was that farming and fishing communities would do just fine, and any displaced worker from the increased use of technology in those sectors would find employment in other areas of the economy. (Blake, 2003: 197)

During the rather dramatic era of economic growth in the 1950s, policy attention focussed even less on questions of rural development. With the exception of Atlantic Canada where some attention was given to the somewhat tenuous economic fortunes of farmers and fishers, many policy-makers felt that the boom in the economy would take care of itself. Further, foreign investment, primarily American corporate capital, began to seep into the Canadian economy. Manufacturing 'branch plants' sprung up across Southern Canada as foreign investors took advantage of the natural resources and educated labour force and avoided tariffs on externally produced manufactured goods. While many championed this approach to generating jobs and economic development, others lamented the vulnerability and dependency upon foreign investment that was inherent in the arrangements (Williams, 1994).

By the end of the 1950s, however, it was becoming clear that this growth was not seeping into many parts of Canada, particularly the rural regions outside of the industrial heartland of Central Canada. As Blake (2003: 198) notes, this concern set the stage for regional and provincial development schemes, make work projects, programs and corporations that still dominate today:

> In fact, many of the poor and depressed provinces in the 1950s created lending agencies such as the New Brunswick Development Corporation, Manitoba Development Fund, Nova Scotia's Industrial Estates Limited and Newfoundland's Newfoundland and Labrador Corporation, each endowed with the power to borrow large sums of money for assistance programs.

The consequences of this attention to what were eventually called 'depressed rural regions' include a legacy of initiatives, schemes and programs; each developed to address a specific problem in a specific place and many existing in different places and with different outcomes, yet with little coordination between them. Perhaps one of the most striking examples of attempts at rural development through policy was the Agricultural Rehabilitation and Rural Development Act or ARDA in 1961. ARDA was the first national program for rural development, designed to focus on rural farms and farm incomes. By 1966, this was expanded to many nonagricultural areas and renamed the Agriculture and Rural Development Act and contained a special $50 million fund called the Fund for Rural Economic Development (FRED).

The instigation and failure of this program is well described by Blake (2003: 199–200):

> ARDA was designed to raise farm incomes and make farm land more productive, and although the Minister [*of Agriculture*] was empowered to develop agreements with the provinces to accomplish his objectives, the program lacked a clear focus, and had a modest

impact. It failed to bring fundamental changes to the rural economy, and there was little co-ordination between the provincial and federal levels of government or between the rural and urban areas. Of the 729 ARDA projects (with a value of $61 million) initiated by 1965, there was little to "suggest that they were seen as part of a comprehensive development program".

In 1969, the creation of DREE (Department of Regional Economic Expansion later becoming DRIE – Department of Regional Industrial Expansion) became a powerful development policy and funding department, attempting to address everything from industrial development to job creation to social housing (Blake, 2003).

By the 1970s, economic, political and social forces had combined to shake the foundations of this arrangement. Building upon the technological revolution that took place with the creation of the silicon chip and its fundamental altering of industrial society, social forces such as environmental concerns and activism, the challenges to American hegemonic power and the threats to energy security through such events as the OPEC (Oil Producing and Exporting Countries) oil embargo, led to economic recession. A subsequent restructuring of the organization of industrial production and manufacturing arrangements were built and fostered in an effort to respond to these forces (Marchak, 1991; see also Teeple, 2000; Bradford, 2004). Marchak (1991) argues that these developments were central to creating a space for the rise of the 'new right' and neoliberal ideology. She notes that the new right, comprised of members of transnational corporations and researchers, were influenced by free market ideology and became 'champions of small business, entrepreneurialism, and nationalism' (1991: 10).

Canada's position as primarily a reserve of natural resources was encouraged by development policies that led to intense resource extraction, but also left many areas relatively 'untouched' in terms of large-scale industrial development. However, the changes in economic arrangements described above, coupled with a growing awareness of the devastation brought on by the extraction of natural resources, had a dramatic effect on life in these predominantly rural areas. Even those areas where industrial development arrangements had been protected were affected by the onset of the Free Trade Agreement (FTA) with the United States as well as subsequent trade relationships. Marchak describes Canada's dilemma by the late 1970s and early 1980s:

> Canada had become a peculiar country in the twentieth century. It was a prosperous, stable democracy, but at the same time, it

possessed scarcely any independent industry, especially outside the heartland of southern Ontario and Quebec. It had the highest level of foreign (mainly American) ownership of industry than any OECD country, the second lowest proportion of GNP invested in research and development ... and an extremely high dependence on exports. Of these exports, the majority were raw or semi-processed materials, or component parts made for the US owned firms straddling the border. When the recession hit the US in the early 1980s, Canada was flattened. (Marchak, 1991: 89)

Subsequent economic restructuring throughout the 1980s and 1990s, coupled with the influence of trade pacts such as the FTA and later NAFTA (North American Free Trade Agreement signed with the USA and Mexico in 1994) created dramatic changes to the Canadian political, economic and social landscape. In 1986, the federal government, under the Department of Employment and Immigration, created the Community Futures initiatives, a largely localized effort to encourage communities to create their own economic development opportunities. Leach and Winson (1995) argued that the impact of the FTA, coupled with monetary policies that kept the Canadian dollar artificially high, created an impossible operating environment for Canadian industrial plants (particularly branch plants of American corporations that were now turning to other parts of the world in search of cheaper labor) to operate in Central Canada. The subsequent deindustrialization of Central Canada and its single-industry towns had a dramatic effect on the communities and their inhabitants, particularly older workers and women (Leach & Winson, 1995).

The most recent iteration of government rural development policies is represented in the Rural Partnership, begun in 1998. It is described by Blake (2003: 203) in the following way:

Since the Partnership was launched, the government's stated objective was to reconnect itself with rural Canadians, and to strengthen the economic and social foundations of rural areas. Its goal has been to promote greater consideration of rural issues and concerns in the design and delivery of federal policies and programs. It encourages federal departments and agencies to scrutinize their policies and programs through the eyes of Canadians living in rural and remote areas, or through the "Rural Lens" as the government calls it.

While many political economists studying the situation in rural Canada agree that there have been dramatic and even devastating economic changes in the past 30 years, Winson and Leach (2002) provide perhaps the most moving and provocative look at the impact 'on the ground', particularly in singe-industry towns struck by the collapse of manufacturing in the 1990s. The authors describe restructuring as a '... complex of factors – technological, organizational, political and ideological – that make up this process [which] have produced a *qualitative* shift in the way the economy is structured' (p. 20). Further, these authors note that the impacts of this kind of restructuring became most evident after 1989, although elements were emerging earlier.

As Roppel *et al.* (2006) note, farming and agricultural policy in Canada was not immune to the impacts of this restructuring. The language of business and global competitiveness also made its way into Canada's agricultural policy as Canadian farmers were encouraged to think like business operators, increase their production and exports, compete on the global market and deal with a reduction of government supports. The following excerpt from Agriculture Canada's report to address the economic changes wrought through the 1980s reflects this shift to a market-led, neoliberal ideology of agricultural policy:

> Our action plan must be guided by some clear principles that give us a sense of direction. Our vision of the future **is a more market-oriented agri-food industry** that aggressively pursues opportunities to grow and prosper. (Agriculture Canada 1989; emphasis in original, in Roppel *et al.*, 2006: 1)

For farming communities in Canada, the result has been a corporatized farming industry, dominated by a few international companies with fewer, bigger farms dependent upon capital-intensive investment and inputs. For many living in these areas, the changes to rural life in those communities have been fundamental and, in many cases, devastating. Current research is just beginning to tell the tale from a gendered, environmental and community power perspective (Roppel *et al.*, 2006; see also Sumner, 2005). Thus, in the last 30 years, rural communities, be they based upon industrial production, agriculture or other forms of natural-resource extraction, have experienced a series of devastating blows, leaving them uncertain about their economic future.

Further, attached to these forces working to shape the economic and social fortunes of rural areas were shifts in the structures of rural governance and local autonomy. While not evenly applied across the country, the 1990s saw a struggle for power in most small communities in Canada. The withdrawal of government support at the national and provincial level meant a 'downloading' of services and responsibilities onto the local municipality. In provinces such as Ontario, as Douglas (2005) has shown, this downloading was accompanied by a dramatic restructuring of municipal governments. Between 1996 and 2004, there were 45% fewer municipalities in Ontario (from 815 to 445) accompanied by 39% fewer councilors or local representatives (Douglas, 2005: 235). Equally dramatic was the reduction in financial support. By 1998, Ontario municipalities became responsible for generating 81.4% of their financial resources from their own coffers (up from 68.8% in 1988). While the representational ability of local, municipal governments, as well as their finances, was reduced, their management purview and jurisdictions were expanded. Now that the dust is settling on this uncertain period, it is clear that the mixture of broad economic and political changes led to real and lasting shifts at the local level.

The conundrum of rural development, then, has been a problem for Canadian policymakers for generations. It is within this context that the drive to tourism-led rural growth must be located in order to better understand the complexities of the situation. As noted above, there is increased pressure on localities to determine the direction of economic growth opportunities for themselves and this is increasingly coupled with the growth in the importance given to entrepreneurialism as well as the easy fit between tourism businesses and the entrepreneur. Thus, using tourism as a tool for rural development has become increasingly popular. While not a significant focus of research in Canada, this relationship has been investigated by some authors (see for instance, George, 2006, 2007; Harp, 1994; Hopkins, 1999; Mair, 2006; Overton, 1996). The next section traces some of the general impacts that these shifts have had on life in rural Canada.

Rural Development: The Attraction of Tourism

Some of the most definitive work in the field of tourism policy analysis comes from Hall. On his own (Hall, 1994) and with Jenkins (Hall & Jenkins, 1995, 1998), this author both laments the dearth of tourism policy analysis and points the way to address this problem. First, Hall and Jenkins make direct links between the transformation in the roles and responsibilities of government and the growth of tourism as a mechanism to help fill the gaps in economic development. The authors write:

> Within Western society considerable debate has emerged in the past two decades over the appropriate role of the state in society. Throughout most of the 1980s the rise of "Thatcherism" ... in the United Kingdom and "Reaganism "... in the United States saw a period of retreat by central governments from active government intervention. At the national level, policies of deregulation, privatisation, the elimination of tax incentives, and a move away from discretionary forms of macro-economic intervention, were the hallmarks of a push towards smaller government and the supposed withdrawal of government from the economy. Tourism is not immune from such changes in political philosophy. Tourism is subject to direct and indirect government interventions primarily because of its employment and income producing possibilities. (Hall & Jenkins, 1995: 36)

The authors also trace the impact of reduced national government activity as it encourages the local state to move into the realm of economic development. The result is a change in the local government's role that is, the authors contend, 'qualitatively different' and more entrepreneurially oriented (Hall & Jenkins, 1995: 37) as it responds to pressure to create employment and investment opportunities for its area. Although their work is describing an urban situation, the overall point of their argument is also valid for our consideration of rural areas. Indeed, the word 'rural' could replace 'urban' in the following quotation as the authors contend:

> Tourism and leisure are an essential part of the economic development strategies of the local state ... In this urban environment, the creation of leisure spaces is both a mechanism to attract tourists and new investment. The city becomes a product to be bought and sold. Therefore, cities and regions in the new entrepreneurial local state constantly seek to image and reimage themselves in order to promote themselves as attractive places to live, work, invest and play. (Hall & Jenkins, 1995: 38)

Mair's (2006) work on tourism in New Brunswick and Ontario illustrates that tourism had long enjoyed a place in the language of development policy in both provinces. In New Brunswick, it had been part of the language of local, provincial and regional economic strategies since before the Second World War. In Ontario, tourism had been utilised by policy-makers to stimulate economic development in so-called poorer regions such as the Eastern parts of that province. Why tourism? Tourism is generally perceived as an industry with easy access; it is perceived as a clean industry and one that doesn't require high skill levels. Murphy (1985) contends that striving for benefits through tourism development has made tourism an agent of change. The research cases discussed in this volume tend to exemplify this notion. Inskeep (1991) stated that tourism is often viewed by communities losing their traditional economic base as their economic salvation. George's (1995) earlier research in Nova Scotia in various rural areas reflects this assertion; many communities in economic crisis situations do turn, in desperation, to tourism as their 'economic savior'. Further, when such economic crisis situations do occur, (i.e. loss of a traditional industry, such as farming, fishing, mining), governments quickly react by introducing a flurry of new programs – training, new skill development and funding incentives – in hopes of reestablishing a new economic industry in these areas. Tourism development appears high on the list of options. In reality, many communities have neither adequate amenities nor infrastructure, and chances for success seem highly remote. George (1995) argues that governments do a terrible injustice to communities in crisis by fostering false and unrealistic expectations, providing large dollars for feasibility studies and quick-fix programs that have little chance for success.

Arguably, Nova Scotia, and much of Atlantic Canada is still 'reeling' from the collapse of the fishery in the early 1990s and the subsequent aftermath. Much progress has been made toward change, but evidence (George, 2004, 2006) suggests that policymakers at national, provincial and local levels are still struggling with economic recovery in the rural areas. Within the political realm in Canada, though, we hear little mention or emphasis of the many negative aspects of tourism, including environmental and socioeconomic. Positive economic benefits are widely promoted and touted, and everyone is encouraged to 'get on the bandwagon'. Tourism presents an opportunity that is extremely appealing to a rural community experiencing economic crisis. In the early 2000s, the Department of Tourism, Culture and Heritage, launched a tourism destination area (TDA) planning strategy targeted towards community tourism development in rural Nova Scotia. But, Murphy warns of tourism's ability to 'sow the seeds of its own destruction' if not planned and controlled properly; there is a real danger that when a community loses its traditional industry, it will embrace tourism to the extent that it merely replaces one dependency with another, thus, setting itself up for another eventual crisis.

Harp (1994) looked at the national level and assessed the efforts of the Canadian government in the promotion of tourism. Identifying the economic context within which provincial, municipal and, where applicable federal, tourism policies are formed and implemented, Harp argues that the election of a Conservative federal government in 1984 led them to ask how Canada could reap greater economic benefits from its tourism industry. This question was operationalized through a concentration upon increasing international visitation and expenditures. As well, research institutes began to consider tourism as an important growth industry. As economic opportunities became fewer and further between in the rural parts of those provinces, the policy language invoking the promise of tourism-led growth intensified dramatically.

Impacts: The Opportunities and Challenges of Tourism and Rural Development

Given the growth in tourism development in rural areas worldwide, it is hardly surprising that there has been much attention paid to the impacts of these changes. For instance, economic studies generally tend to emphasize the potential contribution that tourism can make to a challenged or threatened economy, particularly by way of diversification (see for instance, Gannon, 1994; Weaver & Fennell, 1997). However, there have been criticisms of the assumed economic impacts of tourism in rural areas, particularly in light of how it has been planned and the economic repercussions thereof. For instance, authors such as Galston and Baehler (1995) and Marcouiller (1997; see also Reid, 2003) argue that the economic growth focus of those who encourage tourism in rural areas has placed insufficient emphasis upon determining whether tourism strategies even make sense for the communities and areas in question. Marcouiller criticizes the 'nonintegrative' nature of most tourism planning in rural areas, which inevitably concentrates on marketing and promotion as 'overly myopic'.

> Historically, nonintegrated tourism planning goals have been dominated by business development and economic growth concerns. Inevitably, the market-oriented system will continue to place business and development and economic growth as significant issues around which tourism development goals will be defined. (Marcouiller, 1997: 341)

The warning underlying this lack of integration is, as others have suggested, that there is the ever-present risk that tourism will not be adequately supported (or will be resisted) by locals living in the communities (see for instance, Mitchell, 1998). More broadly, there have also been investigations in terms of tourism's effect on transforming rural social life and culture (see for instance, Bouquet & Winter, 1987; Perdue *et al.*, 1987; Reid *et al.*, 2004). Because businesses are thought to take much of the financial risk associated with tourism development, their particular issues and perspectives have been the hub for much of the tourism planning and assessment process. What is often neglected is the risk assumed by the local inhabitants of the destination itself. The risk to them may be a dramatically altered lifestyle due to overcrowding, inflated prices including land and buildings, as well as noise and other forms of pollution. However, these issues, if given any attention in the development process, are usually subservient to assessments that describe demand for the destination and marketing research.

Further to this, business models are particularly built upon issues of supply and demand and use that information as parameters for decision-making. What are often lost in the equations are issues of production and impact assessments. While hotels in rural and remote areas are the infrastructure that assists visitors to undertake the recreation experience that attracts them to the area in the first place, they are usually not the attraction itself. It is often a unique environment or culture that is the attraction sought by the tourist, therefore, the local community and environment is naturally the producer of the attraction. If that is the case, then the views of the communities need to be a part of the assessment and decision-making process from the beginning of the project and not an after-thought. Finally, added to these considerations are the environmental impacts on rural areas when tourism becomes intense or extends into sensitive areas (see Page & Getz, 1997).

Importantly, it is becoming clear that a synthesized, complex and integrated approach must be taken towards tourism development and also its study. For instance, Sharpley (2004) argues that much of the research on tourism has been overly tourism-centric and thus has not taken adequate account of the 'broader political economy of rural areas' (p. 382), and he calls for increased attention to the relationships between tourism, the rural economy and national policies with respect to agriculture and rural development. Moreover, he argues, considerations of globalization and cultural change are also dynamics that must be taken into account to better understand the complexity of rural change and tourism. Helping to meet this challenge is one of the overarching goals of this book.

Conclusion

Following this brief review of the political economic of rural tourism development in Canada, it is clear that communities are increasingly driven by the need to provide unique and sellable commodities that will attract tourism dollars. Thus, tourism is portrayed as a mechanism for growth in rural areas in that it speaks to the need to generate employment and growth opportunities in the face of rural change and economic restructuring. Throughout this book, we will be arguing that communities need to be in control of both the process and outcome of tourism planning and development. It is the local area and the environment that is critical to making it all work. They provide the opportunity for the infrastructure to exist. In addition, these are communities where the residents will have to live on a day-to-day basis with whatever is developed and implemented. In this sense, this book is not just about tourism, it is about how rural areas are responding to political and economic change at all levels. Thus, no studies of rural change should overlook tourism, and efforts must be made to see how tourism fits into broader questions of rural growth and development.

Chapter 3

The Case of Lunenburg, Nova Scotia

Introduction

This chapter is about one small rural community, Lunenburg, Nova Scotia, Canada and its approach to developing tourism as a response to globalization and change. While previous research tells us of the many dynamics and impacts associated with tourism development, both positive and negative, it is reasonable to assume that the main aim of any potential tourism development is to improve the local economy and quality of life at the destination. Evidence suggests that in many instances, tourism development may be well planned, particularly in developed countries, as often illustrated by 'best practices' stories, however, we repeatedly hear stories of areas, including in Canada, with ill-planned development or, in some cases, no planning at all. In other cases, the concept of tourism development is thrust on a community as a 'quick fix' to address economic woes. In Chapter 1, we outlined and explained an analytical framework to situate various approaches to tourism development. Most approaches to tourism are not clear-cut and cannot be located neatly in one quadrant. While Lunenburg's approach has some dimensions of evolutionary development, it seemed to fit most predominantly in the 'responsive' quadrant. Tourism stemmed from a growing demand generated by interest in the community's new image as a UNESCO World Heritage site and has helped to address a declining economy. Thus, we use this case to illustrate one example of a 'responsive' approach to tourism development, as noted in Figure 3.1, one that was not only initiated by pressures of globalization, including loss of traditional economic base, but also as reactions to a series of fortuitous events.

Key Theoretical Concepts: Commodification of Culture; Gentrification

Commodification of culture

Results from research studies (George, 2004, 2006) suggest a series of dynamics has emerged related to Lunenburg's tourism development,

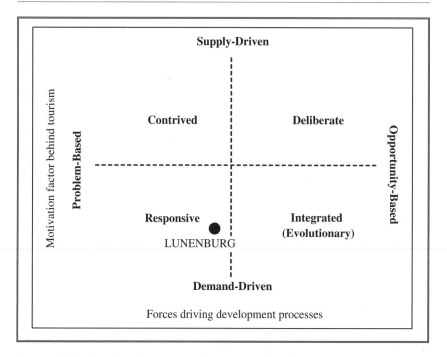

Figure 3.1 Lunenburg's approach to tourism development

which now appear to threaten the community's future and sustainability. First, there is evidence to suggest that widespread commodification of local culture for tourism has taken place in the community. This process transforms a local culture into a commodity intended for exchange for consumption by others. This transformation brings about a totally different philosophy under which a community must operate – one that is quite dissimilar to what, in this case, had underpinned the community's way of life for successive generations. A second dynamic that became apparent in the Lunenburg research was gentrification, a concept that has mainly been applied to urban slum areas, but which is fast becoming noticed in rural areas.

Flora (2001: 9) purported that capital is generally understood as 'a stock of resources with value embedded in its ability to produce a flow of benefits'. Bourdieu refers to *cultural capital* as acquired knowledge, skills and dispositions. However, in contemporary tourism, local culture and its aspects become manifest in object form – a capital asset unto itself. Through tourism, local culture becomes a main asset for economic generation and expectations of providing a continuous stream of benefits to the community that will help maintain its economic viability now and into the future. Prior to commodification processes, culture was not considered a capital asset in an economic sense, but merely as a facet of social development of community life (George, 2004).

Commodification of culture for tourism occurs when a community's culture, developed over the past, perhaps centuries, and created through ordinary spontaneous evolution under principles of *use* value, (i.e. essential element in the social fabric and essence of everyday life in a community), becomes converted into an *object* of exchange value for tourist consumption. Subsequently, culture becomes transformed and reconstructed into a completely different entity, and a consumer value system supersedes a community value system. This consumer value system distorts the original culture and turns it into an artificially created culture. Moreover, when commodification of culture becomes the dominant feature of a community, a metamorphosis process begins to occur where the original community *sheds* its old existence and a *new* community emerges, a *death* and *rebirth* process of community rather than a sustaining process to ensure continuity of community (George, 2004). Triggered by a combination of intervening factors – external, catalytic occurrences and/or internal – a process of commodification can commence that will eventually transform the local culture from its intended purpose and function; first, through a brief stage of maintaining dual value systems, (i.e. both use value and exchange value), and ultimately, accelerating to a point where culture becomes totally subsumed and dominated under relations of exchange value. How this has unfolded in Lunenburg will be discussed later in this chapter.

Gentrification

The Collins Concise Dictionary (2001: 600) defines 'gentrification' as: '... a process by which middle-class people take up residence in a traditionally working-class area'. The Oxford Colour Dictionary (1998: 264) defines gentrification as: 'upgrading of working class urban area by arrival of affluent residents'. But, perhaps Hamnett's (1984: 282–319) definition of 'gentrification' fits best with what has happened in Lunenburg; he states, 'Gentrification is simultaneously a physical, economic, social and cultural phenomenon, [which] commonly involves the invasion by middle-class or higher-income groups of previously working-class neighbourhoods or multi-occupied "twilight areas" and the replacement or displacement of many of the original occupants'. Among the many definitions of the term, the word 'class' is the basic common thread, but Slater (2002) suggests that it is 'perhaps more useful to understand gentrification as a process which brings about change to a neighbourhood based on the influx of "different" people to those there already – a new class of highly educated, highly skilled and highly paid residents are moving in' (2002, Defining Gentrification, para 3: Online Document). In this case study, we argue that gentrification has occurred in Lunenburg as a consequence of tourism. Gentrification is discussed in more depth in Chapter 9.

Research Approach

Much of this chapter has been extracted from George's doctoral work in 2004. The purpose of her doctoral research was to examine the relationships and interconnections between tourism, local culture, community and sustainability in the small community of Lunenburg, Nova Scotia. George's intent was to gain an understanding of the extent to which local culture had become commodified for tourism purposes, and what were, if any, the apparent consequences of tourism development in the community. Field research for the dissertation was conducted during spring and summer 2003. The case study method, following the principles of the interpretative paradigm, seemed most appropriate and was employed for this study. The researcher used a mixed method approach, incorporating both quantitative and qualitative techniques to collect data. Two survey questionnaires were administered, one to visiting tourists in the community and a second to local business owners in the community. Tourists completed 151 out of a possible 300 questionnaires. A survey of the business community generated 39 completed questionnaires. Other data-gathering techniques applied by the researcher included: participant observation, personal interviews, document analyses, audio recording and photography.

In 2006, further research was undertaken in Lunenburg to examine the attitudes of residents towards tourism since its UNESCO designation 10 years earlier in 1995. Two focus groups were conducted, and a survey questionnaire was administered to all households in the community. Two hundred and four questionnaires were completed and provided data to give a sense of residents' views and perspectives on UNESCO-related tourism development in the community.

The Case of Lunenburg

Background

Lunenburg is a small rural community situated on Nova Scotia's Southern coastal region and approximately 100 km from Halifax, the capital city of Nova Scotia (Figure 3.2).

Lunenburg has dramatically changed from its founding days in the 1750s. In our current age of advanced globalization and through its components – capitalism, technology and innovation, movements of people, changing demographics, transformation of many rural areas continues to unfold at an unprecedented pace. From its earlier settlement days, Lunenburg flourished and gained community prosperity, and in its heyday had the most advanced fishing economy in North America. The fishing industry (and related industries, i.e. shipbuilding) was its dominant economic generator, sustaining the community for almost two centuries. With the stark decline and subsequent collapse of the

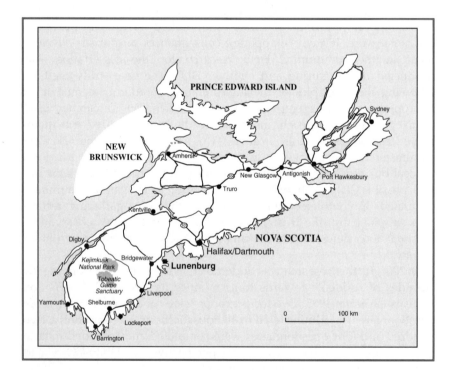

Figure 3.2 Location of Lunenburg, Nova Scotia

fishing industry in the early 1990s, Lunenburg, like many other coastal communities in Atlantic Canada, was forced to consider diversification strategies in efforts to remain an economically viable and sustainable community. In the midst of this reality, a timely and fortuitous event occurred in 1995 – the community was awarded the prestigious UNESCO World Heritage Site designation, which would soon help pave the way to the community's future as an international cultural tourism destination.

History of Lunenburg

Lunenburg was officially founded in 1753. Preceding the settlement of the community, the territory was called Acadia, later known as Nova Scotia, was founded in 1604–1605, and occupied by the French, headquartered in Port Royal (McCreath & Leefe, 1982). Over the next century or so, there were ongoing struggles between the French monarchy and British Empire to colonize new territories, including North America. Documentation analyses from various files at the Fisheries Museum of the Atlantic showed that in 1749, under Lord Edward Cornwallis, Halifax was founded and became the capital settlement of the British-conquered territory. Halifax was to become home of the main governing body of the new British territory. Shortly thereafter, in 1753 Lunenburg was founded, under the command of Colonel Charles Lawrence from the Garrison at Halifax, to become the second major British settlement in the Province. Original documents written by Lawrence are preserved in the Fisheries Museum of the Atlantic.

Although research revealed some evidence of an earlier settlement, the *official* or documented history of Lunenburg began with that period of British colonization commencing in 1753. There was a sense of Britain's domination and control in Nova Scotia, and Lunenburg was considered the second most important settlement in the region after Halifax. Data obtained from the Archived Files, Fishermen's Museum of the Atlantic (2003), in Lunenburg indicated that the British, in efforts to *anglicize* the frontier territory, recruited a contingent of *Foreign Protestants* of German, Swiss and French (Protestant) origin to relocate to Nova Scotia and build a new settlement. Land grants were offered to the recruits, attached with specific conditions that were to be fulfilled over the next few years. The settlers were hand-selected by the British to 'colonize the territory and to counter-balance the more than 10,000 French Catholics then living in Nova Scotia ... the British, continuing their long struggle to establish a firm presence here, believed that these people would be more hard working than the *industrial poor* of Britain, and that, if granted land and assistance in settlement, they could be counted on to become loyal subjects of the British crown' (Moore, 1997).

Many of the residents in Lunenburg today are direct descendants of the early settlers. While the population had remained fairly consistent over the community's 200-year history, it has declined significantly in recent years. From 2001 to 2006, Lunenburg's overall population fell from 2568 to 2317, a drop of 9.7%. Population demographics have also changed, most significantly because of a decline in the community's youth population. Data shown in Tables 3.1 (Statistics Canada, 2001, 2006) and 3.2 (Statistics Canada, 2001) highlights these changes. According to the 2006 Census, the population under 15 years actually dropped by about 24% between 2001 and 2006, while the adult population between 25 and 54 years dropped by nearly 21% during the same period. However, during the time period since the UNESCO designation in 1995, Lunenburg saw an influx of older newcomers, with different backgrounds, characteristics and attitudes. Between 2001 and 2006, the community saw a 25% increase in residents between the ages of 55 and 64, many of them newcomers. The median age of Lunenburg's population in 2006 was 50.1 (2006 Census). These factors have contributed to a significant shift in the demographic makeup and social life in the community (George, 2004).

Table 3.1 Community profile of Lunenburg and Nova Scotia 2001 and 2006

Characteristics	Lunenburg 2001	Nova Scotia 2001	Lunenburg 2006	Nova Scotia 2006
Population	2568	908,007	2317	913,462
No. of families	700	262,905		
Pop. > 15 years	2195 (85.6%)	742,980 (81.8%)	(88.1%)	
Median age	46.7	38.8	50.1	41.8
Children < 15	370		280	
Youth 15–24	225		220	
Pop. 25–54	975		775	
Pop. 55–64	295		360	
Pop. Over 65	705		675	

Source: Statistics Canada (2001, 2006)

Table 3.2 Industry profile of Lunenburg and Nova Scotia 2001

Industry	Lunenburg Total	Nova Scotia Total
Total – experienced labor force	1125	442,425
Agriculture and other resource-based industries	80	29,000
Manufacturing and construction industries	250	70,955
Wholesale and retail trade	160	71,085
Finance and real estate	55	20,620
Health and education	210	80,700
Business services	115	70,270
Other services	255	99,790

Source: Statistics Canada (2001)

Two critical social and political circumstances (external factors) occurred in the later years of the 20th century that would directly affect the development of tourism in Lunenburg. These external factors provided the preconditions for the community's response to pursue tourism. First, there was a collapse of the fishery beginning in the early 1990s, and, second, there was a growing focus and strategic positioning of tourism, in particular, cultural tourism, throughout the entire province of Nova Scotia. These preconditions, coupled with the community's unexpected UNESCO designation, were instrumental in setting the course for tourism development in the community.

Collapse of the fishery in Atlantic Canada

The collapse of the fishery had a devastating impact on many coastal communities in Atlantic Canada, including Lunenburg. The fishing industry was the dominant employer in the community. Industry knowledge and skills came from the fishing industry. These were acquired over the years, not in formal institutions, but through informal learning. Knowledge and skills were passed on from generation to generation, neighbor to neighbor and entry into the fishery was not difficult (Task Force, 1993). Not only did Lunenburg, like other Atlantic Canada coastal communities become dependent on the fishery, nonfishing sectors of the economy became heavily dependent, sometimes entirely, on the fishery for their existence. For instance, suppliers of equipment and facilities, merchants and retailers counted on the fishery to sustain their business operations. Nowhere was this more evident than in the community of Lunenburg. Its fishery was diverse in structure – groundfish, shellfish and pelagic species, with inshore, midshore and offshore fleets – some with fixed gear, some with mobile gear. The fishing industry in Atlantic Canada was broad in scope, included numerous processing companies and employed hundreds of plant workers. In 1990, there were 60,000 fish plant workers processing fish in more than 800 plants in Atlantic Canada (Task Force Report, 1993). Lunenburg was home to one of the largest fish processing plants in North America, National Sea Products, which employed in excess of 500 people. In addition, it was home to a modern fleet of fishing vessels, including several larger 150' stern trawlers. Fishing was a lucrative industry, not only in Lunenburg, but in Atlantic Canada, generally.

However, by 1992, a stark reality loomed. The fishery resource had collapsed and the Federal Government of Canada imposed a moratorium on northern cod, which represented the largest volume of the groundfish species (George, 1995: 9). Several rationalizations for this collapse were put forth. Groundfish stocks had always been subject to cyclical swings. There were ecological changes and anomalies that affect their reproduction or survival, such as changes in water temperature and salinity. Changes in their food supply could have a major impact on replenishment of stocks (Task Force Report, 1993). Many did not buy these explanations and they screamed loudly of mismanagement of the fisheries, including overfishing by foreign vessels. Facets of globalization became obvious and entrenched in a long debate over international fishing rights. But, according to a 1993 Task Force Report, a false vision had been fabricated based on miscalculations of the abundance of the resource, and expectations of governments and communities about the ability of the fishery to sustain coastal communities.

Cultural tourism in Nova Scotia

In 1998, tourism was worth $1.1 billion to Nova Scotia's economy, supporting a total of 33,000 jobs and generating at least $119 million in provincial tax receipts (Economic Planning Group (EPG), 2000). Of the $1.1 billion to the economy, 60% came from *exports*, i.e. non-Nova Scotians visiting the province (p. 11). In 1999, these revenues increased to approximately $1.26 billion, supporting 36,300 jobs and $135 million in tax revenues (p. 7). Total tourism activity in Nova Scotia was 7.5 million person visits in 1998 and 7.8 million in 1999 as compared to 5.4 million in 1994 (EPG, 2000: 6). Further, according to the 2000 report, tourism was a quality industry for Nova Scotia and important to its economic agenda. Such a view has remained consistent and supported by successive governments. In 2006, Nova Scotia welcomed 2.1 million visitors, bringing in an estimated $1.31 billion in revenues (Nova Scotia Department of Tourism, Culture and Heritage, 2007: 1).

Cultural tourism has been increasingly recognized by both heritage institutions and tourism operators around the world as a legitimate component of tourism, capable of increasing tourists visits and generating income (ARA/LORD, 1997). In 1997, ARA Consulting Group Inc. and LORD Cultural Resources Planning and Management Inc. (ARA/LORD), professional consultants, were engaged to do a study on Cultural Tourism in Nova Scotia to 'assess the demand for Nova Scotia's cultural tourism products, and to identify opportunities for developing cultural tourism products in response to market demand' (ARA/LORD, 1997: 1). In their report, ARA/LORD (1997) referred to *cultural* tourism as distinct from *recreational* tourism; other types of pleasure travel had begun to be recognized in the early 1980s as distinct forms of tourism, each with their own products and markets. Although there was now a new focus by governments and tourism operators, research studies on cultural tourism in local regions, i.e. the rural areas of Canada, including Nova Scotia, had been relatively sparse. The ARA/LORD report suggested that there were important differences in average length of stay and expenditures by *cultural* tourists to the province. Cultural tourists were higher spenders and, therefore, a more lucrative market to pursue.

As the fishing era rapidly went into decline in Atlantic Canada, tourism was simultaneously being flaunted for its potential economic viability. Many small fishing communities, devastated by the collapse of the fishery, quickly turned to tourism in hopes of it becoming the 'economic savior'.

Tourism Development in Lunenburg

A 'responsive' approach to tourism development in Lunenburg, Nova Scotia

While Lunenburg today (2007) has a significant and growing manufacturing industry, particularly its composite plastics operations, which produce high-tech products for a global aerospace industry, the community has a well-established tourism industry with a strong focus on its culture and heritage. In 2004, according to Lunenburg's website (August 2004), there were 180 businesses in Lunenburg that offered a diverse variety of retail and wholesale goods and services to townspeople and visitors alike. The fishery, and related industries, although now dramatically downsized and changed, was then still perceived by some to be a significant industry in the community. Others took a more realistic viewpoint; the fishing industry had reached a stage of permanent decline. A Statistics Canada Report (2001) supported the latter belief when it reported that only 7% of employment at that time was related to resource-based industry (fishing).

By 2006, Lunenburg was no longer considered the vigorous fishing community it once was, but instead it had become a well-established tourism destination (George, 2006). Tourism had rapidly grown over 10 years and had directly contributed to changes in the landscapes, seascapes and streetscapes of the community. The waterfront was no longer a bustling fishing or working area as is was in the 1950s to late 1980s. With the development of a sleek new paved street, known as Bluenose Drive, it now provided a core of shops – craft and souvenir, food and lodging and other attractions and activities, providing products and services for the thousands of people who visit the community each tourism season.

Tourism's trajectory in Lunenburg

Based on her research in the community, George suggests that tourism, although not extensive in scale, had been ongoing for some time in Lunenburg. However, tourism development, generally, was neither intentionally planned nor sanctioned in any serious manner initially, nor was it viewed to be of any significant importance to the economic life of the community. According to the study, before the UNESCO designation in 1995, planning for tourism was not a priority item for development in Lunenburg. With no official planning organization or group for tourism development, the community, generally, took a low-key, spontaneous approach to tourist activity, typical of many rural communities in Nova Scotia.

George's research (2004) revealed that local community newspaper editors and prominent local residents promoted tourism as early as 1896. Lunenburg's long path towards eventual full-blown tourism development appears to stem from four main catalysts: (1) the first Fishermen's Picnic, a local social event, in 1916; (2) a restructured Fishermen's Picnic in 1929, which would now include a Fisheries Exhibition; (3) the opening of the Fisheries Museum of the Atlantic in 1967, a Canadian Centennial Project and (4) Lunenburg's esteemed UNESCO designation as a World Heritage Site in 1995. In Lunenburg's earliest tourism years, visitors came from local districts and outlying areas of Lunenburg County to attend the community's Fishermen's Picnic, a cherished social event to recognize and honor local fishermen and their families, which first began in 1916. Generally though, visitors to the community at that time would be considered *excursionists* or *day visitors* – visitors who did not stay in the host community overnight and required special services. However, in 1929, a structural change was made to the annual Fishermen's Picnic, which would quickly alter the entire dynamics surrounding the event and its future. The Fishermen's Picnic, in essence, became a Provincial Exhibition. This newly restructured event would become a second catalyst for tourism development in Lunenburg because attendees now included a wider *tourist market* coming from more distant provincial and regional areas (Atlantic Canada). The duration or *tourism season* around this *new* Fisheries annual event became extended by three to five days, and visitors now required overnight accommodation, food services and other amenities.

A third catalyst for tourism occurred in 1967, with the development of a new attraction, the Fisheries Museum of the Atlantic, a Canadian Centennial Project, and the *tourism season* quickly expanded from 10 weeks in the Museum's first year of operation to six months in 2003. Visitors to the community continued to increase over the next few years (George, 2004).

The impact of tourism on the local economy as a result of the Museum's attraction was immediately obvious. However, the fourth, and perhaps most significant catalyst for tourism development in Lunenburg, arguably, was the 1995 UNESCO designation of the community as a World Heritage Site. This designation came with much prestige and status and placed Lunenburg on the global stage. It was at this point in time that tourism became the dominant force to drive future planning and development in the community. Tourism in Lunenburg grew from a couple of thousand visitors in the early days of the Fishermen's Picnic to today's estimated figure of approximately 300,000 annually (Visitor Information Center, 2003) and an estimated tourism expenditure of $18–$20 million annually (George, 2004), although no official statistics were available to verify this purported information. Figure 3.3 summarizes key periods and events throughout the historical development of tourism in Lunenburg.

The UNESCO World Heritage Site designation process

Lunenburg received UNESCO World Heritage Site designation because it served as the best example of a preserved British Colonial

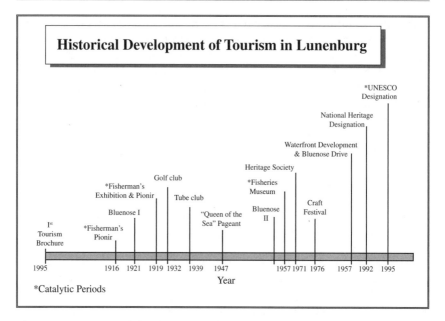

Figure 3.3 Historical development of tourism in Lunenburg

settlement in North America (UNESCO). George's research (2004) uncovered facets of the designation process, a milestone in the history of Lunenburg, one that set a new course for radical social transformation and restructuring of the community. Her research pointed to the Mayor of Lunenburg as the leading proponent in spearheading the designation that resulted in the award for the community.

As previously discussed, prior to 1992, tourism was not a primary objective for development planning in Lunenburg (George, 2004). Although, since the early 1970s, there had been a growing awareness and interest on the part of the community of what unique qualities Lunenburg possessed – preserved architecture, lifestyle and culture, and the larger homes built in the 1920s and 1930s in the earlier days of prosperity in the community. With this increasing awareness and interest, local organizations began to emerge, for instance, the Lunenburg Heritage Society formed in 1971. This small group of residents soon began to focus its attention on the many heritage buildings and unique architecture in Lunenburg. When interviewed, the Mayor of Lunenburg commented 'People, some distinguished professionals, came to view us and said that we really have something special here. When people hear that long enough they probably think, yes, we do and what is it that makes us so special and what can we do to make that idea one that will attract other people'.

The Mayor described how the UNESCO designation came to fruition. His captivating story revealed that it was by happenstance, while on a family vacation and a stopover in Old Quebec City in 1993, that he noticed and became intrigued by a monument with a green crystal in it. Upon closer inspection, he noticed that it was dated 1986, and included an inscription noting Quebec City as a protected site due to its cultural significance. He took several photographs, which were brought back to Lunenburg for discussion about the incident with others in the Town Hall, and what this might mean for the community. 'Prior to that', he noted, 'the UNESCO designation didn't really mean much'. Subsequently, from discussions with other Town Hall officials, the Mayor concluded that the Town Council should further investigate this matter. Initially, there was much enthusiasm about the designation as a potential opportunity for Lunenburg. 'The Town had been trying to find ways to fund a sewage treatment facility for Lunenburg, something the community never had. This seemed to be an opportunity worth pursuing' (Mayor of Lunenburg, 2003).

A collection of additional information and required documents ensued, and talks commenced between the Town authorities and officials at the National Historic Sites and Monuments Board, who showed sincere interest. Dialogue continued with the Federal agency who cautioned against having high expectations; the process of getting listed under UNESCO often took a long time – up to 10 years. Moreover, the process was highly competitive. The Lunenburg contingent assured government officials this was not a pressing issue to the community, however, it was eager to know its chances. Data (George, 2004) disclosed that one particular official of Parks Canada intervened on Lunenburg's behalf, outlining pertinent documents and information required in conjunction with the application for presentation to the UNESCO Board.

To be eligible for designation, the community was required to meet specific property criteria under the UNESCO Operational Guidelines (2002), for the Implementation of the World Heritage Convention (WHC). The final decision was made by the WHC Committee to inscribe Lunenburg Old Town on the World Heritage List on the basis of criteria (iv) and (v) outlined in Section 24, p. 6, because the town was considered:

- (iv) an outstanding example of a type of building or architectural or technological ensemble of landscape which illustrates a significant stage(s) in human history
- (v) an outstanding example of a traditional human settlement or land-use which is representative of a culture (or cultures), especially when it has become vulnerable under the impact of irreversible change ...

The Town Deputy Manager also took on a leading role in preparing required documents and application for the designation process. While the Parks Canada official played an instrumental but less visible role, other interested parties collaborated with Town officials. At a special meeting on 14 December 1995, the Mayor of Lunenburg announced the official designation that would forever change life in the small rural community:

The Old Town portion of Lunenburg was designated a World Heritage Site on Dec, 6th, 1995 by the United Nations Educational, Scientific and Cultural Organization – UNESCO. Old Town Lunenburg is only the second area in continental North America to be designated a World Heritage Site, Quebec City having been listed in 1986. The World Heritage Designation recognizes the uniqueness of Old Town Lunenburg's British model town plan, its architectural, cultural and marine heritage. The town of Lunenburg will be working with the Federal and Provincial Governments to develop the benefits of World Heritage Site designation for our community. (Town Council Minutes of the Special Meeting, 14 December 1995: 6)

The history of events leading up to the UNESCO designation of Lunenburg and its repositioning as an international cultural tourism destination has been intriguing. George's research (George, 2004) indicated that Town authorities were the leading proponents in the designation process with very little or no serious consultation with the community at large, at least, not until after the event occurred. Local *champions* and/or decision-makers are frequently the impetus behind tourism development in a community. In many situations, it is the entrepreneurial segment of a community that takes the lead in driving tourism development (Reid *et al.*, 2001), sometimes to the chagrin of the local residents.

Lunenburg did have a few local champions but, unquestionably, it was the community's Mayor who led the UNESCO designation project. Other advocates of tourism in the community at the time were the local

Board of Trade, the Heritage Society and some key individuals who supported cultural tourism development in the community. Although there had been strong ongoing interconnections between these entities, it was the Mayor, and his Town Council who continue to form the power base (2007), the power base which determines community and economic development policy in the community (George, 2004). George's research clearly indicates that the community-at-large had been left on the periphery of any tourism development planning. By and large, community residents appeared to become involved only when serious issues and concerns emerged and the Town Council was obliged to call special public meetings.

State of the fishing industry in Lunenburg since 1995

As of 2007, the fishery in Lunenburg, arguably, has all but disappeared. The collapse of the fishery in Atlantic Canada in the 1990s, discussed earlier, and its continued downsizing had a devastating impact on the community of Lunenburg. Following trends and advancing globalization, government restructuring of the industry resulted in huge allocations of fishing quotas given to large corporate fishing companies. This, in effect, gave control of the groundfish fishery to the larger commercial conglomerates and international fishing industry, and basically eliminated many of the smaller fleets in Atlantic Canada.

In spite of this, some types of fishing activity by smaller vessels have remained, e.g. lobster fishing and the scallop fishery. Lobster fishing has continued to be fairly lucrative in Lunenburg for those who were fortunate to inherit or secure lobster licenses from their fathers or from other family members. To purchase a lobster license in recent years requires a cash layout in excess of $100,000, not including a vessel or equipment that is a major capital expenditure. In their efforts to survive, many small vessel operators have turned their vessels, formerly used for fishing, into tour boats for tourists. Others have continued to fish in a shorter and restricted fishing season, after which they convert their fishing vessels into tour boats for the tourism season.

On a map of Lunenburg (see Figure 3.4), which is given to tourists and others visiting the community's local Visitors Information Center, a section marked by a dashed line outlines the UNESCO World Heritage Site area, now referred to as Old Town Lunenburg. Much of the area encompasses the historic waterfront, which was previously the working zone for fishermen. Undoubtedly, the UNESCO honor has given the community much exposure and prestige on the world stage, and is a

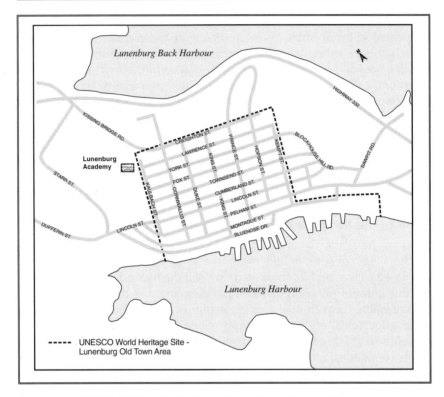

Figure 3.4 UNESCO World Heritage Site – Lunenburg old town area

major factor in the community's strategy for future growth and success as a tourism destination. This, however, has not and will not guarantee any long-term sustainability for the community.

Reconnecting to Theoretical Concepts

Commodification of Lunenburg's cultural assets

Lunenburg's culture and social fabric took approximately 250 years to evolve. Astoundingly, during the last decade, this community's course of spontaneous development has been radically altered by a sequence of events. These include, not only external forces, such as the downturn in the fishery, globalization and technology, but also the unanticipated awarding of the UNESCO designation, the associated prestige and entry onto the world status, and ensuing growth of tourism. The World

Heritage Site designation was a pinnacle of achievement for tourism development in Lunenburg. It came at a moment in time when the community was being economically challenged and forced to consider change if it were to continue to thrive as a community.

The cost of change can be high. The UNESCO designation, along with the series of events that took place in the last decade, led to a process of transforming this small rural community in Nova Scotia and its longstanding cultural heritage into a new community entity. Some may liken this *new* community entity to a *museum without walls* or *a stage on which to perform for paying tourists*. The transformation process has basically removed the essence of local culture from those who formed and owned it, and placed it into the hands of a consuming traveling public and market forces. Arguably, it has thwarted longstanding traditional processes of transmission and accumulation of culture in the community.

It was in the mid-1990s when a handful of individuals in the community recognized that Lunenburg's culture might be a potential asset for tourism – a resource that could be harvested and exploited to stimulate economic activity. In retrospect, questions that might have been asked back then are: 'Is culture as capital not like other resources, subject to the same laws and principles of conservation and management in order to maintain a continuing flow of benefits? When local culture becomes objectified and commodified for tourism, can it still be considered "culture" in the true sense of meaning?' Arguably, living culture and commodified culture for tourism purposes cannot be reconciled as one and the same. Lunenburg, under its qualifying criteria for UNESCO designation, frames itself as a community having a natural and continuing living culture. Perhaps, through the commodification process, the continuity of accumulating and reproducing original culture discontinues; the living culture, in reality, is a brand new culture, one germinated and reborn out of the commodification process itself.

In the case of Lunenburg, external forces beyond the control of the community have triggered a 'responsive' approach to tourism. First, there was the collapse of the fishery and, second, the provincial pull for developing cultural tourism; these forces placed pressures on the community to consider economic development diversification strategies, including tourism. With the intervention of a third and catalytic factor, the UNESCO designation, the transformation process was initiated. Its momentum was further driven by internal forces (Mayor, Town Council, Heritage Society) responding to the external events with a flurry of activities – tourism product development, marketing and a rash of local planning processes. During the process, local decision-makers quickly enacted new zoning policy and laws around controlling and preserving historic buildings and assets. Local residents did not seem to be involved in prescribing these changes. Community involvement in any tourism planning in the community only became evident after the designation had been accepted. When a community begins to commodify its local cultural aspects for tourism development, its local culture could be characterized as having both dual values – use value and exchange value. Over time though, the commodifying process progresses to where the original culturally embedded social construct (use value) becomes dominated by notions of exchange value. Eventually, as in the case of Lunenburg, the community reappears as a brand new transformed entity, one far removed from the longstanding and established traditional rural community it once was. What the UNESCO World Heritage Site designation in December 1995 meant for Lunenburg was to institutiona-lize and legitimize the commodification of its culture. With its interven-tion, UNESCO became the decisive turning point in Lunenburg's evolution, a point where the *old* community would begin to spiral into decline, and a new community would begin to surface. Culture and history – the essence of the old community – were now transcended to abstract levels of heritage and legacy, and, paradoxically, became a *gift* to the 'new' community for tourism exploitation and a basis for its future development. Ashworth (1994: 16) appears to agree; he contends that 'history is the remembered record of the past; heritage is a contemporary commodity purposefully created to satisfy contemporary consumption. One becomes the other through a process of commodification'.

As a local response to global challenges, Lunenburg's decision to pursue UNESCO designation and commodification of its culture for tourism may have resulted in an *iatrogenic* situation in the community, that is, a situation that has been induced by the intervention of unnatural forces. Impacts and consequences have manifested to thwart the natural evolutionary process under which the community's traditional culture evolved and maintained over time. Long-standing mechanisms have since been replaced by new modes of accumulating, transmitting and reproducing culture (e.g. tourism marketers and promoters). Furthermore, one might adamantly argue that what has been commo-dified for tourism may not accurately reflect the *authentic* culture of Lunenburg. Surprisingly, George's research (2004) work on Lunenburg could find no substantial data about the roles and lives of women over its 250 years of evolution.

Gentrification in Lunenburg

Research done on Lunenburg showed that, through the conversion of many of the waterfront areas formerly used by fishermen and industry, and older dwellings and buildings, now used for commercial inns and B&Bs, restaurants and other upscale shops, gentrification has quickly become a phenomenon in Lunenburg (see Figure 3.5). There are several interrelated factors to explain why this was occurring.

First, through the UNESCO designation, the community repositioned itself as a scientific, educational and cultural zone. This has implicitly given Lunenburg an image associated with the upper-middle class. Not only has this image attracted a certain *type* of tourist, as supported by data collected in the research study, it has also attracted a particular *type* of real estate buyer to the community. The local real estate agencies have been instrumental in the gentrifying process. These agencies have taken advantage of the UNESCO designation, the designated historic homes and heritage buildings, and the prestige that this brings, to develop and build a selling

Figure 3.5 From ship chandlery to restaurant

image targeted at an affluent market outside the local area (i.e. international and out-of-province buyers from more prosperous areas).

After the designation, one local real estate agency quickly positioned itself in an alliance with Sotheby's of London and Bermuda, an upscale real estate agency and international selling firm. Its own storefront façade reflects this image and is designed to attract upscale buyers, particularly travelers and tourists who, according to a local businessman working in a local real estate business, ' ... fall in love with the area and want to buy property there' (George, 2004). As a result of inflated prices and increasing sales to more affluent buyers, assessment values and subsequent taxes have risen substantially over the last decade. In fact, the value of real property has outstripped the wealth of the community. Many locals can no longer afford to live there. A different class of resident is replacing them.

> The beautiful old historic homes, one of the major attractions in the town, have reached a point where it was now becoming a negative in driving property values to a point that very few starters could afford to buy properties. In Old Town there are very few who are not affluent or retire who buy here ... drives away younger people to the periphery ... (George, 2004)

A second factor in explaining gentrification in Lunenburg is related to the intensity of 'upscaling' and improvements in local infrastructure by community planners and developers in the community – primarily for tourism purposes. Traditional, once dominant working spaces have now been transformed into tourism zones. The restructured waterfront area, formerly the domain of working-class fishermen, exemplifies this change. Other industry spaces and facilities, including an ice-making plant, docking space for fishing vessels, repair and maintenance marine shops, have been converted into new tourist attractions, including a large museum and aquarium complex, tour bus areas (charter buses), multiple restaurants and touristy shops. Kiosks promoting local tours and other tourist activities now line the waterfront area during the tourist season.

Much of the waterfront area is no longer accessible to ordinary local residents, only those who work that area for tourism. For example, the former wharf and docking areas, which now house the museum complex, are accessible only to paying visitors/tourists who must gain entry through the museum entrance. Infrastructure development also meant a new paved street and parking lot in the tourism zone to accommodate tourists and other visitors as well as numerous charter tour buses that frequent the community during the tourism season from

May to October. Other more recent actions include requests for proposals to develop a Lunenburg Waterfront Master Plan (Halifax Chronicle Herald, Friday, 5 June 2004). The terms of reference highlight the waterfront area as 'the major tourism attraction in town' (Terms of Reference, Town of Lunenburg, 2004: 1): proposals were to address criterion that would 'incorporate heritage uses and structures and create a dynamic waterfront that can accommodate an exciting mix of the often conflicting activities of the fishing/marine industry, increasing tourism and year-round access to the waterfront by the residents of Lunenburg' (p. 2).

A third factor related to tourism-related gentrification in Lunenburg has been the community's shift from a primary resource-based economy (fishing) to a service-based economy (tourism) which produces a different set of occupation options, many requiring other skill-sets and offering lower-paying employment. With lower incomes and fewer employment options available, a future life for local youth wishing to live and work in the local community is rather bleak and unpromising. Traditionally, youth were expected to follow in the footsteps of father, grandfather and forefathers, demanding a different set of skills, mainly related to seafaring industries. These skills are now, for the most part, obsolete in the community's new dominant industry – tourism. Generally, there is a lack of career advancement or high-end employment opportunities in the tourism industry, an industry that is widely perceived to provide low-paying jobs for an unskilled labor force. Cukier, in Sharpley and Telfer (2002: 166) writes, 'It is not difficult to find testimony from "developed countries" concerning the seasonality, servile nature and low remuneration of tourism employment'. Youth have been forced to leave the community to seek employment and affordable quality of life elsewhere. 'Once the rents and housing prices are not affordable to people with lower incomes, people with lower incomes cannot move into the neighborhood' (Wetzel, 2004). The resulting social situation helps shape a setting that is ripe for gentrification and potential displacement by newcomers who *can* afford to buy homes/businesses in the community and reside there.

Such a combination of factors offers a rather bleak and unpromising future for youth wishing to live and work in the community, and has 'fanned the fires' of gentrification. The community has also become attractive to potential outside investors and entrepreneurs who want to seize the opportunity to capitalize on the newfound fame of Lunenburg as a World Heritage Site and tourism potential.

Conclusion

Lunenburg's response – tourism: A shift to a service-based industry

The UNESCO World Heritage Site designation in 1995 became a major catalyst to propel Lunenburg into full-fledged tourism planning and development, and subsequently, to advance a commodification of local culture processes in the community. All too frequently, many small rural communities, losing their historical economic base, frantically begin searching for new types of economic development – they throw out a wide *net* (George, 1995). Often, in desperation, tourism is viewed as the economic salvation of these communities (Inskeep, 1991). Tourism, according to the literature and discourse, is gaining prominence as a prevailing and universal feature of capitalism and economic development in both rural and urban domains. Much of what has happened in Lunenburg's tourism development may have been a matter of good timing and chance. Some may argue that tourism in this community can be described as latent but nonetheless, a spontaneous and organic development. Although George's research (2004) suggests there had been some sporadic tourism activity over the years, it may well have been around that critical time in the early 1990s, when simultaneous events occurred – decline of its mainstay industry, a parallel resurgence of interest in heritage preservation in the community, the global 'cultural turn', the UNESCO designation and other factors, that Lunenburg would inevitably turn to tourism as a response to the challenges it now faced.

Adopting tourism would become a challenge in itself. Tourism is typically a service-based industry, which caters to the needs and demands of a consuming public, and operates under a different set of principles than what the original community had been accustomed to in the past. The Town Council's increasing efforts to market and promote tourism activities, not only to the external world, but also internally within the community, emphasized Lunenburg's unique culture as appealing and competitively advantageous, furthering the notion to commodify this culture. The Council's increasing focus on heritage and architectural controls aimed at achieving its tourism objectives, and on tourism as a diversification strategy for economic development in the community, further accelerated the process. However, as alluded to earlier, it became obvious there was no community involvement in these activities and any serious planning discussion or decision-making was generally done in isolation of local citizen input or participation.

In the case of Lunenburg, the Town Council, as the community's power base, continues today to hold decision-making authority and dominate tourism planning and development in the community. In its earlier enthusiasm, passion and sincerity to achieve economic diversification and community sustainability, the Council neglected to consult the community-at-large to consider potential consequences and ramifications that such a radical shift towards tourism development could bring to the community and its residents. In such situations, when a community is ignored, the residents, who are the creators and owners of community culture, have their ownership privileges revoked. The community is excluded from planning and decision-making processes with intentions to *sell* its culture for tourism. These processes are often spearheaded by a few individuals for personal profit and gain. In truth, this is where a community becomes a victim of cultural appropriation, a growing characteristic of corporate capitalism that perpetuates tourism development.

After it failed to get community consultation in the initial stages to pursue UNESCO designation, Town of Lunenburg authorities later found it necessary to engage an outside expert consultant to survey community residents, to gain their perspectives and input on how to move forward with tourism in the community. Had such a process been introduced before the designation, the subsequent unfolding of developments may have been different. On the other hand, such *ideal* community processes may have prevented the community from achieving the prestigious UNESCO designation so quickly, and, consequently, the community would not enjoy the multiple successes and benefits it has received from the award. For instance, Lunenburg received financial assistance for a new multimillion dollar sewage treatment plant that opened in 2003, and the local business community has enjoyed economic benefits from tourism.

While there was fairly extensive planning by the Town Council around the application for designation, there was an element of surprise and disbelief with the actual announcement of the World Heritage Site designation. The Council had been led to believe that the process to get a community listed would take much longer and that global competition for such a prestigious position was intense. When it did occur so quickly, the Council was elated, but at the same time, somewhat astounded and unprepared for the potential ramifications that it might have on the community. Moreover, with the shift to a tourism industry, many signs have become apparent that suggest the community may be falling prey to another *trap* of dependency – on tourism. George's (2004) research in Lunenburg revealed that several local businesses had become highly dependent on tourist markets and they had a mounting focus on tourism development and related activities. That tourism yields rapid, considerable returns on investments and can be a positive force in remedying economic problems (Mathieson & Wall, 1982), is a view commonly promoted by governments, development agencies, financial organizations, planning departments, local councils and other groups, to counteract economic difficulties that plague rural communities. However, dependency on tourism is a subtle force that tends to befall many communities. If local tourism decision-makers and community planners do not appropriately assess, plan, monitor and control development, this may once again be the case in Lunenburg. This notion is discussed later in this text.

Tourism development in Lunenburg, as a response to globalization forces and change, has not delivered the 'economic savior' that many hoped it would. In a more recent study, (George, 2006) uncovered a stark contrast in the attitudes of residents toward tourism in the community. About half the local residents tend to support tourism and believe that more investment in marketing the community's UNESCO status is critical to the community's future and tourism success. In contrast, many see tourism as destructive to their community. Very few still hold on to a dream, perhaps foolishly, that fishing may return to the community – a fishing industry resurrected. What has become clearly evident, however, is that the community, as a collective whole, does not fully support tourism development. Perhaps this view was predictable because, as discussed, the community had little or no involvement in the consultation processes leading up to the UNESCO designation or subsequent tourism planning. Only after the actual inscription took place did any serious community consultation occur. Many felt the UNESCO scenario had merely been a maneuver of the Town authorities, with little or no regard for the rest of the community.

Reid *et al.* (2002) suggest that when locals are not involved in the planning processes for tourism, tensions and conflicts frequently arise. Evidence suggests that tourism in Lunenburg has not been well-planned at all; it appears to have been a whimsical response to changes brought about by external factors and circumstance. Doxey's Irridex Index (1976) outlines several phases of community irritation and related social and power relationships regarding tourism development. These four stages include: euphoria, where tourists are welcomed and development occurs with little formalized planning; apathy, where tourists are taken for granted and marketing becomes the focus of planning (power); annoyance, where residents begin to have some misgivings about tourism and local protest groups may develop to challenge institutional tourism power; and, finally, antagonism, where residents see tourists as the cause of many problems in their community; there could be remedial planning or fighting against pressures of increased promotion to offset the declining reputation of the destination, and also a power struggle may erupt between interest groups.

Lunenburg's future

From recent research (George, 2006) in Lunenburg, it became apparent that the community has reached the annoyance or even antagonism phase of Doxey's Irridex Index. Social and political power relationships were clearly evident as concerns around the community's culture, identity and integrity had become a serious issue. Disappointed with what was happening to the community and reluctant to accept tourism as its economic mainstay industry, a local citizens' group mobilized in 2004 in efforts to take back control of development and its community's future. The Lunenburg Waterfront Association Inc. (LWAI) was formed as a mechanism to regain ownership of the community's waterfront area with intentions to revitalize it into a working waterfront once again. The LWAI Website (2007) outlines the announcement, which fuelled community outrage and fears that sparked the subsequent conception of the association:

In late 2003 Clearwater Fine Foods announced the planned divestiture of its sizeable Lunenburg real holdings: eight wharves, 24 buildings and approximately 14 acres, consisting of the bulk of Lunenburg's historic waterfront. Every aspect of Lunenburg's economy, identity and culture, and its appeal as a place to live and work is related to the town's status as a working waterfront community. The waterfront is the core economic engine of Lunenburg, not only in direct marine-related jobs, but also as a major generator of visits in the town's successful tourism sector.

The complex role of the waterfront would be compromised if it became something other than an active working place between sea and land. It is the consensus that the area for sale should remain part of a working waterfront. While heritage and cultural issues are also at stake, the ultimate defining issue is the overall economy and most specifically, jobs. In recent years many jobs have been lost or displaced due to a downturn in the fishery. A well-planned working waterfront can help to reverse this trend.

Clearwater Fine Foods, a large international fishing conglomerate, was a major player in the Lunenburg fishery, particularly the scallop fishing industry, and over the years had acquired much of the historic property and buildings on the waterfront since the company moved some of its operations to Lunenburg decades ago. Clearwater began as a small fishing business in rural Nova Scotia by two entrepreneurs who, back in 1976, 'started with a pick-up truck and optimistic vision' (Clearwater: History, 2007). The company had since grown and prospered to become one of the world's leading seafood companies, exerting powerful influence in a highly regulated fishery. The company operated a large fleet of vessels and several processing plants throughout Eastern Canada. In 2002, aiming to position Clearwater as a leader in the international seafood sector, the company president announced details of a $200-million public offering to finance expansion plans. Clearly, Clearwater's corporate success had been achieved from riding the waves of globalization, in which it has 'cultivated and maintained this spirit in its worldwide operations and combined it with innovative product design, marketing techniques and technological advances' (Clearwater: What's New, 2007). In February 2007, the company announced a new Public Offering; net proceeds of the Offering was to be used to enhance Clearwater's capital structure and more importantly to provide the flexibility to allow Clearwater to pursue potential accretive acquisitions that would be a strategic fit with its plan for growth (Clearwater, 2007).

The increasingly inflated value of real property in Lunenburg, largely due to the gentrifying effects of tourism, discussed earlier, had seemingly outstripped the community's wealth and ability to retain many buildings in the community. The community could not afford the hefty sale price tag that Clearwater had attached to the historic waterfront assets, some of which were in a dilapidated condition. The ongoing efforts of the LWAI since 2004 have proved rewarding. In 2005, the Association negotiated an agreement with the Nova Scotia government for a provincial loan, which allowed the community to reclaim some of it historic waterfront properties and guide its future development. According to the Premier at the time (2005), 'The province had to intervene and buy the string of red buildings to prevent them from falling into the hands of questionable developers ... [and] give the community the ability to control their waterfront'. Committed to its goals, the association completed a comprehensive Business Plan (Lunenburg Waterfront Association, January 2007) outlining a proposed future for the properties and the community.

While the waterfront is still considered a major generator of tourism, it is obvious that the real agenda behind its purchase is to develop a working waterfront area to encompass a new marine industry. After the Province of Nova Scotia agreed to give the organization a $5.5 million loan to purchase the waterfront land and property, the LWAI leadership commented, '... first thank you goes to the community, who really understood the importance of our controlling the future and developing it as a working waterfront, not turning it into a residential, tourist or museum activity' (Tradewinds, 2005). Further, the LWAI stated, 'Clearly what the community doesn't want to do is freeze itself in time and become a tourism community or a museum. We don't want to freeze ourselves in time and become a tourist trap' (Tradewinds, 2005).

Ironically, in what appears to be a strange twist of fate, Lunenburg found itself 'buying back' its own original cultural creations, identity and legacy. Dynamics brought about by its 'responsive' approach to tourism development have aroused a new awakening in community spirit. However, this time, it appears this small rural community has become more cautious, not responding so quickly to the 'winds' of change, but rather, taking more time to plan for development in efforts to control its own future and destiny. The question arises, though, 'Will appropriate planning for ongoing tourism development be part of that future?'

Chapter 4
The Case of Port Stanley, Ontario

Introduction

After a slump in tourism activity, Port Stanley is springing back into favor as a tourism destination. This area has had a long history as a popular destination from the 1920s to the late 1960s, when locals began to take longer vacations in more exotic or pristine areas passing up local tired destinations like Port Stanley. Lately, however, local people and visitors from farther a field have reconnected with this area as a tourism destination again. Entrepreneurial efforts to develop new businesses and an environmental clean-up of the surrounding beaches have been strong factors in the reestablishment of tourism in this community. Many of the old private cottages are now giving way to redevelopment that is also contributing to the revitalization.

Interview results from a limited number of town officials and business people suggest that apart from the activities of the local business association, there is either little or no effort to plan tourism development over the long-term or a concerted effort to bring community stakeholders into the process on an ongoing basis and before systemic problems arise again. Hopefully this apparent lack of involvement and planning will change to make tourism in the Port more sustainable. Given that tourism is in a rejuvenation stage following an earlier period, it is integrated into the community psyche and now understood to be a main economic activity of the area (Figure 4.1). There does seem to be a consensus that tourism is always going to be a part of the community and it will mainly be centered on the beach and lakefront with some extension to the shopping area. There is support by tourists for the novelty and beach shops that are sprinkled on the two main streets that are separated from the beach district. Tourism is actively encouraged as a mechanism for attracting permanent residents and rebuilding what was considered to be a dying village. Residents' concerns, including traffic, noise, the tone of tourism development and pollution, are dealt with incrementally as locals initiate petitions and speak at council meetings. Some residents noted that they 'lost their community' in the tourist season, but that

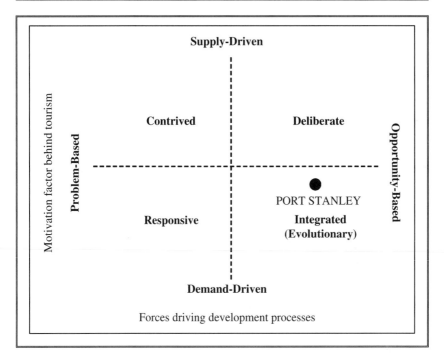

Figure 4.1 Port Stanley's approach to tourism development

community activities in the off season (as organized by service clubs) brought them together and made the trade-off seem justifiable.

There is an overall sense from the respondents in this community that continued tourism development is needed and that improvements could be made to the degree of coordination of tourism and community activities particularly as they affect local residents. Citizens recognize that there is the potential for conflicts over the use of the harbor to meet the needs of natural resource-based industries in the community (a working fishery and agricultural shipments) and the development of that same harbor area for tourists and leisure craft. But, they suggested that government and residents, upon understanding the benefits that tourism can bring to the community, should accommodate and encourage this development.

Communication, trust and an open dialogue to discuss the details surrounding the development of tourism activities was strongly emphasized by citizens of Port Stanley. Because a recent attempt to bring in a tourism activity was perceived by residents to be cloaked in secrecy and owned by people from outside the community, efforts were made to block its development, making it so difficult that the activity was abandoned altogether. Better communication and openness about the project may have produced a different outcome. Respondents expressed that they weren't necessarily opposed to the activity itself; it was more that they felt that the decision-making process had left them completely out of the discussion.

Key Theoretical Concepts: Rejuvenation; Integration

A number of tourism communities provide destinations that receive and give pleasure to many tourists until they lose favor with those same tourists due to changing fashion, or until the communities themselves become tired and rundown through the lack of renewal and rejuvenation. Port Stanley represents such a case. The tourism enterprise in Port Stanley has followed Butler's tourism product life cycle model through its historic development into decline and now into rejuvenation (see Figure 4.2). Butler's (2006: 5) model provides a framework for describing the stages through which a tourism product passes, from early conceptualization to stagnation and decline or rejuvenation starting the cycle over again. Port Stanley presents a classic example of the process of rejuvenation and renewal of a tourism community. This community, once a highly functioning tourism area, passed through the stages of stagnation and decline and is now in the process of becoming refreshed and transformed into an attractive destination once again. This chapter follows the history of this development.

Port Stanley is also a good example of an integrated tourism community given that it has always enjoyed a diversified economy, with tourism incorporated into the overall economy along with other assorted sectors (see Figure 4.7). It can be argued that even the tourism sector itself has become more diversified in this latest round of rejuvenation and renewal.

Research Approach

The research conducted for this project consisted of three separate approaches: secondary analysis of existing data, informal interviews and field observation. Individual members of the research team made several field trips to this site over a number of years for the purpose of producing this volume as well as for other related projects. The intent of the interviews and observations was to come to understand the development

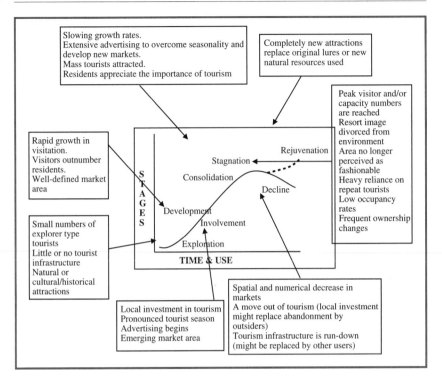

Slowing growth rates.
Extensive advertising to overcome seasonality and develop new markets.
Mass tourists attracted.
Residents appreciate the importance of tourism

Completely new attractions replace original lures or new natural resources used

Peak visitor and/or capacity numbers are reached
Resort image divorced from environment
Area no longer perceived as fashionable
Heavy reliance on repeat tourists
Low occupancy rates
Frequent ownership changes

Rapid growth in visitation.
Visitors outnumber residents.
Well-defined market area

Rejuvenation

Stagnation

Consolidation

Decline

STAGES

Development

Involvement

Small numbers of explorer type tourists
Little or no tourist infrastructure
Natural or cultural/historical attractions

Exploration

TIME & USE

Spatial and numerical decrease in markets
A move out of tourism (local investment might replace abandonment by outsiders)
Tourism infrastructure is run-down (might be replaced by other users)

Local investment in tourism
Pronounced tourist season
Advertising begins
Emerging market area

Figure 4.2 Butler's tourism product life cycle model

process and how the community members perceived the role that tourism played in their community's health. Statistics Canada Census Data (www.statisticscanada.ca), the Village of Port Stanley (www.portstanley.net) and Port Stanley Terminal Rail (www. pstr.on.ca) provided the secondary sources of data for the project. Interviews were conducted with local historians from the area as well as local business people and visitors. Given that there was no intent to test hypotheses, but simply to develop a working understanding of the changes taking place historically in the community, a convenience sample provided the best approach to data gathering during this part of the project.

The Case of Port Stanley

Background

Port Stanley is a rural community that engages tourism extensively in its economic diversification strategy. That said, it has also taken care to include other economic industries in its diversification strategy as well, whether by good luck or by good management. However, this location has had a long and interesting history as a tourism destination.

Port Stanley is situated on the north shore of Lake Erie, approximately half way between Toronto, Ontario, Canada and Detroit, MI, USA. It lies within a populous area of South-western Ontario and has been subjected to changing fortunes over the years because of technological alterations that have affected travel patterns and the changing fads and fancies of travelers. As can be seen from Figure 4.3, Port Stanley enjoys a strategic geographic position on the North American continent and is fortunate to possess the natural amenities that make it a potential tourism destination area.

The Port lies within the catchment areas of one small and one medium-size city, St. Thomas (population 25,000) approximately 9 kilometers distant, and London, Ontario (population 350,000) approximately 22 kilometers from the Port, respectively. It is also 20 kilometers from highway 401, the major transportation route along the Montreal (which includes Toronto) to Detroit corridor. The population of Port Stanley is 2385 (a decline of 4.6% since 1996 according to the 2001

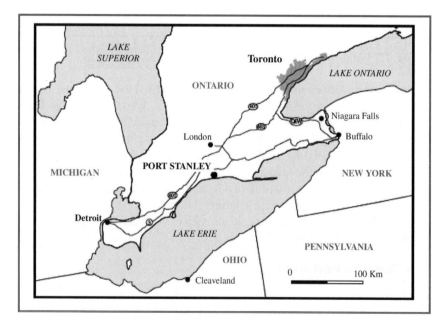

Figure 4.3 Location of Port Stanley within SW Ontario and the USA

Statistics Canada census) with a land mass of 3.9 km². Figure 4.3 provides a closer look at the geographic location of Port Stanley, particularly its situation on Lake Erie. Port Stanley provides an extensive sandy beach along most of the shore line within its boundaries. In addition to having the amenities of a sandy beach and lake that attracts many tourists, the area surrounding Port Stanley has other more subtle attractions as well. Hawks Cliff, which also overlooks the southern shore of Lake Erie adjacent to Port Stanley, provides a collection point for migratory birds, particularly hawks making the long trek south for the winter. This attracts large numbers of birders in the fall to watch this amazing natural phenomenon.

History

Historically, tourism in the Port has been demand driven in that it was sought out by many regional residents for the beach experience and the socialization which naturally transpired along with it. Early on, people visited the destination without the intent or promotion of local officials. It was the only attraction of its kind within close proximity to the two large urban centers in the area. Port Stanley contains a natural resource base with a substantial public beachfront that makes it, an appealing tourism destination supported by abundant (some would argue splendid) natural amenities (Figure 4.4).

Figure 4.4 The beach at Port Stanley
Source: Nikki Gosselin (2006)

The Port was connected to the larger communities of St. Thomas and London by the London and Port Stanley (L&PS) railroad (see Figure 4.5). This was a small independent railway that was initially developed to transport agriculture and natural resource products (i.e. coal) from the Great Lakes ships that visited the harbor, overland to the larger urban centers in the region. It also carried local agriculture produce grown in the area to those same ships to transport to other destinations. According to the present owners' web site (http://www.pstr.on.ca/history.htm), the first passenger train to reach the Port was in 1856. It provided a transportation system to the Port for the holidaymakers in the area as well as for shipping cargo. As the historical sketch of L&P on its web site suggests:

> It was only a short stroll to the beach from the railway station. Passenger traffic plummeted following the Second World War after reaching a peak of 1.1 million in 1943. The end of gas rationing and more use of the automobile caused the end of passenger service on February 1st 1957. From 1915 to this time, over 28 million people had ridden the L&PS. The Railway and its remaining freight traffic were traded in 1966 to the Canadian National Railways, for the CNR car repair shops property at York & Rectory streets in London.

Figure 4.5 The restored London and Port Stanley railroad
Source: Nikki Gosselin (2006)

The boardwalk that paralleled the shoreline along the beachfront was also lined with restaurants and arcade facilities that added another dimension to the holiday experience. Longer stays in a cottage was also possible either through rentals or purchase. There were some small and elegant hotels located at the Port providing additional but limited accommodation. During the late 1930s and early 1940s and into the 1950s Port Stanley was a primary, booming lakeside family resort in South-western Ontario.

Just prior to WWII, the construction on the beach of a pavilion and dance hall (Stork Club) added another dynamic to the destination (Figure 4.6). Focus was on creating an exciting nightlife as a compliment to the sun, sand and water activities that were popular at the time. It was at the Stork Club where many of the highly renowned big bands of the era, such as Duke Ellington and Stan Kenton among others, visited their music on the regional residents during the summer season. The main swing and jazz bands of that era circled the great lakes in both the USA and Canada, particularly rotating around Lake Erie, each summer attracting large crowds of people to their music. During the mid-20th century, the Port provided families of South-western Ontario with their summer playground.

While the 1930s and 1940s were the glory days of the Port, by the end of the 1950s and the early 1960s decline had set in. With the advent of greater ability for long distance travel and increased discretionary

Figure 4.6 The Stork Club

income, Port Stanley went into sharp decline as a tourism destination as visitors' patronized new, fresh, destinations. Would-be visitors were now looking farther a field, particularly to Ontario's pristine north land for their recreation experience. Many of the public and private buildings in Port Stanley became tired and worn and in need of redevelopment, which was not attended to on a large scale or in a systematic way. An additional factor in the demise of the Port as a major tourism attraction was the greater discretionary income of families due to an expanding economy during the 1950s and 1960s, and their new found ability to take longer vacations at greater distances and in more exotic locations. International tourism was also on the rise for middle-class families, who were beginning to replace local destinations like Port Stanley as their vacation choice with long distance destinations. So, as a tourism destination, Port Stanley went into the doldrums.

Port Stanley today

Port Stanley is comprised of 1301 private dwellings that consist of 725 families (Statistics Canada, 2001). That said, and because Port Stanley is a tourism town with a large beach adjacent to the shores of Lake Erie, the unofficial population (seasonal and transient) expands considerably during the summer months.

Port Stanley is a rural port community whose history is one of commercial and sport fishing, harbor facilities for shipping, particularly for coal and oil and for tourism. The community was the regional tourism destination for sand, sun and water tourism during its heyday in the mid-20th century. Port Stanley demonstrates a diverse economy, and it can be argued that it has a healthy industrial infrastructure to support efforts at tourism development (see Figure 4.7).

The median individual income for Port Stanley residents is $24,346 ($24,816 for the Province of Ontario) and for families it is $55,560 ($61,024 for the Province of Ontario) (Statistics Canada, 2001). It would appear that while individual income is comparable to the provincial average, family income is less than the Province's average.

Tourism development in Port Stanley

As a major tourism destination, Port Stanley has been somewhat dormant and has struggled throughout most of the 1970s, 1980s and early 1990s. However, over the past few years, it has undergone a small renaissance and rejuvenation. Perhaps the major development leading that renaissance has been the leveling of the Stork Club by fire and its

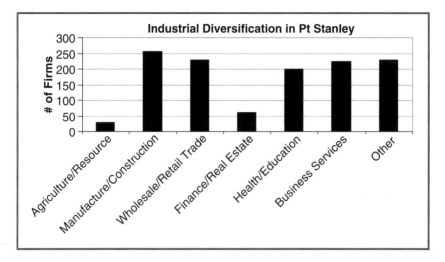

Figure 4.7 Port Stanley's economy

replacement by an upscale condominium development. This is both a feature, symbolizing the redevelopment, and a loss of one of South-western Ontario's greatest historical and cultural landmarks. In addition to the condominium development on the beachfront property which replaced the burned out Stork Club, has been the construction of condominiums on the cliffs overlooking the lakefront area. In addition to the permanent housing stock the condominium development repre-sents, this type of growth is also a good example of the gentrification of rural tourism destinations that has been spoken about extensively in other parts of this book.

In spite of the obvious problems associated with gentrification in maintaining historical conservation, Port Stanley has begun to replace some of the old buildings that have drifted into disrepair with modern day structures. Second summer homes through condominium develop-ment on lakeside properties is often a new strategy for redevelopment. Port Stanley has also been able to maintain its public beach function, including some of its historical private enterprises, which provides a connection with the historical past. Mackie's beachside restaurant and arcade is an example which has been on the beach for several decades and is now a cherished and continuing landmark.

The initial stage of community engagement has been the development of the Port Stanley Business Improvement Area (BIA). Its management board is spearheading the development of Port Stanley. The BIA's mandate is outlined in Section 204(1) of the Municipal Act 2001, which states in part:

> A local municipality may designate an area as an improvement area and may establish a board of management,
>
> *(a) to oversee the improvement, beautification and maintenance of municipally-owned land, buildings and structures in the area beyond that provided at the expense of the municipality generally, and;*
>
> *(b) to promote the area as a business or shopping area.*
>
> *As per Municipal By-law 543, Council designated and established an Improvement Area known as the Port Stanley Business Improvement Area (BIA) in June 2003. A nine member Board of Management has been approved by Council consisting of 5 members who were selected by a vote of the membership of the improvement area and appointed by Municipal Council; 2 Municipal Council representatives and; two municipal staff members who provide financial and clerical support. All members with the exception of municipal support staff have voting privileges.*

With the establishment of the BIA, the stage is set in the municipal system and in legislation for continued development of the citizen participation process. It is important for the BIA to identify and encourage other sectors of the economy beyond the business sector to become active in the tourism development process. Organizations like the Fisherman's Association and a cottagers and residents group now need to be officially identified in the planning process.

Recently, new tourism-related businesses and volunteers have also become more apparent. A group of volunteers has purchased the railway line and restored the long-ailing railway (now called the Port Stanley Terminal Rail Inc.). They have rebuilt designated and vital parts of the track bed and refurbished some of the passenger cars, which has again made the once grand L&PS operative for limited tourism excursions from St. Thomas to Port Stanley. The first of these trips was made in 1983 (see Figure 4.5).

The 1980s saw a rejuvenation of tourism in Port Stanley. While the beach again provided the major attraction, additional ways of engaging that resource were devised. As previously noted, the Stork Club had burned down and was replaced by condominiums. The exciting nightlife of the Port has given way to a more family oriented and longer stay excursions although some local night life still exists and is likely to continue to develop. Additionally, a more sophisticated shopping area, consisting of the usual tourist types of curio and art shops, has been created near the entry to the municipality.

Figure 4.8 The harbor and L&PS in Port Stanley

Along with the natural environment of the lakefront with its sandy beaches, Port Stanley has developed a shopping area on the west side of the bridge and harbor approximately one mile from the beach. The shopping area and the beach are separated by Kettle Creek that flows into Lake Erie. Access to the open water of the lake from the many marinas that are located on Kettle Creek is provided by a lift bridge (see Figure 4.8).

Figure 4.8 not only shows the lift bridge providing access for pleasure crafts to gain open water of the lake, but also the working port with its commercial fishing boats and the restaurants and hotels that line the harbor shore, as well as one of the passenger cars of the tourist railway that is resting at the Port Stanley station. Increased accommodation has helped to provide the needed infrastructure not only to attract but to encourage visitors to stay longer, turning potential day visits into longer stays. Of course, the beach and the lake are the main attractions of Port Stanley. Recreational activities such as beach volleyball have been introduced and provide a facility where young visitors collect.

Rejuvenation, Integration and Tourism in Port Stanley

Given that a community's tourism product is an import of visitors and their capital, rather than an export of goods as is typically the case, these types of communities act differently than districts that are exporting a product to another destination and receiving income in return. In tourism communities, the importation of people is the export. In that way, community tourism development gives a slightly new meaning to import/export theory. The potential problems this difference may generate are inflows of people beyond what a normal municipal infrastructure can accommodate, increased traffic congestion, social stress, cultural tension (particularly if it is a cross-cultural condition), business owners who do not live in the community and are influential in development but do not have to live constantly with the consequences, and the interruption of normal resident activity due to facility overuse and overcrowding.

Any redevelopment must consider not only the tourism product but also the state of housing stock, downtown remodeling, preservation of heritage sites and landmarks, traffic flows and general problems of living. To be sustainable, development must not overwhelm the community either physically or socially. In fact, tourism should be considered as part of an overall multi-sector diversification strategy and not the sole focus for development to the exclusion of other economic possibilities. On the positive side of community tourism development is the potential for increased amenities to be developed in the community that would otherwise not exist without tourism, such as restaurants, museums, attention to cleanliness and increased economic activity. Nevertheless, rejuvenation and development must be 'right sized' and how that is determined is a community affair. Like many other communities Port Stanley is grappling with that issue but has the advantage of having gone through this experience before.

While Butler (2006) applies the product life cycle notion to tourism products, he does not mention the specific application of his concept to tourism communities as a whole. There is no reason why this application cannot be made. However, communities are much more complicated entities than single stand-alone tourism products, particularly if they are not isolated social or physical environments that act as closed systems. Community tourism planning, particularly the principles of renewal, may provide the foundations for rejuvenation and integration. That said, Doxiadis (1996) reminds us of the basic truth during his investigation of renewal principles and renewal projects:

> Thus we are led to the conclusion that, because of the lack of specific goals, urban renewal as a whole has not developed a specific methodology for the formulation of policies and programs. There can be no commonly accepted policies and programs until specific goals for the programs are set and until a specific method has been

agreed upon for the proper estimate of the total size of the problem. Only then can the size of the problem be interrelated with the financial potential of the community that is to undertake the program and with the results to be expected from the implementation of the program.

The lack of specific goals for community tourism development is to be expected given that, for the most part, tourism in any community is usually driven incrementally by entrepreneurs (likely from outside the community) rather than comprehensively, by the community as a whole. Additionally, all communities are unique, so a 'one-size fits all' strategy is likely, in the best situation, to fail and in the worst circumstances, cause irreversible damage to the physical and social environment of the community. It is for these reasons that rejuvenation of tourism communities needs to be undertaken and controlled by all interests in the community and not just the business sector. This collective engagement provides the basis for true integration of tourism where the entire interests and aspirations of community members are included in the process and outcome.

This approach demands creating a clear vision that sets out concrete and achievable goals and principles on which tourism rejuvenation can proceed. Additionally, it must be a communal matter and not left completely to what some would describe as market forces. This model of development gives great consideration to the process of development and not just to product growth. This requirement may be even more vital for rejuvenation and integration of tourism in rural communities because of their reduced physical capacity to handle the issues described above and their increased sensitivity to outside influences.

While Butler's (2006) model, outlined in Figure 4.2, provides a conceptual tool with which to analyze the state of community tourism development, the question of whether or not it can be used as a tool of management as well, requires examination. Certainly, the potential to employ the model in this way is considerable. At the very least, tourism managers and planners can apply the stages of Butler's model as a framework for estimating the place their community occupies on the continuum. Once that estimation is made, then tourism managers have some indication of what is to come in the future and can, therefore, take steps to slow down or alter the trajectory of development taking place. Applying the model as an analytical framework causes tourism planners and community officials to understand the dynamics of tourism development and to realize that it is not a static phenomenon, and the 'golden egg' can tarnish quickly if not continually monitored, managed and directed. The monitoring process requires gazing outside the community for changes in the environment that can dramatically affect the tourism product (tourism and tourists are often said to be faddish) as it did in the case of Port Stanley. Constant evaluation of the tourism product and the social environment in which it is located is also critical to understanding the community's place on Butler's framework. Applying Butler's model can be best accomplished inside a community tourism planning process. The Port Stanley case demonstrates an intuitive understanding of this cycle based on the community's previous experience with tourism.

In addition to the issues that are presented above, the concern of employing tourism to revive a community that has lost its main 'raison d être' is of concern. A community under economic stress because it has lost its main industry may jump into tourism development without understanding the implications and what conditions and processes are necessary to establish a sound and sustainable venture. In the best case, tourism is introduced as an addition to a thriving community that is constituted by an array of other economic activities in addition to tourism. Port Stanley has created a diversified economy, of which tourism is one sector. So, the idea of integration then has at least two meanings. First is the integration of tourism into the community psyche that is achieved by the integrative planning process as outlined above. Second is the grafting of a tourism product onto an economic environment where tourism provides one part among many in the total community economy. A monoculture of any kind, including tourism, is not a healthy and sustainable approach for rural communities that are interested in economic advancement and continued good health and well-being.

In addition to the activities that are associated with sand and water, Port Stanley has created other attractions as well. In addition to the tourism-type shopping, an arts community has sprung up, a theater is situated over the old town hall, the library has been renovated and professional summer theater is now established. Not only is integration of tourism into the overall economy evident, but diversification of the tourism product is also being attempted. These integrations speak directly to the sustainability of the community and tourism development within it.

Conclusion

According to some business owners from the area, the potential for developing tourism in Port Stanley is much greater than most local government and some residents realize. The potential of the harbor (used primarily for fishing and agricultural transport) to become a draw for American boaters was often underscored by many of the residents we spoke to. Yet, this activity has never been capitalized on a grand scale. One respondent expressed frustration that the rest of the community was not far-sighted enough to push for changes in legislation that could open development of the marinas making them more accessible to larger boats and, by extension, wealthy American tourists coming form across the lake. What this respondent considered to be 'government short-sighted-ness' was an identified hindrance to the long-term development of tourism in the area. That said, there have been such schemes over the past that have not materialized for whatever reason. For example, a cruise boat that would cross the lake and dock in a US port was attempted in the 1990s but did not meet with success.

Other respondents recognized the possibility of future problems as the beach attractions could begin to take on a different, more relaxed tone. This outcome may not be consistent with the business model of the upscale boutiques in the village center. While some saw this differentiation as necessary to catch the various market niches, others foresaw that there may be conflict in terms of the image of Port Stanley and consequently the types that would be attracted.

Port Stanley appears to act fairly cohesively in using tourism as a way to attract those who will move permanently to the area. An annual weekend festival is organized and run by local service groups, businesses and individual citizens. These types of events also provide a leisure experience for locals as well as an attraction for tourists. Summer Theater on the second floor of the old municipal building and library seems to be successful. There are others within the community, often perceived to be mainly seniors, some of whom have moved there recently, who desire no more growth and change in the community. It would appear that these views are considered to be in the minority and most respondents felt that the negative aspects of tourism (traffic, crowds and noise) were just part of the tradeoff of attracting new people and income to the community.

With regard to tourism development more directly, the need to coordinate the activities, create partnerships and share resources and information (not just within the community but on a regional scale as well) was often noted as a way to help advance the goals and objectives of tourism in the community. It was felt that the more residents understood these goals and objectives, the more likely they would be to support development.

The research did not identify any mechanism for allowing input into decision-making with regard to tourism planning by community members. It often appeared to residents that tourism plans were made in a closed 'shop'. Respondents noted a division between those benefiting directly from tourism (i.e. businesses and tourism operators) and those who had to deal with the traffic, crowds and noise. In previous summers, residents living near a restaurant/bar on the beach initiated a petition to enforce the village's noise by-law and, on some occasions, resorted to calling the police to enforce it. Reports indicate that the parties met near the end of the summer to discuss the issue, but whether there will be changes made remains to be seen.

Because much of this community's appeal rests with the beaches, the issue of seasonality was commonly mentioned by respondents as a limiting factor in tourism growth. Many considered it quite difficult to earn a living at tourism given the relatively short beach season and were generally supportive of ideas that could help extend the season or pull more people into the area during winter. Currently, not many businesses remain open after early October, but that may change in the future if new events and attractions can be developed.

The environmental health of the beach and lake was discussed as one of the reasons why tourism growth slowed in the area in previous years. While not many respondents mentioned the environmental impact specifically, most acknowledged the value of the beach and the need to keep the natural areas clean and appealing. The latest round of tourism development is a direct result of rejuvenation along the beach, particularly the new condominiums that replaced the Stork Club from years past. While there is mixed feelings about the appropriateness of this condominium development instead of increasing the public beach area, the consensus is that the development was done properly if it had to be created at all.

The physical geography of Port Stanley, especially the village core, creates a traffic bottleneck that while mentioned frequently, was not viewed as an issue that could be handled without great cost. The problems of parking on weekends in the summer and the need for public washrooms were also common issues.

Issues of lack of community involvement during tourism activity development resulted in failure of many initiatives. It was suggested that these attractions were perceived as being developed in the absence of a consultation process or an adequate provision of background information (both about the attraction and the parties involved in the operation and funding) and openness. Respondents were generally suspicious of new initiatives that were brought into the community without transparency and open dialogue. In spite of these continuing difficulties and issues, Port Stanley continues to rejuvenate a long standing tourism destination for the betterment of both the residents and the visitors alike.

Chapter 5
The Case of Vulcan, Alberta

Introduction

With a population of 1940 (Statistics Canada, 2006), Vulcan is located about an hour's drive south of Alberta's biggest (and booming) oil and gas city of Calgary in the Western part of Canada. While the fortunes of Vulcan may not, at least currently, appear to rest with tourism development, community downturn in the mid-1980s pushed a group of community members to take the opportunities presented by tourism development very seriously indeed. This chapter presents the story of the development of *Star Trek*-related tourism in Vulcan, Alberta, insofar as it represents a problem-based, predominantly supply-driven response to economic downturn. Further, research in Vulcan indicates that what is left in the community is a rather contrived, if negotiated, tourism development. To reflect this, Figure 5.1 locates the case of Vulcan predominantly in the 'contrived' area, but also indicates that there were elements of responsive development.

Built around the agriculture industry, Vulcan has enjoyed periods of growth since its formal inception as a town in 1921. By the mid-1990s, there was a deliberate effort to build a tourism draw around the *Star Trek* theme (Town of Vulcan, n.d.). Perhaps this was an obvious choice given the town's name of Vulcan, as it was also the name of the planetary home of the character 'Spock' from the original *Star Trek* television series. After a series of community meetings and small projects that began to tap into the attraction and appeal of *Star Trek*, the nature and kind of development intensified rather dramatically. In 1995, a large replica of a space ship from the television series was built to attract cars passing the community. In 1998, a tourist bureau, the size and shape of a *Star Trek* space-station, and reportedly costing a million dollars, was officially opened. Since then, a variety *of Star Trek*-related activities and imagery has been used throughout the town to build on this theme. Pictures of characters from the show and its various spin-offs have been painted on the outside and inside of many downtown buildings and little green aliens are pictured on the directional signs along the main streets (Figure 5.2).

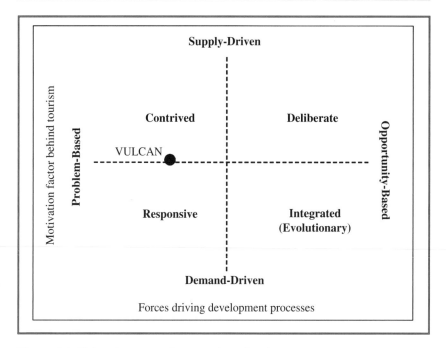

Figure 5.1 Vulcan's approach to tourism development

In this chapter, the events that frame the particular type of tourism crafted in Vulcan provide an intriguing and exemplary case study of rural tourism development. For example, assessing this case allows us to ask: how are television, film and fashion influencing the creation of themed consumption spaces for tourism in rural and urban areas? While movie and television themed tourism is growing, there have been relatively few efforts to investigate these developments (see Busby & Klug, 2001; Mordue, 2001; Riley *et al.*, 1998) nor to help us better understand how the creation of media-themed tourism settings plays out in local communities. The case presented here allows us to build on these understandings.

Key Theoretical Concepts: Contrived Tourism Developments; Contested Meanings of Place

The purpose of this section is to introduce key theoretical ideas that can be used to better understand the ways in which *Star Trek*-related tourism was negotiated in Vulcan. While the case of Vulcan is

Figure 5.2 Image of directional signs in Vulcan, Alberta

undoubtedly complex, two main theoretical ideas can be utilized here. First, the notion of a contrived tourism development offers essential insight into the kind of tourism development undertaken in Vulcan as well as the impacts thereof. As Paradis (2004: 198) notes, more and more communities are undertaking efforts to create themed experiences in their communities in order to attract businesses and tourists alike. He points out that '[t]hemes are social constructions, contrived and applied to the landscape by certain individuals with their own unique perspectives'. While there has been growing attention to the broader issue of contrived tourism, mostly through attention to simulated tourism environments, fantasy-based and even themed cities (see for instance, Forrester & Singh, 2005; Gottdiener, 2001; Hannigan, 1998; Paradis, 2004; Sorkin, 1992), there has been relatively little effort thus far to discuss rural communities directly. Paradis' (2002) work on Roswell, New Mexico, the fabled site of a UFO crash in the 1950s, and Mordue's discussion (2001) of Goathland (the film set of a very popular British television series about life in a rural community in the 1960s) are important exceptions and are discussed in more detail later. Moreover, Paradis (2004: 199) argues that community conflict over contrived themes may be 'particularly acute' in smaller towns and cities.

To a certain extent, all tourism settings are contrived. Great debates about the *authenticity* of attractions and communities engaging in tourism development have raged in Anthropology, Sociology and Cultural Studies. Moreover, recent developments in the social sciences push us to question the right of representation that underlie all tourism attractions; be they historical reenactments, museums, themed events or any other of the key tools used to manufacture things to draw visitors in from outside the community. Who decides how a community looks to tourists? How are these decisions made? Whose voice and perspective is privileged? Who is left out? Authors such as Morgan and Pritchard (1998) question the power relationships that enable some to make these decisions, thereby shaping the construction of the identity of the tourism place, leaving out other voices and interpretations that may be contradictory or seen as less attractive. Mordue (2001: 237) describes these relationships clearly:

> To talk of contestation over valuations of place, place identity, performance in place or indeed the integrity of any symbolic aspect of "tourist space" (MacCannell, 1976), is to flag the *cultural politics of tourism*. (Emphasis added)

McKay's study (1994) of the tourism industry in Nova Scotia offers an excellent example of an investigation into how culture and identity are selectively created in an effort to develop a tourism industry. His work shows how the owners and operators of Nova Scotia's tourism industry manipulated and created a more profitable image of the province; an image that rested upon 'the rural ideal' while masking existing violence and gendered inequalities. He writes:

> All of this, the ruggedly virile men, the virginal but accessible women, the romantic courtships, the happy families – constituted a way of reading gender relations in Nova Scotia. The fishermen with tuberculosis, the hard-pressed women who did at least half the work of the fishing economy, the unhappy families, the abused children – these anomalies were ignored. (McKay, 1994: 263)

Mitchell (1998: 89) describes the pressure in rural heritage-based tourism to capture the 'best of both worlds'. That is, there are 'carefully crafted products of a preindustrial society (e.g. quilts, pottery or stained glass)' combined with modern conveniences including parking, washrooms and air conditioning. While the case presented here is of a rather different flavor in that the tourism draw is not exactly based upon some sort of contested conception of the rural idyll, these ideas are still valuable in that they shed light on ways in which all identities are contested, valuing one person's or group's perspective over others. Indeed, Paradis (2004: 206) makes a distinction between 'heritage theming' and 'enterprise theming' and these ideas will be taken up again towards the end of the chapter.

Further, given what Mordue and others have described as a very political struggle over the contested meanings and representations of place, it is not wise to assume that this development of a contrived tourism experience/image is completely in the hands of the producers of that experience/image. As this case makes clear, it is the continually changing attitudes and actions of everyone who takes part in the life of Vulcan: those who want the *Star Trek* image to be an all-encompassing theme for community, the various tourists who visit (e.g. fans of the series as well as others) and the locals who live in Vulcan, which leads to a very nuanced, multifaceted experience of place. Mordue (2001) for example, calls our attention to the way the spaces of the community are experienced and created by all actors, not just tourists or tourism developers. He argues that even the tourists cannot be lumped into one category and that residents may be comfortable with some aspects of tourists behavior and not others (e.g. walking or hiking may be viewed as a less intense form of visitation, while driving, bus touring, shopping and parking in the downtown may be seen as more of a frustration for locals).

Research Approach

Time spent in the community of Vulcan made it clear that this was a town determined to survive economic hardships and to carve out an enduring image for itself. Two research trips were made to the community in 2006. During the second trip (December), in-depth interviews were conducted with key informants and lasted between 40 and 90 minutes. To add depth to the study and to help identify key informants for interviews, articles printed in the local newspaper, *The Vulcan Advocate*, were evaluated to gather a sense of the number and tone of the reports about tourism-related developments as well as community reactions. While spending time in the community, many informal conversations were had with locals in the downtown area. In addition, photographs of *Star Trek*-related images were taken. The interviews were tape recorded, transcribed verbatim and returned to the participants for additional comments and clarification. Key informants included: two members of a group called the Vulcan Association for Science and Trek (VAST) which was instrumental in launching the *Star Trek*-themed tourism; a member of the local government and owner of a downtown business; and individuals working in tourism and economic development-related areas in the town of Vulcan and surrounding County of Vulcan.

The Case of Vulcan, Alberta

Background

Unlike many rural communities and primarily due to the boom in the oil and gas industry in Alberta, Vulcan enjoyed a 10% increase in its population from 2001 to 2006. However, with 1940 residents in 2006, this is still a relatively small, homogeneous community with an aging population (Statistics Canada, 2006). The most recent statistics on income are from the 2001 Census data (Statistics Canada, 2001) and tell us that the median income for individuals in 2001 was $20,487 (as compared with $23,025 for all Albertans) and the median income for families for the same year was $49,335 (as compared with $60,142 for all Albertan families). Thus, the income levels in Vulcan are below the provincial average. Table 5.1 illustrates the industrial diversity of the community as compared with the rest of the province.

History

Voisey's (1988) book on the history of Vulcan traces its past as the center for wheat production and shipping. Vulcan played a very important role in early national development Strategies and was part of government policies to populate the Western part of the country, particularly through extension of the railroad. Thus, farming was a very successful undertaking in the West, especially for Vulcan and it became the center for grain production and shipping. Vulcan's legacy as the 'wheat capital of Canada', is forever captured in the emblematic and enduring image of nine large grain elevators along the railway tracks (referred to as the 'nine in a line'), which, while no longer in existence, stands as a testament to Vulcan's successful agricultural past.

While the fortunes of farming are chequered at best, consistent economic downturn throughout the latter part of the 20th century hit Vulcan as hard as any other community in the region. Indeed, as is described in more depth later, it soon became clear to members of the community that farming was not enough to sustain it. While today's relatively recent and dramatic boom in oil and gas production is undoubtedly changing the fortunes of many communities surrounding the city of Calgary, in the 1990s, Vulcan's residents were very worried about its future.

Table 5.1 Economic diversification in Vulcan, Alberta

Industry	Vulcan Town			Alberta		
	Total	*Male*	*Female*	*Total*	*Male*	*Female*
Total – experienced labor force (41)	860	455	405	1,681,985	913,385	768,595
Agriculture and other resource-based industries	80	60	15	184,105	134,380	49,725
Manufacturing and construction industries	110	90	15	264,940	213,885	51,055
Wholesale and retail trade	175	75	100	258,740	133,770	124,970
Finance and real estate	35	15	25	84,335	34,640	49,695
Health and education	190	50	140	259,050	58,095	200,955
Business services	120	65	35	316,265	190,780	125,490
Other services	150	75				

Source: Statistics Canada (2001)

It is also important to note that alongside financial downturns in farming in Canada, particularly at the small-scale level, there was an ideological shift influencing the nature of government involvement. As Marchak (1991) notes, neoliberalism and the language of down-sizing, restructuring, government efficiency and the withdrawal of the 'nanny state' were becoming pervasive throughout the 1990s and, as Mair (2006) has argued, helped set the stage for an encouragement of tourism-related answers to the conundrum of economic growth, particularly in rural parts of Canada. It is within this context that the case of Vulcan's tourism development trajectory must be understood.

Tourism Development in Vulcan

The Rural Initiatives Program: A community-visioning session

As researchers and academics concerned with encouraging participatory or community-based approaches to all forms of planning, tourism included, it is somewhat heartening to know that the seeds of Vulcan's tourism-related destiny were planted during early attempts to have at least a representative, participatory process for finding solutions to the economic challenges faced by the community. Each of the participants interviewed identified one or two key meetings in the early 1990s, when community leaders were brought together to hold a visioning process (supported and facilitated by the local community college).

It was at these meetings where the ideas about tourism, and *Star Trek* tourism in particular, came to the forefront – at least for a few people. While the idea of *Star Trek* wasn't a big hit at first, what came out of those meetings, at least for our purposes here, was a core group of individuals committed to building on the connection between the highly popular television series and the serendipity of the town's name. Stories of *Star Trek* fans driving to Vulcan to have their pictures taken in front of the cement town sign pushed this group to consider the television connection as an untapped resource and an indication of latent tourism demand. And so this group formed an association called the Vulcan Association for Science and Trek (VAST) and started to build a series of science and *Star Trek*-related projects and images in their community.

By the mid-1990s, a large replica space ship was built by a local and positioned close to the edge of town to lure traffic into the community, and at some later point, lights were put on the structure to make it visible in the night sky to oncoming traffic. Many local store-owners on Main Street had agreed to paint (or allow someone else to paint) *Star Trek*-related imagery on window fronts and building' walls. By 1998, a large

Figure 5.3 Vulcan Tourism and Trek Station

center, in the shape of a space station and housing some science-related materials was built as a tourism center just South of the community (costing, in the end, a million dollars) (Figure 5.3).

In addition, ongoing efforts to host *Star Trek* conventions, and to bring fans of the television show into the community for shopping and other activities were made throughout this time period. The conventions, ultimately called VulCons to reflect the town's name, were hosted annually and this event celebrated its 17th year in 2007. Over the last few years, this VulCon (now called Galaxyfest) has been held in conjunction with Spock Days, an annual festival that has been through a number of iterations (described in more depth later), but remains a family-oriented festival held in June.

Building a (Contested and Contrived) Tourism Image

While many of the discussions with research participants as well as more informal conversations with other locals revealed a humorous, almost whimsical approach to these developments, when one looks more carefully at the evolution of these events, one can see how adopting such a contrived (even alien) theme can lead to trouble. Indeed, it is perhaps not surprising that among the first and most consistent visitors to Vulcan were avid fans of the television shows, and research participants identified nearby fan clubs as being key supporters of *Star Trek*-related events. The 'Klingons'[1] and others, came to Vulcan dressed in character costumes from the shows and were acting out, or performing (Edensor, 2000), the *Star Trek* image in ways that made some locals uncomfortable, particularly those unfamiliar or unsupportive of the show. Early efforts to encourage the broader community to attend and support these tourism activities resulted in some difficulties, even physical aggression, as was the case during an early attempt to host a Klingon-style dinner as well as a dance for both the fan-tourists and participants in a rodeo at the same time. According to interview participants, while the fan-tourists were keen and perhaps even a bit too enthusiastic about playing their role as Klingons and other characters from the show, the community members were very uncomfortable and reacted negatively to the experience, once resulting in fights. Thus, while the connection between the community's name and the television series was apparent to this particular group, it was actively resisted by others in the community who felt it did not reflect who they were.

The members of VAST who participated in the interviews expressed regret that they had not realized that the local population might be unprepared for, or uncomfortable with, the way these visitors would behave. This caused the members of VAST and other community groups to separate the rodeo and other non-*Star Trek* events from events such as VulCon. Figure 5.4 shows the type of events that were held at Spock Days/Galaxyfest in 2007. From the various events, it is clear that the organizers are trying to create spaces where fans of the television show (and the community's tourism theme) can coexist and enjoy activities (such as the Klingon Fear Factor) with others who are merely looking for community-based activities they can enjoy with their families (e.g. the slow-pitch tournament).

Over the course of interviews, reviews of the local newspaper and observations in the community, it is clear that much has been invested in developing the theme of *Star Trek* in Vulcan. However, it has not been embraced widely by the rest of the community and interview participants expressed unhappiness with how uncoordinated and inconsistent the theme is; desiring a much more comprehensive *Star Trek* experience. When asked how they thought the rest of the community might be feeling

List of Events:

Friday June 8, 2007 - Around Town:

9–4:30 PM	Trek Station open regular business hours
4:30–6 PM	Station Closed
6–6:30 PM	Registration @ Trek Station
7–9 PM	Meet and Greet Reception at the Trek Station Featuring: The Official Launch of the new Vulcan Space Adventure Virtual Reality Game; Special appearance by this year's celebrity guests: Klingon Fear Factor (Round 1); Cash Bar & Appetizers.
	*NSA Sanctioned Slo-Pitch Tournament *Free BBQ Sponsored by Vulcan County *Fireworks

Saturday June 9, 2007 - Around Town:

	Telus World of Science Star Lab @ Vulcan Prairie View Elementary School - throughout the day
9–4:30 PM	Trek Station open regular business hours. Dealer's Tables in Patio Tent
10 AM	Parade
11:30–1:00 PM	Klingon Fear Factor Downtown (Round 2)
1:30–2:30 PM	Q&A Session @ Vulcan Trek Station Tent
3–5 PM	Autograph Session @ Legion
5:30–8:30 PM	Galaxyfest Banquet (featuring celebrity entertainment, constume contest, and Klingon Fear Factor finals) *Cabaret featuring: Live Entertainment TBA @ Vulcan County Central High School

Sunday June 10, 2007 - Around Town:

10–4:00 PM	Trek Station open regular business hours
10–12 noon	Take a traveller Breakfast/Video Conference @ Vulcan Prairie View Elementary School featuring an interactive Video Conference with Marie-Josee Potvin - a Research Engineer from the Canadian Space Agency who will explore: "Science Fact and Science Fiction". A Continental Breakfast Concession will be available.
	Slow-Pitch Finals

Figure 5.4 List of events for Spock Days/Galaxyfest
Source: Mair (2006); Town of Vulcan (2007)

about these developments, participants suggested that after 20 years, most residents have just resigned to the fact that it has developed this way. Moreover, there is no real indication that the influx of tourists to the area is translating into any meaningful economic development for the community. The workers at the Tourism and Trek Station estimate that 15,000 people come into the center every year (it is open year round), but also admitted that the numbers of people who then spend time (and money) in the rest of the community (just a short walk up the street) is far less than this. In fact, no real effort has been made to determine what the economic impact of these developments might actually be.

Newspaper analysis shows that during the first few years of the Tourism and Trek Stations' existence, great pains were made to record the number and address of visitors and to publish those results weekly. It does not appear that this has been continued to any consistent degree, although one interview participant expressed a desire to contribute to the paper, perhaps by writing a column to highlight and communicate developments at the Station and to report on the economic benefits. In addition, a new, large and reportedly expensive ($250,000) virtual reality game has just been built at the Tourism and Trek Station and given that half of the funding comes from the Town (Dickens, 2007), explanations and rationalizations will undoubtedly have to be forthcoming.

Reconnecting to Theoretical Concepts

Contesting and negotiating the meanings of community

Developing a theme for a community, as Paradis (2004), following Hannigan (1998) argues, is a way of transforming areas into destinations and centers of consumption; it should be noted that consumption is a fundamental theme underscoring this case and all of the cases in this book, although it may be clearest here in the discussion of Vulcan. As Paradis (2004: 200) notes:

> In a market economy based increasingly on consumption rather than production, contrived meanings and identities become all the more important to create perceived differences in products that are in actuality quite similar. In short, themes are designed specifically to promote the virtual and experiential consumption of places.

Of course, it is worth understanding the impact that this might have upon those who travel there. However, it might be even more valuable to begin to understand what impact this might have for those who live there, particularly for those in a small town embarking upon such a journey. While there has been much important work, which permeated early tourism studies and suggested that themed or contrived environments were some sort of effort to 'trick' tourists into thinking they were in a fantasy world (for a summary, see West, 2006), it is important to remember those who live in these communities and the stress that can be caused by living in such a fantasy (or alien) environment.

As the above case study discussion illustrates, there is a careful negotiation of this contrived tourism image at work in Vulcan and thus it is clear that there has not been an all-powerful, one-sided effort to brand this community. Indeed, there are many perspectives and motivations at play in Vulcan not least of which include: the members of VAST (now defunct but the key members of that group are still keen to continue to build on the *Star Trek* image); those concerned with drawing attention to the community to attract new residents and other forms of investment; locals who live there and do not connect with the imagery or events; and the tourists who may or may not come to the town to partake in *Star Trek* events and experiences. Navigating these varying motivations is a difficult task.

Further, the move to what Paradis (2004) calls 'enterprise theming' as opposed to 'heritage theming' may be important in terms of explaining the on-going resistance to the developments in Vulcan. While themes based upon heritage are also socially contested and privilege one perspective over another, perhaps building upon some version of history would be more acceptable than a completely fabricated, alien, identity. While some may see *Star Trek* imagery as whimsical and fun, others may read the theme as being sacrilegious (Paradis). In short, does it matter that this theme has no real connection to life in Vulcan?

Conclusions

In the 1980s, the jump to tourism seemed like a valid response to the economic realities facing Vulcan. The particularities of that jump, that is, the choice to follow a tourism development trajectory that many in the community found to be alien and alienating, however, can teach us many things about the way a tourism project can affect the identity and meaning of a community. This case is remarkably similar to Roswell, New Mexico, a community also experiencing economic downturn from its resource-based economy and where, as we learn through Paradis' (2002) work that the alien imagery accompanying the UFO theme in this community has elicited a wide array of community reactions, from support to embarrassment and resistance. These cases should help us to realize that reacting to a political economic situation with a tourism-related solution in a small town requires a much more careful and grounded approach. Voices of the community members, as many as possible, must be heard so that the decisions made to 'brand' a town are not met with resistance from those who have to live there. Also, it would help address some of the inevitable disappointment felt by those who dreamed of this theme taking off only to be unsatisfied with the results when the rest of the community failed to come on board. In Chapter 13, we present an approach that may help to plan, manage and perhaps even alleviate some of these tensions.

Ideally, what this case illustrates is that it is not a simple one-way process of an identity or an image (however alien) being imposed onto a community and being either accepted or outrightly objected by those who live there. Instead, we have a nearly 20-year process of negotiation and acceptance; where even the most outlandish and contrived images and ideas can be brought into the community and made its own. We don't know what the future holds for Vulcan, its short-term oil and gas fortunes probably make discussions of tourism-led growth seem dated and even unimportant. Nonetheless, it has crafted an image for itself that may well endure as long as the 'nine in a line'. Whether the community comes to celebrate or regret this decision, is a matter for another study sometime in the far distant future.

Note

1. Klingons are a race of very aggressive and distinct characters that have played major parts in all of the *Star Trek* series. With a fully realized culture, language, style of dress and social history, Klingons are probably the most identifiable and enduring characters from the series.

Chapter 6
The Case of Canso, Nova Scotia

Introduction

In this chapter, we discuss another small community in rural Nova Scotia, Canso that took a different approach to tourism development as a response to globalization and change, in an effort towards achieving community economic sustainability. The case of Canso discusses how one remote community, at a time when its future looked grim and in spite of having a lack of resources, deliberately created an attraction that would draw international tourists to the area and, subsequently, become a major economic generator for the area. Canso is placed in the quadrant labeled 'deliberate approach' indicated in Figure 6.1. This quadrant represents tourism development that has been a problem-based and supply-driven response.

Like Lunenburg, discussed in Chapter 3, Canso had depended on the fishery to sustain its local economy over several decades. When the Atlantic Canada fishery collapsed in the early 1990s, this remote community was perhaps one of those regions that were hardest hit. Generally, the entire community had totally depended, directly or indirectly, on the fishery for its mainstay livelihood; thus, the impacts of the fishery collapse were immediate and severe. In spite of not having the necessary infrastructure and other components to sustain a tourism industry, the community turned to tourism in hopes of alleviating its economic woes. Several theorists (Gunn, 1988, 2002; Pearce, 1981; Mill & Morrison, 1985; Nickerson & Kerr, 2001) claim that a destination must have critical components if it is to sustain any successful tourism development, for instance, necessary infrastructure, facilities, attractions, support systems, etc. Unlike Lunenburg, though, as previously dis-cussed, Canso did not purposely position itself as a tourism destination area; rather, it focused on a quick and short-term economic strategy. The plan was to open a short 'window' of economic opportunity during the summer period, one that would draw significant numbers of tourists to the area for a brief period of time. Initially, the festival was a one-day event but very quickly grew into a three-day tourism activity. Even so, because of this short-lived timeframe for tourism, Canso was what we

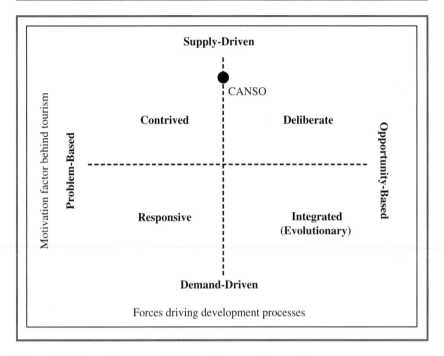

Figure 6.1 Canso's approach to tourism development

might refer to as an ephemeral or provisional 'destination'. Such a tourism development strategy undoubtedly can have both advantages and disadvantages for a destination. For example, any negative impacts would likely have limited impact on the area and can be mitigated more easily. On the other hand, the potential to maximize economic benefits from tourism would also be extremely limited.

Canso's tourism development strategy involved creating an attraction based on a particular cultural aspect, but, ironically, one that had very little relevance to the community's history or tradition. This attraction materialized as a festival event built around a singer/songwriter and his particular genre of music. To visitors and outsiders, the event has since become symbolic of a 'suffering' and resilient community, and its overwhelming struggle to survive. To the locals, however, it has become a symbol of community identity and a springboard to heal their wounded community spirit. Ten years since the festival's inception, the festival has achieved fame and acclaimed success. Canso's tourism development appeals to a specific niche market of tourists – musicians and songwriters – both domestic and international, and its popularity and reputation are growing. This case study chronicles Canso's 10-year journey to becoming a tourism destination.

Key Theoretical Concepts: Tourism Destination Development; Community/Place Identity; Cultural Tourism (Creative Cultural Industries)

Against all odds, this small remote community in Nova Scotia, Canada, has used the creative arts – music and song writing – to build a focal tourism attraction, which has now positioned Canso as an international cultural tourism destination. The attraction has not only helped to stimulate and revive the local economy, it has also lifted the community out of the doldrums and restored its dignity. This case leads us to challenge traditional theories explaining tourism development, and it raises questions about what have been considered essential components to developing sustainable and competitive destinations. It also supports and reinforces other perspectives, for example, how we measure and determine tourism 'success'. Arguably, tourism 'success' cannot be measured in economic terms alone, but must include the enormous social and cultural benefits it can also provide. Such benefits include: strengthening social cohesion and social sustainability, motivating volunteerism, building community capacity, enhancing/restoring community pride, fostering collective optimism and developing coping skills and resiliency. It, indeed, invokes other questions about the role of the creative cultural arts in tourism, in this case, music, not only for its utility in tourism product development, but also as a mechanism to expand old and new social relations and, in turn, reimage a new community identity.

To sum up, this case study serves to illustrate how, by contriving a culture-based festival attraction of music and song, borne from community struggle, resistance and perseverance, Canso has used tourism as a force to rejuvenate and rebuild its community, economically, as well as its pride and collective spirit. This alternate form of tourism might be considered social or civic or transformative tourism. The literature about tourism destination development and its role as an economic development strategy aimed at achieving community sustainability is fairly extensive; a few widely noted perspectives are highlighted in the following section. Also discussed are several other factors that emerged in this case study, including: community capacity and sustainable communities; social cohesion, social relations and social sustainability;

place (community) identity; and the notion of creative culture (arts and music) as a mechanism in tourism and cultural/social transformation.

Tourism destination development

The term 'destination' is often interchanged with other terms, such as 'destination zone', but basically it is the point of arrival or receiving area for tourists. The concept of a 'destination zone' as a tourism attractor and economic generator encompasses several elements: major access and gateway, community (with its infrastructure and services systems), attraction complexes and linkage corridors (between other attraction clusters and community) (Gunn, 2002: 222). Ideally, these elements need to be integrated for tourism to be successful. The destination zone is also referred to as a 'tourism destination area'. A destination may be a country, region, community or site. The geographic boundaries defining a destination zone or area are often blurred to tourists because, generally, they do not perceive or distinguish distinct borders in their concept of destination.

Albeit purporting minor variations, tourism theorists (Gunn, 1988, 2002; Pearce, 1981; Mill & Morrison, 1985; Nickerson & Kerr, 2001) generally agree that a tourism destination area requires several essential components. These components include: a focal attraction(s), hospitality services, complements to the focal attraction(s), supplementary activities, access system, community and integrating characteristics, which includes the overall ambiance and scale of tourism development in an area and how well these are integrated into the social and economic life of the community.

'One of the great challenges facing tourism is to clearly understand the factors that motivate individuals to choose one particular destination over the myriad of other possibilities' (Ritchie & Crouch, 2003: 110). Ritchie and Crouch argue that it really boils down to the core resources and attractors in an area that ultimately motivate the traveller to visit a particular area. It is the promise of an exciting and memorable experience. These resources and attractors include: the physiography of a destination, its culture and history, a range and mix of available activities; an adequate superstructure; entertainment and market ties. Even so, they note that while entertainment is often a complementary activity, it may be the primary appeal of the destination (Ritchie & Crouch, 2003: 111).

Many authors have heralded both the positive and negative impacts of tourism development, and its success or lack of it, particularly relating to how well it is planned and managed, and most importantly, how well the stakeholders, including community, were involved in the planning and development processes. Others have put forth notions of alternative tourism that might be considered gentler forms of tourism than the dominant traditional approaches to tourism development (i.e. mass tourism).

Community/place identity

One form of alternative tourism that is not so common is sometimes referred to as civic tourism. At the heart of this concept is the idea that tourism is a *means* for community development and not an end in itself. Tourism is viewed as an enabler of healthy place-making; tourism is an activity that might foster civic activity; tourism is a way of bringing citizens together (Shilling, 2006). Local involvement and community control contribute to successful tourism development (Chambers, 2006) and are critical to its long-term viability (Commission for Environment Cooperation, Canada).

Following a study on a Maori community in New Zealand, McIntosh *et al.* (2002) put forth another approach to tourism development; they presented the notion of 'attraction-based identity', where a community's identity would be purposefully constructed or 'adapted' to provide a cultural tourism experience; this was done in order to achieve sustainable tourism. 'Attracted-based identity, derived from Proshanksy's place-identity, is an attempt by members of a culture to portray their identity and values in a tourist recreation experience' (McIntosh, 2002: 42). According to McIntosh (2002: 42), three premises behind this notion are: (1) place-identity is a means for articulating cultural identity; (2) cultural identity can be consciously reproduced (commodified) within the purpose-built setting of an attraction (cultural identity is consciously constructed by proponents of the culture as a tourist experience, and/or may be modified to meet tourist demands) and (3) tourists will seek to understand and appreciate the significance of cultural values and identity. This concept may well be expanded further in its application to communities undertaking various forms of culture-based tourism aimed at achieving a sustainable economy. Ultimately, the driving factor behind any type of tourism development strategy is economic generation.

Proshansky's (1978) theory of place [community] identity refers to 'those dimensions of the self that define the individual's personal identity in relation to the physical environment' characterized by individually or collectively constructed attitudes, values, thoughts, beliefs, meanings and behaviour (Proshansky *et al.*, 1983: 62). This theory, based on the work of Relph (1976), as noted in McIntosh (2002), conceptualizes three main components of identity: static physical setting (physical features), activities (observable activities and functions) and meanings (or symbols). 'A sense of place or of identity is expressed and endures in the fusion of these interrelated elements' (McIntosh *et al.*, 2002: 41).

Renshaw (2002) presents some interesting revelations about how the processes of globalization are revolutionizing our world and are viewed as threats to many individuals, institutions, localities and traditions. In many cases, the globalizing phenomenon is seen as the root cause for dislocating and destabilizing many smaller (and larger) communities. Some argue it is the primary factor in the decline of traditional industry-based economies such as fishing and agriculture communities. Further, 'Globalization has strengthened the rise of individualism', he states, 'but this has not been accompanied by the social bonds necessary to sustain a stable and meaningful life' (Renshaw, 2002: 1). As a result, many people suffer from anxiety, insecurity and rootlessness and a sense of loss of individual and collective [community] identity. Thus, a community's social fabric, social capital and collective identity becomes weakened and dismantled, threatening its future sustainability. How to respond to this new reality and potential vulnerability is a major challenge for smaller communities, especially those in rural regions.

Cultural tourism and the role of the creative cultural industries (arts and music)

Much of the existing literature on cultural tourism generally refers to what is often defined as cultural heritage tourism – culture based on dimensions of the past, such as museums, local cultural traditions and unique ways of life, historical architecture and restorations, heritage and cultural landscapes and so on. This kind of tourism is touted for its many positive impacts – employment opportunities, preservation of important heritage and cultural markers, protection of heritage buildings, renaissance of lost or threatened cultural aspects, such as crafts, language and so on. There appears, however, to be far less research available that focuses specifically on another distinct form of cultural tourism, one that considers and draws on the creative cultural industries, for example, arts and music, as valuable assets for tourism development.

By adopting tourism as a response to globalizing changes, several local communities are creative and innovative in applying new approaches that will showcase their uniqueness and set them apart from other tourism destinations. In some instances, this includes placing an emphasis on the arts and music as core tourism demand generators. In the midst of the woes of globalization and economic crisis, Renshaw (2002) examines Mundy's (2000) work, which explores some of the ways in which the local 'arts and culture' world, the creative class, might respond. According to Renshaw, it is within the globalization context of blurred boundaries and contested assumptions that new horizons can be extended to provide new opportunities for innovation, ingenuity and creativity through the flexible use of collaborative networks. It is within this changing landscape, which includes varying positive and negative impacts resulting from advancing communication technologies (e.g. internet) that he argues the arts and music have a dynamic role to play. Change has given rise to:

> ... the creation of new industries which are dependent on knowl-edge-sharing and collaborative innovation within more localized areas (Leadbeater, 1999: 144–148). Given initiative and imagination, such developments can open up new possibilities for artistic ventures with local communities. (Renshaw, 2002)

With the potential danger of social and psychological disconnected-ness arising from the obsession with new communication technologies, noted above, Renshaw (2002) suggests that 'musicians are challenged to ensure that participatory music-making and live music in all its forms remain at the heart of any cultural life'. Matarasso's views (1997: 84) tend to support this notion:

> The greatest social impacts of participation in the arts ... arise from their ability to help people think critically about and questions their experiences and those of others, not in a discussion group but will all the excitement, danger, magic, colour, symbolism, feeling, metaphor and creativity that the arts offer. It is in the act of creativity that empowerment lies, and through sharing creativity that understand-ing and social inclusiveness are promoted.

The preceding theoretical discussion provides some context for examining the case of one rural community in Nova Scotia, Canada, and how it has contrived a music-based festival attraction designed to draw tourists to the region in response to some of the consequences and threatening impacts of global change. Next, we provide a brief overview of our research approach and background on Canso, and its particular situation.

Research Approach

The genesis for this research study came from revisiting an earlier study done in Canso shortly after the collapse of the Atlantic fishery in the early 1990s. For her Master's thesis, George undertook research that would investigate this single-industry community and the resulting plight when its mainstay industry failed. This industry failure led the community to consider tourism as a potential economic revitalization strategy. Conclusions drawn from that earlier study suggested the community had no potential whatsoever for tourism; consequently, the researcher criticized the Provincial government of the day for misleading Canso, and many similar rural communities, with false promises and hopes of tourism successes. In a reactive political approach, the government of the day hastily introduced a flurry of tourism development programs and incentives for those communities affected by the fishery collapse. Ten years later, however, it has become evident that Canso has, indeed, against all odds, achieved a remarkable degree of success with tourism. This revelation challenged the author's earlier research conclusions and renewed her interest in the community, hence, initiation of a reexamination and case study of the community and its situation 10 years later (2006–2007). Various primary and secondary research methods were used to collect data for this study, including: document analysis (newspaper clippings, books, articles, press releases and thesis), audio-recordings analysis (previously recorded public interviews), digital photography, field-observation, participant-observation and personal conversations. Data were collected over a one-year period from May 2006 to July 2007.

The Case of Canso

Background

Canso, a small coastal community in Nova Scotia, Canada was one of the many rural coastal communities on the East coast of Canada affected by the collapse of the Atlantic fishery in the early 1990s. The small community, situated on the North-east tip of the Province of Nova Scotia (see Figure 6.2), is somewhat isolated and remote because of its distance from the Trans Canada highway and Antigonish, its nearest significant commercial center located about 114 km away. Historically dependent on the fishery, Canso quickly fell into a state of crisis with disruptions to and the ultimate collapse of its traditional fishery. In 1991, the population of Canso was about 1200, but with the eventual collapse of the fishery, the

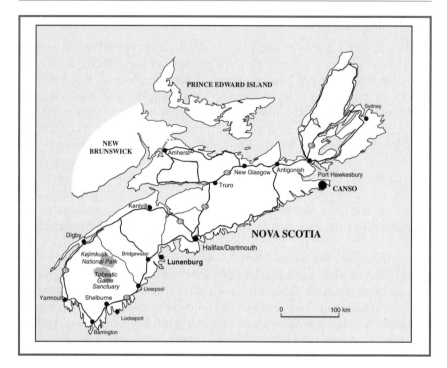

Figure 6.2 Location of Canso, Nova Scotia, Canada

number rapidly declined leading to other social consequences and challenges for the community.

History

In 1987, Canso's largest employer, a fish plant then owned by National Sea Products (NSP), a well-known seafood conglomerate in Canada, along with its four offshore trawlers that supplied fish to the plant for processing, employed about 700 local people (Benedetti, 1994). Provincial government funding had heavily supported the plant over the years to keep it operating so as to sustain the local economy and employment base in the region. In spite of receiving 'special' financial treatment earlier in 1984 when the Provincial government loaned NSP $35.5 million in hopes of providing 1100 jobs at Canso (Meek, 1994), the company, noting declining profits, announced permanent closure of its year-round operations in 1989 (George, 1995). This startling move threw the community into a state of shock and despair. The plant was shut down putting more than 700 workers and trawlermen in the area out of work (Canso Historical Society, 2004).

Shortly thereafter, in 1990, after much protest and lobbying by the community and local politicians, the Provincial government entered into an agreement with another seafood company, Sea Freez Foods, to purchase and continue operating the plant. The deal resulted in the company assuming the previous owners' debt with no interest payable to the government for three years. In return, the new owners promised to provide 500 jobs for 10 months of the year at the plant (Meek, 1994) and, according to the Fisheries Minister at the time, long-term employment for 20 years. This forecast would prove to be overly optimistic and unrealistic (Canso Historical Society, 2004). A groundfish moratorium in Atlantic Canada, put in place in July 1992 by the Federal government, aggravated any hopes of reviving economic stability in Canso based on the fishery (George, 1995). The ground fishery, according to government scientists, had become unsustainable and had collapsed. Fish quotas and restrictions that were imposed by the government severely hampered Sea Freez' efforts to keep the processing facility operating as planned.

For over a century, fish plant workers and sea-going fishermen had traditionally provided the backbone of this rural community's economy. The entire community, basically, had been reliant on one single industry – fishing. It was now faced with a new cruel reality stemming from the severe impacts of plant closures and subsequent loss of its mainstay industry – this economy was gone. Canso, like many coastal communities in Atlantic Canada that have historically relied on the fishery for their livelihood, was confronted with the task of diversifying to create much-needed local jobs (Canso Historical Society, 2004: 316) if it were to survive.

Responding to the demise of one of Atlantic Canada's primary and significant economic industries, which impacted so many small rural communities in the region, the Federal government intervened with a flurry of new programs and incentives aimed at promoting tourism as an economic generator (George, 1995). The community of Canso, emerging from an intense grieving process, took up the challenge and responded and, despite not having what tourism planning theorists (Getz, 1986; Gunn, 2002; Inskeep, 1991; Murphy, 1985; Mill & Morrison, 1989; Crouch & Ritchie, 2003) would argue are necessary and critical components for destination development – infrastructure, resources and expertise – set about to develop tourism in efforts to save its dwindling economy and community. Tables 6.1 and 6.2 provide industry and community profiles of Canso.

Table 6.1 Industry profile of Canso, Nova Scotia

Industry 2001	Canso Town			Nova Scotia		
	Total	*Male*	*Female*	*Total*	*Male*	*Female*
Total – experienced labor force	440	230	210	442,425	234,445	207,985
Agriculture and other resource-based industries	65	65	0	29,000	23,600	5,405
Manufacturing and construction industries	120	75	50	70,955	55,845	15,105
Wholesale and retail trade	65	25	40	71,085	36,020	35,070
Finance and real estate	0	0	10	20,620	8,140	12,480
Health and education	80	10	75	80,700	19,660	61,040
Business services	20	20	0	70,270	42,210	28,065
Other services	80	35	45	99,790	48,970	50,820

Source: Statistics Canada (2001)

Table 6.2 Community profiles of Canso: 2001–2006

	Canso Total	Novia Scotia Total
Population and dwelling counts in 2001		
Population in 2001 (1)	992	908,007
Population in 1996 (2)	1127	909,282
1996–2001 population change (%)	− 12	− 0.1
Total private dwellings	437	403,819
Population density per km²	183.6	17.2
Land area (km²)	5.4	52,917.43
Population and dwelling counts in 2006		
Population in 2006	911	913,462
Population in 2001	992	908,007
2001–2006 population change (%)	− 8.2	0.6
Total private dwellings	429	425,681
Population density per km²	168.1	17.3
Land area (km²)	5.42	52,917.46

Source: Statistics Canada (2006)

Tourism Development in Canso

A 'deliberate' approach to tourism development in Canso

Findings in this study were quite fascinating. In spite of previous skepticism and departure from generally accepted tourism development theories outlined earlier, Canso has achieved some reasonable measure of success with tourism. Findings revealed longstanding struggles in the community and a dedicated determination to cope with the numerous challenges that had threatened its survival over the years. Having been heavily dependent on the fishery, corporate interests and government support/intervention for decades, the community was now confronted with a new and stark reality – it had to change. It had to diversify somehow. Through years of ongoing struggle and hardship, the community had become known as 'the symbol of coastal communities being oppressed by industrial giants who had squandered their resources' (Canso Historical Society, Canso, 2004: 304).

In 1997, under the inspiration and leadership of a young 'champion', just returning home with his university degree in hand and hoping to help 'save' his dying community, Canso was mobilized to organize and implement its first major tourism attraction – an International Music Festival – in an effort to stimulate economic development in the community. According to Reid *et al.* (2005), having a champion to spearhead action is a critical component in any community tourism development process.

The tourism event/attraction and Stan Rogers

Research data showed the music festival concept was first conceived in 1994, the brainchild of its local emergent 'champion', who would later become the event's artistic director. The original notion was to construct a festival that would draw tourists and promote the region – tourism could bring substantial economic benefits to the community. The festival was to be constructed as a memorial to a popular Canadian songwriter, artist and folk music icon, musician Stan Rogers, who had been killed in a 1983 airline tragedy while returning home from a folk festival in Texas, USA.

Stan Rogers was born in Hamilton, Ontario, Canada. Although he didn't live there, his mother was a native of Canso and he spent many of his early summers visiting this region of Nova Scotia. '[His] songs chronicled life in Canada from the East Coast to the West Coast and all points in between' (Canso Historical Society, 2004). Rural people related to his songs, which 'gave a voice to the people in this country who worked in the fisheries, mines and on the farms'. His fame as a folk musician and songwriter grew over the years from his songs and music about the Canadian experience, which particularly appealed to rural folk and the working class. Rogers' songs and music, stemming from his earlier visits to the Canso region of Nova Scotia, conjured up images of folk people and the more simple rural country ways of life.

In a public interview recorded by Radio UPEI (Greencorn, 2006), Canso's newfound young 'champion' revealed three conditions that had triggered his inspiration and motivation to pursue the festival attraction concept: (1) he was young, full of vigor and freshly educated, returning home in 1996 and wanting to help; (2) he thought it would be fitting to pay a tangible, living tribute to singer and songwriter, Stan Rogers and (3) he saw the desperate need for economic development in his home community. At that time, however, as he pointed out, the primary focus of the project was to stimulate economic development in the area, not the artistic component. In that same year, (1994), the East Coast Music Awards (ECMA) was held in Nova Scotia. According to the data, Canso's 'champion', full of vim and vigor, attended the awards event and approached Rogers' widow who also attended, and presented his 'festival' event concept to her. She thought it was a good idea and one that could, if done properly, honor her late husband's memory. Mrs Rogers, who held all copyright agreements to her late husband's music and songs, agreed to the idea but with certain conditions attached: (1) there must be evidence of adequate funding, (2) the community must hire someone with solid experience (she recommended a person well-known for previous experience) and (3) the event must be an international festival for songwriters (Rogers, Radio UPEI, 2006). Within a year or so, the first festival took shape and was implemented in summer 1997. In her public recorded interview (2006), Rogers' widow stated that she has attended every annual festival since its inception. According to one community official (Anonymous, 2006), the festival attraction now considered an international songwriter's event, called the Stan Rogers Folk Festival, also known as StanFest, is continually growing, drawing as many as 10,000–15,000 visitors annually, some from as far away as New Zealand and contributes in excess of $1 million to the local economy.

Data analysis and research show the progressive development and growing success of the 'event' as a tourism attraction over ten years. With the help of government support, the music festival has significantly helped the community diversify its local economy and achieve its original objectives. The Chedabucto Bay Folk Society, a local group, is responsible for administration of the annual festival. When it was first initiated in 1997, the community only had 11 hotel rooms in the entire community to accommodate visitors to the 1-day event. In its inaugural year, the festival drew 3000; in 1999, attendance increased to 8000, and in 2000, 13,500 people participated in the extended three-day event. In 2007, there were reports that sales of festival passes increased by 20% over previous record sales in 2006 (Halifax Chronicle Herald, July, 2007).

Visitors to the festival do not have access to five-star accommodation; for the most part, they reside in tents in a camping-ground setting on the 15-acre site. Basically, Canso and the festival site becomes a 'tent' city (see Figure 6.3). Others camp out on local residents' lawns, stay in nearby B&Bs or find accommodations in outlying areas.

Although the festival is still reliant on government funding support, Canso has attempted to 'wean itself off government help' (Matheson, 2000). Recognizing the value of tourism as a means to diversify local economies and the need to support its growth pace, the Government of Canada injected financial support in 2002, including $148,400 from the Atlantic Canada Opportunities Agency (ACOA) under a special program

Figure 6.3 Stan Rogers Folk Festival site – a tent city
Source: George (2006)

that supports economic diversification in rural communities formerly
dependent on the fishery. In addition, $41,186 from HRDC and $17,000
from the local Chedabucto Bay Folk Society helped provide funding for
site improvements - new washrooms, showers, storage facilities and a full-
time professional manager (ACOA News Release, February 2002). Private
sponsorships for the event, by such corporations as ExxonMobil Canada,
grew from $17,000 in its first year to $60,000 in 2000. The Canada Council
and Heritage Canada have also provided financial support for the event.

In 2007, with the completion of a new fixed stage and infrastructure
improvements, projects enabled by a tourism infrastructure investment
of $215,962 from ACOA, the Canso attraction now has the potential
to expand its scale and musical performance timeline from a weekend
event to a year round series of events. 'The local arena, which has also
been used as an entertainment venue for the festival over the years, will
also be available to host a variety of community events year-round'
(ACOA Press Release, 2006). Festival organizers are also developing new
partnerships and alliances that will extend the concept of the celebration

of music and songwriting further out into the larger Eastern Shore region of Nova Scotia. For instance, the first Sherbrooke Now Songwriters' Music Camp has been introduced in conjunction with the 2007 Festival in the nearby community of Sherbrooke, Nova Scotia (Figure 6.4).

For three consecutive years, 2002–2004, the festival won the prestigious East Coast Music Award for event of the year. By 2007, it had grown into one of Nova Scotia's premier cultural events. Figure 6.5 shows the line-up of international performers for the 2007 event. In a Canadian Heritage Report (2005):

> The Stan Rogers Folk Festival has come to be a major cultural event for Nova Scotia. Annually, the festival hosts more than 50 artists and groups in an exciting, six-stage event … have received East Coast Music Awards for Event of the Year for the past two years running. Audience numbers have grown to approximately 5,000 people per day. Economic impact of the event has been estimated at $1.5 million. (Canadian Heritage Report, 2005: 1)

Figure 6.4 The 2006 Stan Rogers Festival in Canso
Source: Francey

Figure 6.5 Promotional poster for the 2007 event
Source: StanFest website (2007)

> [It] ... has taken nine years to build infrastructure we need ... has
> office complex, washroom and shower complex, concessions build-
> ings and several complexes to sleep performers ... developed nearly
> 15 acres of camping grounds. (Mason [SOCAN], 2006: 1)

Reconnecting to Key Concepts

Community participation/volunteerism

According to the data, over 700 local volunteers help implement the
event; the festival has bonded the community, which takes ownership

of the event. Community ownership is considered a critical factor in community tourism development (Reid *et al.*, 2005) if success is to be achieved. Ideally, residents need to be involved in the planning process from the beginning. Canso's organizers appear to have adopted a slow-growth strategy and have considered the event's fit with the community. 'What is crucial is that we don't grow at a pace the community isn't comfortable with' (Greencorn in Matheson, 2000: 2). To sell the initial 'festival' idea to the community back in 1997 and to garner support and volunteer help, proponents made approximately 600 phone calls to Canso residents (population less than 1000). And they bought into the idea.

> [Using] ... their "guerilla inclusion strategy," people have to volunteer just so they don't feel left out ... people feel a social responsibility to pitch in ... from the start they realized there was a lot at stake ... think they bought into the dream partly because they were scared of what would happen if we failed, but then people got caught up in it, and now feel a real ownership of this festival.

> There's no question this is a Herculean community effort. And the volunteering started long before many of the thousands who now attend could even find Canso on a map. ... We were faced with turning what was basically a couple of large grown-over hills and a field into a major festival site, with all the necessary infrastructure ... Canso has always been an industrial town. People here know how to work with their hands, so there was an incredible amount of talent we could tap into, everything from electricians to guys with chainsaws. Ninety percent of the effort and expertise to build this was volunteered. (Greencorn in Matheson, 2000: 2)

But, community participation and volunteerism are certainly not taken for granted by festival organizers.

> ... while volunteers are cheap labour, they do require maintenance and the organizers are careful to make sure they feel appreciated. Each volunteer is expected to work 10 hours over the three days, and for this, they get a pass to the rest of the festival and a T-shirt that identifies which volunteer crew they are on. It's functional during the event, and popular the rest of the year; kind of a uniform that shows someone is part of the team. As well, the volunteers are invited to join with performers ... for after-hours parties ... [and] brought together for an appreciation bash ... army of volunteers is a big reason why the festival has been successful ... couldn't do it without them. (Greencorn in Matheson, 2000: 2)

Arguably, in Canso's case, such participation and volunteerism have not only been instrumental in the festival's success, they have fortified and enriched the community's social capital capacity, a concept discussed earlier. '... the festival works because the whole community pulls together' (Mason, 2006). As Woolcock (2001: 12) commented, 'Communities endowed with a rich stock of social networks and civic associations will be in a stronger position to confront poverty and vulnerability, resolve disputes and/or take advantage of new opportunities'. Such a position can only help enhance a community's ability to achieve sustainability. Evidence in Canso strongly supports earlier community planning theory (Reid *et al.*, 2005), which argues that community buy-in and involvement is a major factor in any community development planning.

Community and identity

Notions of community identity from two different perspectives became apparent throughout the data collected for this study. First, there is a strong sense of identity and pride felt by the community. Canso, the community, has become a symbol of overcoming struggle and strife in difficult times. It was one of the rural coastal communities in Atlantic Canada most devastated by the collapse of the fishery. 'The past decade has involved a major community effort to diversify the local economy away from the fishery and into such new sectors as cultural tourism. The festival has come to be the banner success story of this effort' (Greencorn, RadioUPEI, 2006). Excerpts from various news articles give a sense of what the festival event has meant to the community.

> ... not just because of its economic impact, but also for what it has done for the collective attitude of the community, stands as a key ingredient of Canso's renaissance (Matheson, 2000). ... has done wonders for the spirit of the people here over the last ten years... has been a spiritual lift and confidence builder for the community ... Stan Rogers Festival put Canso on the map. (Mason, 2007)

Second, a collective identity has been developed by the musicians and songwriters themselves. One of the conditions that Ariel Rogers gave to Canso festival organizers when giving them permission to use her late husband's legacy as an icon for the event was that it would be an international festival for songwriters. David Francey (David Francey Letters, 2003), musician and songwriter, gives a sense of this communal identity:

As much as the festival is built around the memory of one man, it does indeed celebrate the singer songwriter, and the community that music itself creates.

The event brings old and new songwriters together annually to share, create and celebrate their crafts and art of making music. Musicians and songwriters, representing every genre of music, have come from countries as far away as New Zealand, Australia, United Kingdom, China and Denmark to perform or take part in the event. The provincial newspaper, The Chronicle-Herald (2 July 2007 Issue) refers to StanFest as the 'true UN of music... where most StanFest attendees are lost in a United Nations of music, with brilliant songs issuing from every corner of the field'. Most importantly, the festival has provided Canso with a new image – a space to celebrate songwriters and songwriting.

Sociability effects of cultural (arts and music) tourism

The sociability effects of the Stan Rogers Festival became evident from analysis of the data. Cultural activity generates new models of sociability, which is an important source of the value of culture (Dayton-Johnson, 2003: 16). According to Dayton-Johnson, in attempts to explain sociability effects, cultural activity, such as a festival, has two dimensions – first, the content (message) of the activity– the content effect, and second, the shared experience of the event itself – the conviviality effect.

> The content of the activity – what the singers are singing about – offers social criticism, political commentary, raucous storytelling and other material that serves as the fodder for conversation and deliberation about a community's values... the shared experience can generate conviviality among the members of the audience, which they might carry with them when they return to their homes. (Dayton-Johnson, 2003: 16)

The musical content of the Canso festival portrays an obvious theme – loss, social strife and survival. With a long history in facing adversity and struggle for survival – industrial shutdowns and collapse of the fishery – Canso can identify well with Rogers' musical lyrics. He wrote a lot about loss – loss of jobs in the fishery, of a way of life, of youth itself (Meek, Chronicle-Herald, 2007: 1). Meek's article caption, 'Mood upbeat but songs so sad' expresses a general sentiment instilled by the musical content of the Stan Rogers Folk Festival:

> ...it's about a soldier returned from the war, a man who ruins his life and hurts his family because of a drug addiction he can't shake... all

sang what seemed to be sad old songs. Here in the storied but ill-fated town of Canso that means songs about a fishery that died or a kid that had to leave town and then got homesick... annual festival is about things and people that left the world before their time ... give you some sense of how StanFest feels – kind of joyful and irreverent – even if one big theme seems to be loss. (Meek, Chronicle-Herald, 2007: 1)

Vast numbers of places have been immortalized in song lyrics (Gibson & Connell, 2003). Tourism in many such places has capitalized on musical allusions. In addition, movies, television and other forms of media have induced tourism to specific places. Gibson and Connell (2003) provide several examples of 'lyrical places', for example, the song, Mull of Kintrye. Arguably, taking somewhat of a different twist on this notion, the types of musicians and lyrical messages portrayed in the musical storytelling and songwriting performed at the Canso festival, and the overall event itself, tend to immortalize the community's life struggles and perseverance as a rural coastal community in Atlantic Canada. Thus, Canso becomes a 'lyrical place' associated with collective and personal struggles of rural folk or others struggling with life in the 21st century. The festival may, indeed, attract certain types of performers and tourists who identify with these notions. The data suggests that much of the music delivered at this unique festival is very personal in nature. In reference to the kinds of music performed at the Stan Rogers Festival, producer and performer, Mills said, 'Personal songs have a huge impact... about agony dispersed with joy' (Mills, RadioPEI, 2006).

Interestingly, the data suggested a strong common bond and shared experience between the community and the songwriters themselves, in what Dayton-Johnson (2003) may call a form of 'conviviality effect'. He states, 'There are good reasons to suspect that there are network effects in the consumption of cultural commodities; the enjoyment of listening to a live musical performance might be enhanced if one can talk about it later with someone who witnessed it' (p. 17). In Canso's case, this appears more apparent between the participating professional performers and community volunteers rather than other festival attendees. For instance, after each festival performance, the community volunteers and amateur musicians mingle and take part in after-hour parties and 'jam' sessions with the professional performers and songwriters, thus enhancing social relations and enabling sociability opportunities, as well as strengthening a 'common bond' that appears to exist among the festival goers.

Conclusions

Canso's tourism development defies what researchers have previously argued as the necessary ingredients for successful tourism – ample accommodation, amenities, infrastructure, services and so on. In spite of not having these resources, the community has, over 10 years, successfully created and grown an international tourism attraction. Long viewed as a depressed economic area, Canso has taken on a new 'persona' as a cultural tourism destination, one that is unique to other destinations. While not the 'saving grace' for Canso, the festival is a big economic piece. The community organizers have a longer-term objective of expanding the event to a two to three-week 'Festival of the Arts', using the Stan Rogers Folk Festival as its big demand generator. This is aimed at realizing a grander vision of 'becoming the cultural engine for this region' (Greencorn, RadioUPEI, 2006). Perhaps Canso's success, as the research suggests, is due to the strong involvement, solid commitment and enthusiasm of its people. The festival is a leading example of community ownership and animation (Greencorn, RadioUPEI, 2006). Although Canso has relied on government funding over this first 10 years of the festival project, what is different now is the funding goes directly into the community coffers for decisions in disbursement and not into the pockets of large corporations and conglomerates on whom the community had formerly been dependent. Canso residents appear to have taken collective ownership of their community, and are clearly making decisions regarding its future direction. This shift from previous government intervention breaks a longstanding dependency cycle in Canso, instilled by large companies and outside corporate investment and control, which had, basically, dominated the community for decades. A new shift in thinking and mindset have also released the community from the grip of learned helplessness, a state, according to Seligman (1995) that occurs when there are continuous failures – in this community's case, numerous plant failures, industrial shutdowns followed by the devastating collapse of the fishery (George, 1995). Such a state prevents individuals from helping themselves to solve problems – a passive acceptance of a situation.

The people of Canso, Nova Scotia, historically known for their determination and perseverance, have risen again with a renewed hope and collective spirit. Canso's economy and future are looking ever brighter these days as a unique tourism destination. The community will serve as a role model for other rural communities in efforts to achieve community sustainability in the face of global change. We will discuss the positive actions of Canso in our recommended planning model in Chapter 12.

Chapter 7

Synopsis: From Case Studies to Premises

Introduction

In writing this book, our intention has been to marry theory and somewhat abstract concepts with the very real situation of tourism in small communities across Canada. To this end, we sought to introduce and discuss some very evocative and instructive case studies. By presenting those cases, we aimed to describe 'practical' or 'on ground' examples of rural tourism development in action. Sprinkled throughout those cases were key concepts that we considered vital to understanding each case. The purpose of this brief chapter, then, is to look *across* the case studies to pull out major themes and key conceptual issues that are relevant to all of the cases and to the study of tourism development in rural areas more generally.

Cross-case analysis

Once the case studies were completed and written, it became obvious there were some predominant themes that related well to, and could help us to better understand, what was going on in the other communities. For instance, the issue of gentrification, of obvious relevance to the case of Lunenburg, could be seen at play in Port Stanley. The notion of theming and branding, while central to the discussion of what is happening in Vulcan, could also help explain some of the processes at work in Canso and in Lunenburg. Once we began to see the broader themes at work across our cases, we started to craft a set of foundational concepts – or premises – upon which we could build our overarching argument for what we see as healthy, responsible and appropriate tourism development in rural areas (see Table 7.1). Further, we present full chapters on these major themes.

Table 7.1 Foundational premises behind responsible rural tourism development

Premise No. 1:	The role of tourism in local culture is complex and not well understood
Premise No. 2:	Tourism changes the rural landscape
Premise No. 3:	Community is a central component of rural tourism
Premise No. 4:	Sustainable rural tourism and sustainable rural community must be synonymous
Premise No. 5:	Tourism is not an add-on but should be an integral part of rural development policies
Premise No. 6:	Planning is essential for successful tourism development

From Case Studies to Premises

To set the stage for this second half of the book, it is useful to introduce each premise in turn.

Premise No. 1: *The role of tourism in local culture is complex and not well understood*

The first major premise is fundamental to the overall purpose of this book, while at the same time, it is hardly surprising. Besides relaxation (especially sun and sand), there are no bigger attractions to tourists than cultural experiences. Experiencing and learning about cultures that are different from our own are central motivators for travel. This leads, of course, to considerations as to the impacts of travel for cultural consumption. The challenge, however, is that we often think of the cultural relationship within tourism settings as a one-way set of experiences or relationships, best captured in the dichotomy 'host/ guest'. Much early research in tourism argued that the power to change culture through tourism came from the activities, desires and expectations of the tourist. Certainly these are important considerations imbued with power relations, especially within the context of commodification and exploitation (most clearly exemplified in child sex tourism), but these issues are much more complex. In the rural areas of Canada, for example, the culture may well be based in ways of life (e.g. fishing, agriculture) and therefore can be both quite well-established and resistant to change. The attraction of travel to a small community is often based in exploring and understanding those ways of life; a nostalgia for the past. To this end, there may be power in the hands of locals living in these communities to decide how their local 'culture' is expressed and even consumed by tourists. In many senses, becoming a tourism destination can lead to the protection and even celebration of this way of life.

It is important to note that we are by no means suggesting that tourism can become a replacement for these rural ways of living (see the following premises for more discussion in this area), but that the cultural exchange between rural host and guest is complex and has many opportunities for power and control. As in the case of Lunenburg, the ways in which culture has been created and re-created over time in that community reflects the multifaceted nature of cultural change and development. Moreover, the particularities of each community mean that we cannot adequately generalize about the ways these changes take place.

In Chapter 8, we explore this complexity by discussing the myriad ways that tourism can impact the culture of the host community. After engaging the notion of culture by outlining some of the major conceptual developments in this area, we move more directly to a consideration of tourism by discussing the cultural economy. A major theme throughout this book is the argument that many communities undertake tourism development in response to broad economic changes (namely restructuring), and so the discussion of the culture economy is timely and necessary. Next, instead of merely making the often-heard argument about the benefits and challenges presented by tourism in small communities, we organize the discussion around the notion of continuity and rupture. This perspective allows us to embrace the complexity of this issue rather than trying to oversimplify it, and it provides an opportunity to introduce some new concepts. Tourism continuity is discussed in terms of the role that tourism can play in such areas as cultural revitalization, protection and enhanced understanding. Rupture is discussed in terms of conflict, loss of control and diversity, acculturation and other concepts that are important for better understanding the power relationships at work. In addition, one of the most exciting developments within the study of tourism and one that fosters a much more critical and sophisticated way of thinking about cultural impacts is introduced through the idea of transactions.

Premise No. 2: *Tourism changes the rural landscape*

A second premise is that tourism changes the rural landscape. Again, this is unlikely to be a surprising statement. We've all visited a place from our past and been surprised at the amount and nature of change it experienced, either through tourism or, more likely, through tourism-related development. Tourism development, especially in rural places, so often driven by local business and industry forces, trades on making the landscape and even the community, look and feel like something that tourists want to see and experience. As in the case of Vulcan, this is not necessarily what the locals want to see and experience and this can cause great tension in small places. Ideally, these tensions are worked out before the community changes too much – beyond what either the locals and/or the tourists desire. Moreover, the successful attraction of tourists can lead directly to gentrification, as interests in downtown buildings as tourist attractions and even upscale living spaces lead to their refurbishment and prices are driven up. These points were made clear in the discussion of Lunenburg as well as Port Stanley. Acknowledging that tourism is such a force in small places is an important first step towards understanding how to prevent a situation where those who live in the community feel they are excluded and/or marginalized.

In Chapter 9, we engage the notion of gentrification in some depth, paying special attention to the inherent power relationships. We explore the many ways of defining gentrification and account for its growing role in certain kinds of development, both rural and urban. We then move toward a critical look at tourists and the role of tourism as a force for gentrification. While many communities yearn for a successful tourism enterprise, one of the perhaps unintended effects of this success can be that prices for land and housing increase beyond what many in the community can manage. Moreover, this process of gentrification is intimately connected to ideas of place branding and theming through tourism and so we take up these concepts in some depth towards the end of the chapter. In the last few sections, the rather complicated idea of sense of place is explored as it relates to the impacts of tourism upon rural development and planning. In particular, we include an emphasis on the extent to which rural areas are becoming 'playgrounds' for outsiders, particularly Caucasian, wealthy urbanites. As with the discussion of culture, the extent to which tourism changes rural landscapes is portrayed as very complicated and its study must be grounded in specific communities.

Premise No. 3: *Community is a central component of rural tourism*

While 'the community' is often merely considered the setting for tourism in small places, our analysis of the case communities makes it clear that it is much, much more than that. Community can make or break a tourism development initiative. Tensions stemming from an unsupported tourism initiative or development can and will be felt by tourists and will, ultimately, taint the tourist experience. Many tourism researchers have made this point clearly and we've all heard the idea that tourism development *should not harm the goose that lays the golden eggs*. We take these ideas very seriously as we seek to put the idea of community at the forefront of any tourism-related discussion.

In Chapter 10, we deal with the notions of community and community development, tracing back their conceptual roots and outlining their potential role in rural development more broadly. While we point out that defining community is inherently challenging, the task is worth pursuing. In addition, we outline the modern tensions between community, individualism and even notions of democracy as we seek to explore what this means in terms of the role of community in rural tourism development. Understanding community and community development, more particularly, gives us the depth of understanding as well as the conceptual tools required to ensure that we can take the steps needed to make certain that the tourism development undertaken is reflective of, not contrary to, the needs and wants of those who live there. We complete this discussion with a more practical look at *how* we might bring community more deeply into the world of tourism. To this end, we highlight the role of community participation and involvement in tourism development through a brief introduction of planning.

Premise No. 4: *Sustainable rural tourism and sustainable rural community must be synonymous*

The notion of sustainability is frequently brought into the discussion of tourism development, but much work needs to be done as we continue to add flesh to the discussion of exactly what is being *sustained*. Many times the goals of sustainable rural tourism are merely concerned with *sustaining tourism*, and not sustaining the social, political, economic and environmental health of the community in question. As is argued in many places throughout this book, our perspective is that *sustaining community* by focusing on the health of its social, political, economic and environmental capacities is an essential, long-term plan for sustaining any kind of tourism development.

In Chapter 11, we argue that focusing on sustaining tourism at the expense of the rest of the community risks ruining both. To ground this argument, we move through the, by now, well-known and highly influential discourse on sustainable development, and illustrate the extent to which the key ideas of sustainable development have, at least in principle, been adopted by many large-scale tourism organizations. Many organizations have adopted important operating principles and codes of ethics to try to instill practical considerations of sustainability into the tourism world. A critical review of the impact of these principles and codes, however, asks how much of these ideas trickle down to actual tourism practice. Because we argue that community and sustainability cannot be divorced, we identify five key factors that must be taken into account when discussing sustainable rural tourism and sustainable rural communities: economic, social, political, environmental and cultural. We develop these concepts in some depth and reflect on what they mean for a broader discussion of sustainability, especially as regards issues of social cohesion and 'community capital'.

Premise No. 5: *Tourism is not an add-on but should be an integral part of rural development policies*

Surprisingly, only a small number of tourism researchers have stated directly that policy affects tourism and vice versa. Our analysis of the cases, however, as well as our understanding of the broader political economic context within which all rural development decisions are taken, reveals that this link is central. Tourism development does not happen in a political vacuum and a close inspection of these developments can help to reveal the ideologies and values that frame the assumptions of policy-makers. For instance, once you begin to look closely at policy formation, you can see how tourism has become increasingly popular as a mechanism for stimulating economic growth under many national, provincial and local governments because of its focus on competition, private investment and entrepreneurialism. These three facets fit well within the broader ideological tenets of neoliberalism. Thus, rural development policies (largely agricultural policy in this country) that are formulated in this neoliberal era, can have a deep and long-lasting impact on the types of tourism development opportunities and challenges that are undertaken. The danger, however, is that if we miss this linkage, we risk seeing tourism as an 'add-on' or an afterthought for rural development policy. This would thereby allow these neoliberal assumptions to dominate our thinking in regard to what kinds of tourism should be undertaken, and tourism would continue to be dominated and led by business and private interests – often to the exclusion of the rest of the community.

In Chapter 12, we introduce the notion of policy and investigate the concept of public policy in particular, linking it to issues of rural and tourism development. We also broaden the discussion to include the policies of many large and small tourism organizations, to consider the extent to which there are effective tourism policies in place and where they might be found. However, while from a public policy perspective it cannot be said that there is really a tourism policy *per se*, there are very few policy decisions (or lack of decisions) that do not have an influence on tourism development, especially in small communities. We argue for the need to deal much more directly with tourism at the public policy level, especially if we are earnestly concerned with developing sustainable rural tourism.

Premise No. 6: *Planning is essential for successful tourism development*

While it makes intuitive sense when we say that planning is essential for success in tourism development, in most cases, efforts to understand planning in this context is limited at best. Like the policy discussion, ignoring the planning part of tourism development means we are at risk of accepting uncritically the assumptions regarding who should be doing the planning and how it might proceed. Further, this means that many power relationships go unchallenged and, ultimately, the tourism product is developed almost exclusively by private interests through business. As is argued throughout the book, leaving out the other parts of the community invites failure.

Chapter 13, then, is a rather different chapter. Building upon our experiences in planning tourism in many small communities across Canada, we will outline some steps for a participatory, community-led approach to tourism planning that we argue goes far in terms of helping to answer the concerns of sustainability, integrated policy making, community power and even cultural change. Thus, after a brief outline of why this approach is important, we move straight into outlining a very practical, step-by-step discussion of community-led tourism planning and development.

After touching on the ideas of planning more generally in Chapter 13, Chapter 14 synthesizes our discussions and reinforces the main arguments presented in the book; it provokes us to question the ways we think about and plan rural tourism development and points towards a future alternative.

Conclusion

In this chapter, we did an analysis of our four Canadian cases to pull out apparent themes and key conceptual issues that seemed germane to all of the cases and which, we argue, are significant to the study of tourism development in rural areas more generally. The remaining chapters that follow are more lengthy expositions on these key concepts. As with the case studies, each chapter is presented as a stand-alone discussion. However, it should become clear very quickly that these ideas are deeply interrelated.

Chapter 8

The Complex Role of Local Culture in Rural Tourism[1]

Introduction

When considering any tourism development, the host community and its local culture should be given precedence as the foundation on which all action is grounded. Culture is the basis on which individuals and communities interpret the world, and as such, preservation of this fundamental human construction must be given primacy. And, while culture is dynamic and not static, it must be given room to grow and develop naturally and not determined by outside influences or economic imperatives. Local culture, and its many forms of expression, is often the lure that attracts tourists to an area in the first place, particularly in traditional rural communities, and the 'goose that has laid this golden egg' should be nurtured to continue in productivity for the long term. Some argue that without culture there is no tourism (Jafari, 1996). Tourism provides 'spaces' where encounters between different cultures occur – where a host culture interconnects and interacts with a visiting culture. Increasingly, researchers discuss relationships between tourism and culture, focusing on cultural heritage tourism and its potential appeal as a development tool in many regions in the world. Tourism today, as an operative of globalization, brings the stage for encounters between different cultures to the doorsteps of formerly less-travelled regions and local rural communities. The advancement of our current form of globalization is predicated upon the dominance of corporate capitalism and neoliberal development policies. These have encouraged homogenization, have brought us to our current global/local nexus, and have changed the way we communicate, do our business and live our daily lives. This challenges us to now reflect on the potential consequences of these changes, particularly in the rural regions.

With tourism growing exponentially to become one of the world's leading industries (UNWTO, 2006), a major challenge that confronts us is to take a more critical approach in understanding this phenomenon. Paralleling the spread of globalization and growth of tourism, sustainable development has also become a critical global concern. While sustainable development has received extensive and wide-ranging coverage in recent years, it has largely been framed in global environmental terms (Overton & Scheyvens, 1999). Rural community sustainability is discussed in more depth in Chapter 11.

Arguably, a dominant focus of research has been the economic benefits of tourism. Until fairly recently, the research has tended to ignore the subtler and less transparent negative impacts of tourism on the social, environmental and cultural milieu. Overton and Scheyvens (1999) claim the social perspective still seems a subordinate player in the sustainable development coalition. Further, they suggest that even less attention has been given to cultural diversity in the sustainable development equation and the local perspective is frequently subordinate to the global. Culture, brought to life through its many forms and expressions, is a core component in the tourism product. Increasingly, it is being exploited and utilized primarily for economic gain and, in many cases, its form and purpose, which evolved as a social construct for life in a community, have been destroyed (George, 2004). The relationship between tourism and culture is a dichotomous one. While it has high potential for achieving positive dimensions of cultural 'continuity', as argued by previous researchers (Var & Ap, 1998; Yu & Chung, 2001; Mubarak, 2002; APEC, 2000; UNESCO, 1996; Robinson, 1999; McIntosh et al., 2002; Proshansky et al., 1983; Barthel-Bouchier, 2001; Taylor, 2001), tourism is also said to result in serious negative consequences (Robinson, 1999; Jafari, 1996; Reid et al., 2001; Cooper et al., 1998; Davidson, 1993; Ziff & Rao, 1997; Kroeber, 1948; McIntosh et al., 2002) that often 'rupture' or frustrate a community's local culture.

As tourism extends into rural and more remote regions where local cultures have long been robust and protected from external influences, questions arise about the potential consequences it may have on the cultural dimension of local areas. This chapter discusses the complex role of culture in rural tourism development.

Key Theoretical Concepts: Local Culture; Culture Economy; Commodification of Culture

Tourism

As globalization expands, tourism needs to be understood as both a 'cause and effect' variable, affecting life in contemporary society. That is, it is both an instrument in perpetuating globalization and is an outcome of the globalizing process. The growth and invasion of tourism to new regions carries major consequences and impacts, both positive and negative, as noted above. Tourism, with its complex inward and outward functions and structure, is a socioculturally embedded phenomenon. It has diverse dimensions and untold influences of which economics is only one (Jafari, 1996). Nonetheless, Jafari points out that the economic forces of this mega-industry and the study of its potential have been instrumental in bringing tourism to the national and international forefront, as an attractive economic opportunity.

Mobility is central to the concept of tourism, involving movement from one place to another where interaction and exchange can take place. Other tourism theorists have highlighted notions of spacelessness, timelessness, identity seeking and nomadism, as characteristic of modern or postmodern conditions for tourism (Kovac, 2001).

Parrinello (2001) depicts tourism mobility as a circular process portrayed through the construction of a tourism travel experience. Most models of tourism illustrate this circular process with a point of departure (origin, and tourist's culture), a place of arrival (destination, and host's culture) and return to point of origin. This concept of tourism as a circular process may have broader application than just the mobility aspect. In tourist and host encounters, a circular transformation process occurs where two different cultures interact and exchange knowledge, customs and values. The tourist and host (destination community) meet and interact in the 'encounter zone' and a social transformation process begins to take place. Arguably, both tourist and host 'give and take' something to and from the other through this encounter, which results in some level of cultural transformation in each other (see Figure 8.1). This transformation process may result in either, or both, positive and negative outcomes for the host (destination community) and the tourist.

Contemporary tourists travel to other places for various reasons, some to seek 'escape' from mundane and everyday lives. Research suggests that commodification of 'escapism is the core of today's tourism industry' (Urry, 1995). Tourism is about selling dreams and is related to the 'eternal search for the meaning of life'; it is about experiencing beyond the ordinary (Schouten, 1996). It is as if there is a search for the 'roots of existence'. Increasingly, in light of our globalizing world, economic prosperity and fast-paced lifestyles, these 'dreams' and 'search for meaning' are sought by tourists in the rural countryside where they can experience the perceived idyllic setting, and often, in doing so, cause disruption to local life.

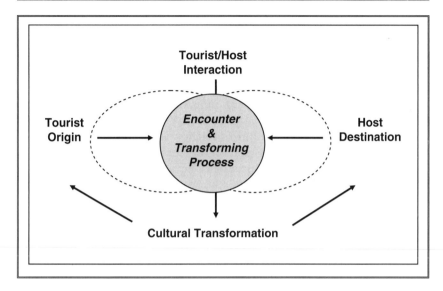

Figure 8.1 Circular transformation process

As tourism achieves significance as an economic generator, many rural communities have adopted it as an economic development strategy. Lacking any concrete understanding about the complexities and dynamics of the tourism system and proper planning processes, many have been unsuccessful. As tourism continues to develop within a globalizing context, such theories become 'living realities' in many countries, regions and communities. Most importantly, essential to the understanding and development of successful tourism is to understand culture (Robinson, 1999).

What is Culture?

Culture, as a dimension of tourism, is discussed from the anthropological perspective. According to Keesing and Keesing (1971), culture refers to the totality of man's [sic] learned, accumulated experience. It refers to those socially transmitted and distinct patterns of behavioral characteristics belonging to a particular social group, i.e. Canadians or Japanese. Smaller local social groupings might include: Inuits, Newfoundlanders, French Acadians and Mennonites, among others. Tylor's (1871) often quoted definition defines culture as, 'that complex whole which includes knowledge, belief, art, morals, law, customs, and any other capabilities and habits acquired by man as a member of a society' (in Burns, 1999). For Kroeber and Kluckhohn (1952), culture is 'patterns, explicit and implicit, of and for behaviour acquired and transmitted by symbols, constituting the distinctive achievement of human groups, including their embodiments in artefacts' (in Keesing & Keesing, 1971). To Burns, culture is '... a linked set of rules and standards shared by a society which produces behaviour judged acceptable by that group' (Burns, 1999).

Burns (1999) argues that culture's relation with tourism begins when tourism enters and becomes part of an already ongoing process of symbolic meaning and appropriation. Burns points out that through tourism, culture becomes a commercial resource, especially culture that is perceived to be unique or unusual by many actors (including tourism planners and potential tourists). This notion of uniqueness to attract tourists is what underlies the 'commodification' of culture, including cultural landscapes and cultural heritage buildings. Understanding the various links between tourism systems and a destination's culture seems necessary to prevent or minimize negative impacts on a host culture occurring through the act of receiving tourists (Burns, 1999: 57).

A culture economy

Ray (1998) refers to the commodification of the countryside and aspects of its culture as the creation of a 'culture economy', which consists of strategies to transform local knowledge into resources or 'capital' available for exploitation. According to Ray, this knowledge is simply comprised of 'ways of doing things and ways of understanding the world' identified through various cultural markers. These cultural markers include: traditional foods, music, craft, folklore, local landscapes and architecture, and history. Such knowledge and cultural markers become objectified and commodified under the guise of cultural tourism. Thus, as new forms of tourism advance into long-established isolated regions and rural societies, local cultures become subject to intrusion, turmoil and change.

Arguably, most researchers would not disagree with the notion that one fundamental characteristic of current social conditions is a changing relationship between the economy and culture. Social change, generally, occurs as a result of contradictory and/or conflicting social relationships. Contradictions and conflicts reside in tourism where cultural and economic values often clash, both in tourism development planning processes and direct interactions that take place between hosts and visiting tourists.

Increasingly, in what is now commonly referred to as the postmodern era, culture, composed of symbolism and representation, imagery and other intangibles, has become reified and constructed into a commodity for monetary exchange. A community can 'sell' aspects of its local collective culture to any tourist who is willing to pay for it. Ideally, tourism is based on the premise that interactions occur between two human variables: the tourist or visitor, and the destination host, with the intention that both will receive desired benefits – visitor satisfaction for the former and economic gain for the latter. This encounter of two different cultures is part of the circular process discussed earlier (see Figure 8.1) that provides a setting for social transformation to occur. However, as alluded to earlier, the dynamics and outcomes of this transformation process are not necessarily positive, but rather, are more likely to unfold in a dichotomous and contentious relationship.

A dichotomous relationship between tourism and culture

While tourism promises the idea of 'continuity' for community and cultural wellbeing through economic development, research shows that it can also be a force of 'rupture'. Tourism is frequently touted as an alternative to achieve economic sustainability, but little attention has been given to notions of cultural sustainability. Table 8.1 outlines the potential outcomes of tourism's relationship with local culture that portray the dichotomous nature of this growing phenomenon. The following is a brief explanation about each of these outcomes.

Tourism as Continuity

Through peace, cultural understanding and appreciation, cultural revitalization, affirmation and promotion of cultural identity and

Table 8.1 Potential outcomes of the host–tourist encounter relationship

Continuity	*Rupture*
Peace	Cultural conflict
Cultural understanding/appreciation	Acculturation/loss of diversity
Cultural revitalization	Cultural appropriation
Affirming/promoting cultural identity	Staged authenticity
Economic revitalization/sustainability	Leakage/loss of local control

Source: George (2002)

economic revitalization and sustainability, tourism provides a mechanism towards building continuity for communities.

Peace

Tourism plays a major role in international relations and world peace (Var & Ap, in Theobald, 1998: 44–47). In 1980, the WTO Conference in Manila declared that 'world tourism can be a vital force for world peace and the role of tourism as a vehicle of international understanding and peace derives from the notion that interaction between hosts and guests makes understanding possible among peoples and cultures' (p. 44). International tourism is regarded as a catalytic force for tension reduction and peace building (Yu & Chung, 2001). Mohammed Hosni Mubarak, President of Egypt (2002, Web site: para 6) states, 'Tourism and peace are intertwined. Tourism fosters understanding and peace, which support one another and enable continuity'.

Cultural understanding/appreciation

Tourism broadens opportunities for cultural exchange and encompasses nations from all parts of the capitalized world (Mubarak, 2002); it can be a bridge to an appreciation of cultural relativity and international understanding (Smith, 1989). The Asian-Pacific Economic Cooperation (APEC) (2002) assembly

> recognises and values the many non-economic benefits that tourism provides ... in particular fostering cross-cultural understanding; promoting local and indigenous cultures, arts and heritage; highlighting the need to preserve the social and cultural fabric and integrity of host communities; and promoting world peace by developing international cooperation in a spirit of friendship, dialogue and understanding.

Cultural revitalization

Tourism can contribute to cultural revitalization, drawing from authentic sources and stimulated by an increasing market of postmodern tourists who are searching for 'meaning and truth' in culture (UNESCO, 1996). Tourism, as a mechanism in the globalizing process, creates new spaces for new cultural encounters and alliances. When a 'tourist' and 'host' meet, each carries within them a meaning of his/her own identity and each gets something new from the experience. Cultural diversity provides a wide range of unique tourism products that are authentic and original. One of the main attributes of tourism is to provide diverse experiences through contact with new cultures and cultural expression. As heritage and cultural attractions become highly demanded commodities, the focus of political and economic agendas is shifted towards their revival, preservation and maintenance. Increased profits made from the culture industry may help support preservation of cultural artefacts and landmarks.

Economic revitalization

As demand for cultural tourism products and new spaces increases, promising opportunities present themselves for economic revitalization, particularly in economically depressed areas. Tourism creates job opportunities in local communities and provides indirect as well as direct benefits to the local economy. Tourists are increasingly seeking exotic and unique cultural spectacles and experiences and will often pay premium prices to do so (Robinson, 1999). Potential opportunities for local entrepreneurship and self-empowerment are created. Flexible specialization, a more recent development theory, is more conducive to smaller enterprises and communities where tourism products can be customized to meet the diverse and ever-changing tastes of modern tourists (Milne & Ateljevic, 2001). Communities, each with their own distinctive culture and characteristics, can 'package' exclusive product offerings.

Affirming and promoting community identity

Cultural identity is founded on tradition, lifestyle, values and protocol and can be associated with 'place identity', a concept introduced by Proshanshy (1983). 'Place identity' refers to 'those dimensions of the self that define the individual's personal identity in relation to the physical environment', characterized by individually or collectively constructed attitudes, values, thoughts, beliefs and behaviour (pp. 57–83). It is the sense of cultural identity and belonging that one seeks to pass on to succeeding generations (McIntosh *et al.*, 2002). This sense of identity can be affirmed and promoted through the tourism experience, depending on how it is constructed by a community and offered to tourists.

In tourism, authenticity is often expressed as some accurate reconstruction of the past (Barthel-Bouchier, 2001). Authenticity in the present must pay homage to the conception of origins; sites, objects, images and people are positioned as signifiers of past events, epochs or ways of life (Taylor, 2001: 7–26). Taylor notes that the capacity of such a strategy to create the impression of temporal distance adds value to tourism and is an important feature when commodifying culture. However, there is much debate around the notion of authenticity.

Authenticity is a social and symbolic construct that can be reflective of a community's identity and culture, its past and its present, its heritage and its living culture. Not just individuals but communities have distinctive identities (Barthel-Bouchier, 2001). A host community, represented by individuals with diverse opinions and values, can negotiate and construct what is considered to be authentic and acceptable for the community. This 'impacts the very identity of the community and how it is interpreted to tourists' (Barthel-Bouchier, 2001: 221–239). This notion relates to the concept of 'attraction-based identity' where cultural identity may be consciously and purposefully commodified through tourism (McIntosh *et al.*, 2002).

Tourism as Rupture

As pointed out earlier, while tourism can contribute to notions of 'continuity', we recognize it has destructive powers that can lead to 'rupture' in the social fabric of a community. This can occur through cultural conflict, leakage and loss of local control, staged authenticity, acculturation and loss of diversity, and cultural appropriation.

Cultural conflict

Tourism often results in cultural conflict. Robinson (1999: 22–23) states,

> Its very presence (tourists) can chip away at the local culture and essentially re-invent or define it to fit the exigencies of the tourism industry. The result is that host communities find culture and traditions under threat from the purchasing power of the tourism industry. Neither are tourists better off from a cultural viewpoint. Instead of getting rich and authentic cultural insights and experience, tourists get staged authenticity ... (UNESCO Courier, 1999, July–August)

Assumptions that tourism generates cultural harmony, and is a vital force for peace have been exaggerated (Robinson, 1999). According to Robinson, there has been little evidence to support the view that tourism is bringing the world together. Further, he states, 'tourism is one globalizating influence that can initiate dramatic and irreversible changes within the cultures of host communities' (p. 22). The idea that we should sustain and protect cultures is not yet fully developed. Robinson notes that the most obvious conflict is between tourist and host, engendered in part by the fundamental difference in goals – the tourist is engaged in leisure, the host is engaged in work.

Leakage and loss of local control

Another source of conflict arises between a host country and the often persuasive and economically powerful developers and operators of international corporations, mainly in First World countries, and the tourism industry (Robinson, 1999). The flow of tourism receipts and transfer of capital from developing countries to the developed world, where the majority of the tourism businesses and agents are located, fuels this type of conflict. Conflict is also found among different sectors of a host community, where residents, for example, the tourism entrepreneur and the local farmer, may have differing goals. The case for attracting hard currency relatively quickly and often with minimal investment is a powerful argument for governments in both developing and developed countries (Robinson, 1999).

Loss of community control often results from tourism. In many cases, communities, whose cultures are being commodified and exploited, have not been included in the planning processes in any substantial way. This seemed evident in the study of Lunenburg, discussed in Chapter 3. In addition, St. Jacobs, a small village in Canada, provides a clear example of 'cultural commodification' where tourists have been seduced by images, social representations and symbolic constructions, to travel to the village and 'gaze' at the Mennonite community and its unique way of life. Previous research (Reid *et al.*, 2000) suggests that the local Mennonite community had little or no involvement whatsoever in the 'commodification' process. While tourism produces economic benefits for rural communities, it often brings discord and other tensions, and cultural disharmonies within the local community emerge as a serious issue. Often, this can be attributed to a lack of understanding of tourism, or with having little or no local involvement in the planning processes.

Staged authenticity

Tourism turns local cultures into commodities where religious rituals, ethnic rites and festivals continue to be reduced and sanitized to conform to tourist expectations, resulting in 'reconstructed ethnicity' (Robinson, 1999). Part of the problem stems from the packaging of 'cultural experiences' by foreign companies residing outside the country where these experiences occur. This is another feature commonly attributed to globalization. 'Cultures are reduced to a two-dimensional world carried by glossy brochures which depict idyllic locations and superficial narratives' (Robinson, 1999: 23). Tourism is the prime threat to indigenous homelands and culture through exploitation, dislocation and desecration (McIntosh *et al.*, 2002). McIntosh *et al.* emphasize if tourism and culture are to have a sustainable relationship, they must be developed in harmony with the community interests. To ensure authenticity, culture must be protected and preserved. The community that owns it must negotiate and approve what is or is not authentic culture.

Acculturation/loss of diversity

An even larger contradiction and potential threat emanating from tourism and increasing global economic activity, is the demise of cultural diversity on a world scale due to acculturation. On one hand, tourism thrives on its ability to offer diverse and exotic attractions and experiences, but on the other hand, it contributes to acculturation of host cultures. This notion of acculturation is more often applied to broader societal cultures rather than to local communities. Acculturation comprises those changes in a culture brought about by another culture and will result in an increased similarity between the two cultures (Kroeber, 1948). Although this type of change may be reciprocal, it is more often an asymmetrical process resulting in the absorption of one culture into a powerful other. Through globalization processes, languages and ethnic dialects have succumbed to the English language, and many have become, or are in danger of becoming, extinct (BBC, 2001). The intensity of the acculturation process is dependent on how strong indigenous traditions are in sustaining a distinctive local identity.

Cultural appropriation

Tourism is an industry where the notion of cultural appropriation, the borrowing or taking from others, appears pervasive. From stories to music to architecture and landscapes, community culture is appropriated and commodified by others for the purpose of making a profit. For example, a touring company often advertises a 'product' to tourists which includes sightseeing of a community's architecture and surrounding local landscapes and exposure to the local folklore and myths. If it does so without the community's knowledge and consent, or without any benefit to the community, it can be said to be appropriating that community's culture. As tourism extends into rural communities, ownership concerns and cultural appropriation may become contentious issues.

A Cultural Turn

Research and discourse that integrates the social and cultural with economic dimensions of tourism reveals the complex nature of this phenomenon. This notion of complexity must be addressed and embraced if we are to gain an understanding of the links that exist between tourism and the broader processes of development (Ateljevic, 2001). Tourism must be viewed as a transaction process, incorporating both exogenous forces and the endogenous powers of local residents and entrepreneurs (Chang *et al.*, 1996). Cultural and environmental dimensions are crucial to understanding development processes. More attention needs to be given to the impacts of tourism on the natural environment, cultural attributes and people's broader quality of life.

The crossing of boundaries and the integration of cultural politics into the formation of knowledge have been marked as the 'cultural turn' in the social sciences (Chaney, 1994). As rural communities struggle with issues of change and work to achieve sustainability, this view of the 'cultural turn' has significance. Because rural communities are historically embedded in local culture, this resurgent interest in culture may present opportunities for sustainable economic development through the mechanisms of tourism. On the other hand, it also poses serious threats to cultural sustainability.

Conclusion

Challenges for rural communities

Three main challenges seem evident: understanding the complex relationship between culture and tourism, redefining the concept of commodifying culture and deciding what aspects of culture to commodify.

Understanding culture and tourism

Understanding the power of tourism as a force for transformation is crucial; the transformation process can bring about both positive and negative elements. The challenge for rural communities adopting tourism as a strategy for sustainable development lies in how they will respond to the paradoxical nature of the change process that often occurs when hosts interact with tourists. In light of this, challenging questions arise, for example, 'How can rural communities achieve economic sustainability while retaining and maintaining cultural sustainability?'

Redefining the concept of commodifying culture

The concept of commodifying culture requires more examination. McIntosh *et al.* (2002), in a study of indigenous people in New Zealand, applied notions of cultural/place identity and attraction identity to explain a commodifying process of culture there. Aspects of culture, heritage buildings and architecture, folklore and history, festivals and customs, etc., can be bundled and packaged into unique commercial items that will attract tourists to destinations. This 'cultural bundle' becomes the attraction for a community. However, there is a sacred part of a community's culture that needs to be protected and preserved, including the community's cultural or place identity – its integrity, values, beliefs, everyday living experiences and freedoms of local people, its soul – which cannot be for sale. Packaging the 'cultural bundle' and building the attraction should be a matter of community negotiation where the community determines what it considers inviolable, and can preserve and protect this from the 'cultural bundle' offered to tourists.

Determining what aspects of culture to commodify

Perceiving and understanding culture from two perspectives – that which is inviolable and that which can be an attraction, perspectives which can be separate but yet not exclusive to each other – may be a key factor in achieving cultural sustainability in light of tourism. Communities need to negotiate and decide which aspects of local culture to commodify and which aspects are 'not for sale'. Using this approach to tourism development, communities initiate a self-assessment process to construct, manage and control commodification of their own cultural assets, a process aimed towards achieving, not only economic revenue generation, but also cultural sustainability in the community.

With advancing globalization, increasing concerns about sustainability, a resurgent interest in cultural tourism and a 'cultural economy', tourism development becomes appealing to many rural communities now in the throes of change. However, as was emphasized at the EGIS Conference, *Impact of Globalization and Information on the Rural Environment* (January, 2000), 'There are few issues more important – or more contentious– than the impact of globalization and technology change on global food production and the rural environment'. It is highly desirable to promote and stimulate the maintenance and development of a diversity of land uses to achieve rural sustainability, including agrotourism as well as cultural tourism in regions with historical or cultural value (EGIS, 2000). But, we emphasize once again, to understand the consequences of implementing tourism as a mechanism for achieving rural sustainability, it is first essential to understand culture (Robinson, 1999).

In response to the many changes taking place in the local economic climate that have stemmed from globalization and other political factors, notions of rural tourism and commodified culture are increasingly being discussed and promoted as a potential mechanism for social and economic revitalization and rural sustainability. In Canada, where much of the country is rural, many small communities have evolved with strong cultural traditions and ways of life. In the midst of change, many are now striving to achieve a sense of sustainability; some are using traditional cultural heritage assets for tourism development purposes, such as in Lunenburg. Further, others are also drawing on contemporary cultural aspects in more creative and innovative approaches, as shown in the cases of Canso and Vulcan, where expressions of modern popular culture are being commodified for tourism development. Whether culture is traditional or modern, highlighting some of the dynamics that occur between tourism and culture provokes serious thought and questions: Do rural communities have the potential to develop and implement tourism strategies using their cultural assets and capacities as a way of achieving sustainable development? Can Canadian and other rural communities successfully position themselves as tourism destinations in a global 'cultural economy'? Can they deliver marketable and unique local cultural products for tourism and, at the same time, sustain continuity of community and culture for the locals? Are rural communities able to manage the apparent, as well as more subtle, transformation processes that tend to occur from intensive encounters between hosts and tourists? Some insights related to the latter question are brought forward in Chapter 9.

Notes

1. This chapter is a reworked version of a previously published article, *Tourism and Culture: A Dichotomous Affair* (George, 2002). It is used here with permission from the publisher.
2. This conference, *Impact of Globalization and Information on the Rural Environment*, was organized by Harvard University – David Rockefeller Center for Latin American Studies, and the Scientific Committee for the Study of the Environment (SCOPE) – EGIS Project. Cambridge, USA. January 13–15, 2000.

Chapter 9

Changing the Rural Landscape

Introduction

In this chapter, we address how tourism may have an impact on both the physicality of the rural landscape as well as the social and psychological experience of place. In particular, we discuss important and interrelated notions of tourism-related gentrification and the growing tendency to create themed and branded spaces in many rural areas. More broadly, we draw attention to the implications of the tendency to position rural areas as 'playgrounds' for the ever-expanding urban population. While some of these impacts certainly include positive benefits, for example, property refurbishment can visually improve the aesthetics of an area, our collective research in various parts of Canada suggests that tourism can alter the 'face' and nature of traditional rural landscapes and negatively affect those living there. The aim of this chapter is to look more closely at tourism and its influence on rural areas. As Shaw and Williams (2004) note, tourism places are constantly being created and re-created; we seek both to better comprehend how this phenomenon is changing the rural landscape and to set out ways to ensure that the community stays in control of these processes.

Key Theoretical Concepts: Gentrification; Branding and Image

What is Gentrification?

Generally, the literature on gentrification (Glass, 1964; Smith, 1979b, 1996; Hamnett, 1984, 2000; Slater, 2002a, 2002b; Kennedy & Leonard, 2001; Lees, 1999, 2000; Ley, 1981; Wyly & Hammel, 2001; Wetzel, 2004) has focussed on cities and more specifically on neighbourhoods within these cities. Gentrification is frequently theorized as a development strategy for urban renewal and revitalization in many larger cities where core areas have been negatively affected by various impacts of urban sprawl, for instance, the loss of core shopping areas and the corresponding reduction of the tax base. 'In many cases, if not an explicit intention of cities' redevelopment efforts, gentrification can be a by-product, particularly in cities with little vacant land or few unoccupied buildings' (Kennedy & Leonard, 2001: 1). Evidence from previous research on urban gentrification suggests that, in spite of the benefits it is purported to bring, 'gentrification can impose great financial and social costs on the very families and business owners who are least able to afford them' and 'it creates noticeable changes in neighborhood character in a matter of months' (Kennedy & Leonard, 2001: 1).

There are several contrasting definitions and interpretations of the term gentrification, depending on the philosophical and political framework in which it is being discussed. Philosophical positions threaded through the discourse on gentrification vary, including: realist (Bridge, 1994), feminist (Bondi, 1991), postmodern (Rose, 1984) and poststructuralists (Mills, 1993; Lees, 1996, 1999, 2000). Betancur (2002) discusses the politics of gentrification and contends that early literature focuses on the middle class and the so-called 'pioneer' perspective in rehabilitating the inner city (Wolf, 1975; Lipton, 1977; Ley, 1978; Clay, 1979; Berry, 1980; Kasarda, 1982). In attempts to define gentrification, Slater (2002a) turns to the term first coined by Ruth Glass in London in 1964:

> One by one, many of the working-class quarters of London have been invaded by the middle-classes – upper and lower. Shabby, modest mews and cottages ... have been taken over, when their leases expired, and have become elegant, expensive residences ... once this process of "gentrification" starts in a district it goes on rapidly until all or most of the original working-class occupiers are displaced and the whole social character of the district is changed. (Slater, 2002 – Defining Gentrification, para 1: Online Document)

As discussed in Chapter 3, Hamnett (1984) states, 'Gentrification is simultaneously a physical, economic, social and cultural phenomenon, [which] commonly involves the invasion by middle-class or higher-income groups of previously working-class neighbourhoods or multi-occupied "twilight areas" and the replacement or displacement of many of the original occupants' (Hamnett, 1984: 282–319). Among the many definitions of the term, 'class' appears to be the basic common and dominant thread, but Slater suggests that it is 'perhaps more useful to understand gentrification as a process which brings about change to a neighbourhood based on the influx of "different" people to those there already – a new class of highly educated, highly skilled and highly paid residents are moving in' (Slater, 2002a) – Defining Gentrification, para 3: Online Document.

'Working class neighborhoods that are at risk of gentrification are generally those that have features that make them more desirable' (Wetzel, 2004, para: 17, Web Document). These features might include interesting architecture, historical aspects, cultural uniqueness, landscapes/seascapes or some other attraction. 'Displacement is a change in the class composition of a neighbourhood over time' (Wetzel, 2004, para 18: Web Document). Wetzel (2004) further contends that 'displacement, whether through urban renewal and the bulldozer or by market forces, is an act of force nonetheless. It is anti-democratic because it denies self-determination to an existing community' (Wetzel, 2004, para: 19, Online Document).

Kennedy and Leonard (2001) suggest that gentrification in urban areas is driven by an imbalance in housing supply and demand. Subsequently, this imbalance leads to many positive benefits, such as a revitalized economy and increased tax base, but it also leads to affordability problems, displacement and unanticipated changes in the character of a neighbourhood (Kennedy & Leonard, 2001). They define gentrification as 'the process by which higher income households displace lower income residents of a neighbourhood, changing the essential character and flavour of that neighbourhood' (p. 5). Further, Kennedy and Leonard (2001: 6) define revitalization and reinvestment, terms that are often used interchangeably with gentrification, respectively as:

> [Revitalization] is the process of enhancing the physical, commercial and social components of neighbourhoods and the future prospects of its residents through private sector and/or public sector efforts. Physical components include upgrading of housing stock and streetscapes. Commercial components include the creation of viable businesses and services in the community. Social components include increasing employment and reductions in crime.

> [Reinvestment] is the flow of capital into a neighborhood primarily to upgrade physical components of the neighborhood, although re-investment can also be made in human capacity.

Although many developers interpret the terms 'revitalization' and 'reinvestment' as implicit merits of gentrification, Kennedy and Leonard (2001: 5) argue there is a difference. In their study, they state there are three conditions specific to their definition of gentrification:

1. Displacement of original residents
2. Physical upgrading of the neighbourhood, particularly of housing stock
3. Change in neighbourhood character

In short, when these three conditions become evident in a community, it is not revitalization or reinvestment but, rather, gentrification that is underway. What causes gentrification? Shaw (2003: 1) offers a blunt perspective, suggesting that gentrification is caused by:

1. Big profits for the suppliers of gentrified real estate
2. Consumers who want to be where the action is
3. A well-oiled media industry that keeps the whole merry circle turning

Shaw (2003) also applies stage theory to gentrification, stating that it can occur in four stages with varying intensities: marginal gentrification, early gentrification, gentrification proper and advanced gentrification. These stages are not necessarily sequential. Communities may experience only one or all of the different stages. However, she alludes to the notion of an inverse relationship between the different stages and associated impacts, i.e. in its early stages, gentrification can provide numerous positive benefits to a community, such as historic and cultural protection and preservation, an increased tax base, community improvements, etc. As it accelerates, however, positive benefits tend to become overshadowed by increasingly negative impacts, such as displacement, unaffordability and changes in community make-up.

Gentrifying Rural Landscapes and Rural Communities

Evidence from research in the Lunenburg and Port Stanley cases indicates that gentrification, is taking place and consequently changing the population composition and physical nature of these rural communities. Previous studies on gentrification have tended to focus on urban centers, or larger cities in Britain and the USA. More recently, however, the 'process of gentrification, which initially emerges as a sporadic, quaint, and local anomaly in the housing markets of some command-centers of Europe, North America or Oceania, the impulse behind gentrification is now generalized; its incidence is global, and it is densely connected into the circuits of global capital and cultural circulation' (Smith, 2002: 427).

While little discussion on gentrification in the rural community appears in the literature, this gap should not be interpreted to mean that gentrification is not occurring in the countryside. This could not be further from the truth. Whole communities are being gentrified and mainly through tourism. The terms 'revitalization' and 'reinvestment' previously discussed is not new to rural community economic development discourse. In fact, governments across Canada frequently promote and tout tourism development as a prime contributor to rural community revitalization and reinvestment. In a News Release (February 2, 2001), The Honorable Brian Tobin, then Premier of Newfoundland/Labrador, commented:

> For the past four years, the Canada-Newfoundland Comprehensive Economic Development Agreement has supported more than 260 projects in diverse areas such as tourism, technology, community economic development, human resources and entrepreneurship, and investment and trade. These investments have contributed to the revitalization of our economy.
>
> Of the $11 million allocated for tourism development and cultural and heritage industry initiatives, $4.5 million has been designated specifically for cultural and heritage industries. As this province has moved into the global market with its tourism product in the past decade, it has become increasingly obvious that our culture and heritage not only make us unique, but it is also a source of economic strength ... Our investment in tourism, culture and heritage through this agreement will contribute to the further development of these important sectors to our provincial economy.

George and Reid (2005) argue that tourism may be a prime force behind gentrification in rural communities and consequently, can initiate radical structural and social transformation. Further, these changes may not necessarily benefit the communities as intended. Indeed, upon closer examination, it appears such changes may threaten the communities' future sustainability. In this instance, as was illustrated by our case studies on Lunenburg and Canso, and to some degree in Port Stanley, traditional resource-based industries such as farming, mining and fishing that have been dominant in rural areas for generations have declined and are now being replaced by a new industry – tourism. This new industry requires reconstruction of infrastructure, both public and private, and frequently relies on historic culture as the guide to that development. This is not much different than the pattern identified in cities with the exception that the redevelopment is in some ways attempting to emulate or freeze a built environment in a certain time period. Gentrification is occurring not just for the purpose of upgrading homes but with the hopes of creating or maintaining an economic industry – a tourism industry based upon a local culture – and of rejuvenating a dwindling economy. Whatever the purpose, the main result of gentrification processes is to replace working-class areas with new ones, those associated with a more affluent, middle-upper class lifestyle.

Some argue that gentrification of the rural countryside is not such a new concept after all. Phillips (1993, 2002: 284) contends that gentrification 'is a term which has had quite a long history of use in a rural context, although it has not been subject to the same degree of reflection and contestation'. Cloke and Little (1990: 164) interpret gentrification as connected to 'class-dictated population movements, which lead to an immigration to rural areas of middle-class residents at the expense of the lower classes'.

Others (Murdoch & Marsden, 1994; Urry, 1995) have examined the movement of middle-class people to the rural countryside, and Shucksmith (1991) has examined how low-income groups are being displaced from the housing market in some rural areas. History indicates that early elites and the wealthy frequently acquired lands and large estates in far-away rural areas for a getaway, personal leisure and privacy. For example, several of Hollywood's rich and famous purchased properties or built private retreats and luxury lodges in rural areas of Africa or other exotic remote locations. These early gentrifiers, however, did not bring the same conditions to a neighbourhood, as do contemporary gentrifiers nor were the earlier invasions as intensive as they are today. What is different now is the scope and pervasiveness of this phenomenon and its consequences on entire rural communities due specifically to tourism development. Phillips (2002: 285) attempts to distinguish the difference between urban and rural gentrification.

> Whilst class colonization and social displacement are significant themes in both rural and urban studies, rather less attention has been paid in rural studies to the issue of the material refurbishment of properties ... emphasis in many rural studies is on house building rather than refurbishment ... the urban context, in contrast, has long been seen as centre on the refurbishment of existing housing. This emphasis on residential refurbishment has not gone uncontested and has spawned two lines of debate that act to further differentiate urban studies of gentrification from rural ones.

One view is that there are particular agents of gentrification or gentrifiers. Smith (1992) emphasizes the 'popular image of gentrifiers as people who buy a property, do it up themselves and then live in the refurbished property' (in Phillips, 2002: 286). According to Smith (1996), these owner-occupier developers can be said to be the true gentrifiers.

However, Smith (1979a, 1979b) has more appropriately identified four types of gentrifiers:

1. professional developers, who purchase property, develop it and then resell it for profit (1979b: 546).
2. landlord developers, who rent properties after they have been refurbished.
3. sweat-equity owner-occupier developers, where prospective owner-occupiers buy a house, finance its rehabilitation privately or with a construction mortgage or loan, and carry out the work with their own labour (1979a: 27).
4. unmediated owner-occupier developers, where a new occupier buys a property and then employs a developer to rehabilitate it (1979a: 28).

Increasingly, in many rural communities, the older, historic homes have become a focus for refurbishment and purchase, as exemplified in Lunenburg. However, according to Phillips' (2002) interpretation, Hamnett (1991, 1992) and Warde (1991) criticize Smith's view of gentrifiers, outlined above, because of its all encompassing nature; Hamnett and Warde argue that schemes of 'large developers do not involve the refurbishment of existing housing stock but the construction of new properties, albeit with some simulated historicity built into their design' (p. 286). This is the situation in Port Stanley, where former beach areas have been utilized for upscale condominiums.

A viewpoint that has been generally ignored within the rural studies literature on gentrification is the notion to 'stretch the concept of gentrification from a focus on the (re) construction of residential space towards encompassing a range of consumption activities' (Phillips, 2002: 286). That is, the construction of new products and services for consumption, accompanied by inflated prices, are part of the gentrification process. Researchers (Beauregard, 1986; Mills, 1993; Featherstone, 1991) have noted how residential gentrification has often been accompanied and stimulated by the development of retail, leisure and entertainment facilities, such as restaurants, bars, clubs, fashion boutiques, art galleries, museums and sport facilities (Phillips, 2002: 286). Coincidentally, this same kind of development merges with tourist destination development to meet the needs of tourist markets.

Tourism as a Force of Gentrification

As previously discussed, governments are adopting tourism as a strategy for revitalization of and reinvestment in rural areas. There is compelling evidence to support that tourism provides numerous benefits to a community – job creation, community improvements, new investment, increased economic income, etc. However, there is evidence to suggest that tourism is also a prime force of gentrification.

Less prosperous rural communities undertaking tourism often concentrate heavily on upgrading and improving local conditions to attract and provide experiences that meet the expectations and demands of tourists. In this instance, tourists, with high demands and expectations, provide incentives for gentrifiers. It can be argued that contemporary tourists, although different from early privileged elite travellers of the 'grand tour' era, nonetheless belong to an affluent, leisure class (Veblen, 1896; MacCannell, 1999). A tourist is one who has *discretionary* time and income to travel and spend that income on leisure activity. With a myriad of leisure activities and tourism experiences available, contemporary tourists are increasingly choosing to escape to the idyllic rural countryside in pursuit of novel experiences to counter those associated with the fast-paced humdrum of modern urban societies and workplaces.

One of the most important elements in this process of gentrification is the role of private investment. In this era of growing commodification of leisure experiences, rural areas are fast becoming play spaces for golf, hiking, skiing and other recreational activities. Private investment is often first on the scene to capture and package these opportunities to potential visitors. For example, Intrawest is a large Canadian corporation known for its large-scale resort community developments. With 11 ski resort communities to its credit, some in the biggest ski areas in Canada (e.g. Whistler Blackcomb in British Columbia and Blue Mountain in Ontario), Intrawest is a key exemplar of this form of investment. The following illustrates their strategic approach to resort building:

> We start with a mountain and enhance the skiing. Then build an animated place so that people stay longer. All this attracts more skiers who come more often, spend more money and bring their friends. More real estate is built and attractions are added, drawing yet more people … [which] leads to the expansion of year-round facilities, maximising the value of shops, hotels, convention facilities and restaurants … As occupancy and room rates climb, so does demand for resort real estate, creating a surge in real estate values. All this results in a total resort experience which brings year-round destination visitors, generating the financial critical mass which … leads to more resorts. (Cited in Whitson, 2001: 154)

Tourists have become gentrifiers in more direct ways. Many become captivated by the slower paced, 'traditional' country 'folk' ways and perceived rural purity and quality of life, which lend to notions of a past era and simpler lifestyle. Some are motivated to desire, seek and purchase a 'piece' of this rural 'fantasy', something perceived to be absent and/or different from their everyday lives and routines. While visiting rural communities, affluent tourists often visit local real estate agencies, seeking information on the availability of land and property for sale in the local area. Local real estate agencies respond to this increasing interest and demand from tourists by highlighting and promoting traditional heritage/historic homes and buildings, unique architecture and other cultural landscapes, reminiscent of a past era, which might be available for purchase. Communities themselves, as noted earlier, and other commercial interests, also respond to this growing fascination and demand by restructuring former workplace areas into newly created tourism zones, for example, old mills, factories and waterfront areas, which once belonged to the working class of the community; these become transformed into tourist attractions or upscale accommodation. Numerous communities and hamlets in rural Canada have restructured their former working 'waterfront' areas specifically as new zones of tourism and leisure development. Similarly, old mills, such as in Aberfoyle and Elora, both small communities in rural Ontario, have been renovated as upscale restaurants or inns and, more recently, as condos, to serve tourists and leisure consumers. Our research in Lunenburg, Nova Scotia and Port Stanley, Ontario, strongly supports the notion that tourism is a force of gentrification, evidenced by the alterations in their physical landscapes.

In Port Stanley, which has, over past years and still today, maintained a significant fishing industry, the most obvious sign of gentrification also became evident from examining the local real estate property. In this case, much of the sandy beach property, which drew the leisure and family recreation market for decades, has now been replaced by a slew of upscale condominium developments overlooking the lake; this has dramatically changed the beach landscape. Smaller, run-down seasonal dwellings in the area have also been upgraded to fit the more affluent image. A series of art galleries and upscale shops are evident as a new class becomes more apparent in the community.

In the more advanced stages of the gentrification process, newcomers displace local rural residents; as suggested earlier, many are drawn to the community for leisure or pleasure and not necessarily for active community membership. In Lunenburg's case, these newcomers are frequently tourists who have become enchanted with the community or are optimistic entrepreneurs who see the opportunity to cater to a new and growing tourist market. As a result, a new image of the rural community may take shape, one that portrays a leisure and affluent community and one far different from the longstanding images associated with the rural working-class.

Lunenburg's new image as a tourism destination takes root in the notion of rural community as a blended mix of affluent newcomers who have acquired a 'piece of the rural ideal' for personal or business purposes. Most, arguably, have no cultural or social attachments nor share any collective memories of the traditional community. Landscapes have been converted for affluent leisure-class residents and tourism, replacing the former working landscapes. A series of dynamics affecting social structures, including escalating house prices, higher tax assessments, building limits/restrictions and unaffordable housing, have occurred to expedite a social situation where local residents can no longer afford to live in the community; they become displaced by newcomers. These newcomers are often well-off 'outsiders' who seize the opportunity to purchase real estate for a small business (e.g. a B&B) or as a second home they occupy as seasonal residents. Evidence from George's (2006) work in Lunenburg suggests the 'second home' phenomenon has become a real issue in the community; many residents feel that 'seasonal' residents offer very little to the local life and signs of resentment have surfaced. These dynamics perpetuate a revolving circle of inflating prices, affluent buyers, increasing taxes and inability of locals to own real estate. Marjavaara (2007) and others (Sharpley & Sharpley, 1997; Fountain & Hall, 2002; Gallent *et al.*, 2003, 2005; Visser, 2004) argue that in the case of second home tourism, permanent residents are often displaced due to high demand for second homes, especially in exclusive locations (Lunenburg is a UNESCO World Heritage Site):

> ... based on local price inflations of dwellings, generated by external demand for second homes in the area. Buyers and owners of second homes in attractive areas are often recruited from upper-class segments of society, with a higher socio-economic status than permanent residents, forcing the latter to buy dwellings elsewhere, even forcing them to leave due to escalating property taxes ... is the case in many attractive rural areas where price levels have recently skyrocketed. (Cited in Marjavaara, 2007: 27)

Others (Keen & Hall, 2004; Selwood & Tonts, 2004) argue that the depopulation trend in many rural communities is caused by a restructuring of a local economy as a result of a decline in a traditional industry such as farming or fishing. This has resulted in rural unemployment and outmigration, leading to empty dwellings or potential second homes (Muller *et al.*, 2004). While this argument may explain depopulation and second-home purchases in many rural communities in Canada, it does not appear to hold true in Lunenburg's situation.

Following the World Heritage Site designation of Lunenburg, local real estate agencies 'jumped on the bandwagon' with aggressive marketing strategies targeted toward affluent 'potential' buyers. Most of this marketing effort was directed at international markets. Tourists visiting the community were frequently drawn to one local agency's polished, upscale storefront on the main street that showcased the best real estate 'buys' in town, including many of the beautiful heritage buildings. Further, the gentrification of the town ensures that children of long-time local residents have little hope or prospects for staying and making a living in the community of their parents, grandparents and great-grandparents.

Paradoxically, the reshaping of the original community's social fabric and image appears to have altered its uniqueness, which attracted the newcomers in the first place, thereby conflicting with their perceived rural 'fantasy'. Thus, one can argue that extensive tourism development leads to gentrification, which can invoke radical social and structural change processes that ultimately reframe and reimage the 'rural' community.

Gentrification: Future trends

Gentrification is reshaping a new demographic mix in both Lunenburg and Port Stanley. Aside from its original and naturally ageing population, data from the Lunenburg case show that the community is receiving an additional influx of older, but more affluent and highly educated residents, who are no longer of childbearing age. Many come from other countries, i.e. the USA and Germany, and/or other urban areas of Canada. The number of local ancestral families living in the community is declining. Data also indicate that family incomes for those that do live in Lunenburg are declining (Statistics Canada, 2001), thus making life increasingly unaffordable for locals. Recent data from Statistics Canada (2001) show there is an extremely high ratio of older people to younger people in the composition of Lunenburg's population. The school population is now in decline and with fewer children being born into a community dominated by older residents, a bright and sustainable future appears uncertain.

With the influx of newcomers, comes a whole new mindset – new attitudes, perspectives, customs and philosophies – quite different from those longstanding and traditional in the community. As part of the displacement process, old customs, traditions, beliefs and community values deteriorate and inevitably will be lost and replaced by new ones. Gentrification also results in loss of cultural diversity (Kennedy & Leonard, 2002). These demographic and social changes associated with gentrification carry potentially negative consequences for a community and its future sustainability – deteriorating human capital, declining social capital, disrupted social cohesion and community identity, as well as loss of traditional conduits that ensured authentic cultural and social reproduction in the community.

Supported by the literature and our research data, gentrification is well underway in both Lunenburg and Port Stanley. Further, evidence suggests that tourism is a major contributor to the gentrification process. All three elements composing Kennedy and Leonard's (2001) definition of gentrification are clearly evident in Lunenburg's current situation. First, there is evidence of displacement of its original residents. Second, there has been intensive physical upgrading of the neighborhood, particularly of housing stock and other historic buildings and landscapes; and third, there has been a radical change in neighborhood character.

Gentrification can affect demographic, social and cultural dimensions in a community, unbalancing community capitals and compromising the community's ability to maintain or achieve sustainability. Although tourism is frequently promoted and undertaken as a revitalization or reinvestment strategy for dying communities, little or no research discusses tourism-related gentrification and its potential impacts on the community. Tourism-related gentrification is usually well underway when signs of tension and conflict begin to appear. This phenomenon is becoming increasingly apparent in rural communities adopting tourism. Further, it also appears that the concept of gentrification is widely associated with urban development issues, but is generally not known or seriously considered as a rural community development issue. This may be a tragic oversight that could be overcome with appropriate planning and intervention. In many rural communities, gentrification often surfaces as a subtle, creeping process that tends to occur gradually over time, but quickly gains momentum when specific features and attractions in the community are highlighted and publicized. In Lunenburg's case, it was its prestigious UNESCO designation and subsequent tourism development. This follows Shaw's explanation (2003: 1) that one of the causes of gentrification is, 'a well-oiled media industry that keeps the whole circle turning'. Since the UNESCO designation, there has been intensive commercial marketing activity and massive publicity of Lunenburg from media that continue to draw new affluent tourists and consumers to this tourism destination.

As previously pointed out, earlier stages of gentrification can provide multiple benefits to a community. Planners and citizens alike are generally unaware of the dynamics and negative impacts until they become substantial and apparent in the community. Such communities often have to respond by taking reactive or remedial actions. Thus, more research and public awareness about the potential consequences of encroaching gentrification in rural communities is imperative. Only then can community planners and officials be proactive and consciously intervene to help reach a balance of community capacity necessary to maintain a healthy and vibrant society. Moreover, new approaches to tourism development as revitalization and reinvestment strategies need to be developed, which will consider the wide-reaching consequences of gentrification and allow communities to plan and implement appropriately to thwart or mitigate negative or undesired impacts.

Gentrification is not just particular to urban areas and its neighborhoods, as previously emphasized. We need only to take a look at rural communities in our local areas to get a sense of dramatic changes taking place. Further, gentrification in rural communities is a phenomenon that appears to be closely aligned with tourism development. As in urban areas, gentrification is a force with the power to revitalize, renew, change or eradicate rural communities, depending on how it is understood and planned or not planned by community decision-makers, planners and developers. Critical to the community development process, planning is the subject of Chapter 13. Next, we discuss an interrelated process: the growing tendency towards theming and branding of rural areas.

Building the Rural Brand: Theming and Imaging the Countryside

This discussion of rural branding and theming takes in many dimensions that have been brought out so far in this book. First, our current era of economic restructuring has left many communities, urban and rural, struggling to attract investment for development. Further, each of the communities we describe in the case studies highlights the varying dimensions of this particular struggle. This is a new era for community and economic development, and authors such as Paddison (1993) developed the notion of 'the new urban entrepreneurialism' to explain this frequent and often frantic search for investment. Brought out in their book on place promotion, Gold and Ward (1994: 2) define place promotion as, 'the conscious use of publicity and marketing to communicate selective images of specific geographical localities or areas to a targeted audience . . .'. It is important to note, however, that not all place promotion takes the form of such a deliberate strategy (as is the case with Vulcan, Alberta, described in Chapter 5), and some places are 'promoted' through no effort of their own (e.g. through literature, film). Morgan and Pritchard (2004) outline the various components of place promotion and point out that it involves not only publicity and marketing, but also 'flagship' developments and 'spotlight' events in the arts, media, leisure, heritage and sport. Nonetheless, place promotion, particularly in the form of theming and branding, are obvious approaches used by those concerned with enhancing tourism development. Further, the cases of Canso, Lunenburg as well as Vulcan have a strong element of this type of promotion.

Branding and theming

Olins (2004: 24) describes branding as an unsurprising outcome of business practices:

> Well, there is no doubt that business is about making money. But to make money, business people have to exploit and attempt to manipulate human emotions just like political leaders. Businesses have to create loyalties; loyalties of the workforce, loyalties of suppliers, loyalties of the communities in which they operate, loyalties of investors and loyalties of customers. In creating these loyalties, they use very similar techniques to those of nation builders. They create myths, special languages, environments that reinforce loyalties, colours, symbols, and quasi-historical myths.

There are four key ways that we can think of brands: as communication devices, as perceptual entities, as value enhancers and as relationships (Morgan & Pritchard, 2004: 61). Brands are used to convince the consumer (or potential consumer) that there is no substitute for this product. In our case of tourism, experience and branding plays on emotions as well as the extent to which an entire array of ideas or attributes can be conveyed by a sign, an image or a slogan. Of course, branding for a tourism community (or any other destination) is an incredibly difficult challenge and the relationship between governments and business becomes crucial here. As Morgan and Pritchard (2004: 63–64) argue:

> Nowhere is the paradox of public policy and market forces more sharply defined than in destination branding. Political considerations have compromised many a creative execution. . . . In this sense, successful destination branding is about achieving a balance between applying cutting-edge solutions to a marketing problems and the real politick of managing local, regional and national politics.

To be successful, a brand must create an emotional attachment and still be credible, deliverable, differentiating, convey powerful ideas, be enthusing for stakeholders and partners, and resonate with the customer (Morgan & Prichard, 2004: 70). Shaw and Williams (2004) note that the tourism industry gives more powerful meanings to its products when it is able to associate them with particular places and themes. In their discussion on theming, MacDonald and Alsford (1995; in Shaw & Williams, 2004: 246) summarize the key elements of the ultimate experience in themed environments, Disneyland:

- high-quality visitor services . . . which satisfy the postmodern tourists who are "playful consumers of superficial signs" and spaces
- multi-sensory experience, which involves:
  - simulated environments (natural, cultural, historical, and technological)
  - humanizing of these environments by live interpretations and performances
  - state-of-the-art films
  - themed exhibits and eating places
- a highly structured experience, which attempts to counterbalance the risk of information overload through the structured programming of visitors
- the constant reinvention and upgrading of experiences, with the latest technologies

While these topics don't describe explicitly the cases in this book (rural communities rarely have the resources to develop such an intensive and coordinated approach to theming), they are useful because they highlight the effort to satisfy the desires of tourists for what they know are not authentic experiences. Further, they highlight the extent to which the theming of community may extend far beyond what the residents are willing to accept.

Interestingly, this theming and branding approach may even be a drawback in terms of the whole tourism industry. As Coles' (2003: 212) work on Leipzig points out, following a rather systematic approach to developing a place promotion/branding strategy leaves many places looking and feeling the same, or what he calls 'an indistinct heritage mix with limited opportunities to exploit other market segments'.

Gruffudd (1994: 247–248) argued that the promotion of places, rural places in particular, involves a transmission of 'enduring values' built upon aesthetic, social and moral ideals founded primarily in Victorian England. While the role of these values in the construction of place may be clear (one thinks of rural places as pure, unspoiled, un- or anti-industrial, etc.), places like Vulcan, it might be argued, are fostering an alien image of community (based upon the *Star Trek* imagery) yet are still founded on morals and ideals, including the benefits of intercultural communication, respect of difference and nonviolence.

Hannigan's work on the Pacific Rim (1998) suggests that there are two main 'models' of theme park development:

> "Buffet-model" within which the visitor is given a mixture of choices (attractions) covering both global and replicated traditional culture. The "local model" where theme park is developed around a local culture – usually strongly commodified albeit around local themes.

Thinking back to our case studies, it might be argued that both Lunenburg and Canso, Nova Scotia, are building their themes upon local history and culture – even if it is somewhat fabricated and enhanced. In these communities, the theming stems from the area's history and heritage and taps into the nostalgic desires of many tourists for access into the past – a simpler time. The case of Vulcan, however, is a bit more puzzling. To understand this case, we can turn to Shaw and Williams (2004) as they argue that there should be a third model: global culture promotion. As the case study of Vulcan identified, the appeal of the community, as attempts were made by a few members of the local community to develop its theme, was built upon a global phenomenon as they worked to tap into the enduring, international appeal of the *Star Trek* television series. This is much less about local heritage and history as it is about globalization and the spread of popular culture through television and other media.

There are many unintended impacts of place promotion, branding and theming and while our focus is on rural areas, it is also useful to highlight the important research on the impact of these approaches on urban areas. As Hall (1998; see also Morgan & Pritchard, 1999) makes clear, the long-term impacts of place promotion using things like mega events or large, flagship developments, are rarely considered, nor are real efforts at consultation part of their development. These developments are not only often very exclusionary, but can have enduring and potentially unalterable impacts on a community's sense of place. This may be especially true for small communities where the impact of large projects (such as the Trek and Tourism Station in Vulcan) is undeniably important.

In Hoelscher's (1998) excellent study of the creation of a themed community in rural America, he points out that there is very often an exclusionary process at work. By choosing one particular theme around which the tourism destination image is to be built, aspects of local life and culture are, by definition, left out. Therefore, tensions exist, what Hoelscher calls an unstable 'dialectic of public memory ... inevitably susceptible to political manipulation and commercialisation by both official and vernacular interests' (Hoelscher, 1998: 22). Moreover, he highlights the challenges implicit in the 'conspicuous construction' of these themes, as their success may mean the community's identity may become 'other-directed' and reflect the desires and wants of tourists to the exclusion of community members. This notion of other-directedness leads us to a broader concern with the tendency of change in rural landscapes away from productive places where people make their lives to 'playspaces' for (urban) visitors.

Rural communities as urban playgrounds

Law (2001) argued that tourism has the potential to change communities, especially small communities, into playgrounds for the middle class. While this change is not completely one-sided and communities resist and negotiate their playground status, powerful forces are at play, particularly when a small community decides to sell itself as a leisure space for wealthy tourists. Moreover, Law points out not only that this complex process has been oversimplified within tourism research, but that there are ways to use the opportunity to determine the image of a community to cement community power. Law (2001: 82) concludes his study on Collingwood, Ontario, in the following way:

> It was argued ... that pressures of gentrification and commodification, spurred by global dynamics of demography, attendant consumption patterns, and the spread of global capital do not necessarily result in the sort of cultural annihilation often found in contemporary

literature. Rather, these same threatening processes can serve as catalysts for conscious negotiation of identity explicitly conducted at the iconic level.

Aguiar *et al.* (2005) argue that while relatively understudied, many smaller communities are redesigning and reinventing themselves as particular kinds of playground and living spaces for wealthy tourists and workers looking for a change. Their work traces this reinvention process in Kelowna, British Columbia. In Kelowna, these authors identify four 'discourses' at work in constructing this community in order to attract economic attention: an ideal retirement community, a playground, a 'white' or 'familiar place' and a site of advanced technological development (thereby attractive to the new 'creative' class).

Whitson (2001) has traced the impact of the relationship between rural development and the growing search for nature-based recreation and puts this situation in historical context. He writes:

It represents a significant departure from our past as a nation of agriculture and resource extraction as most Canadians now relate to nature primarily as a place of leisure and many rural regions are now more valuable as 'recreation resources' than for the farming and forestry once associated with them. However, for those that do, new economic possibilities have opened up. (p. 146)

Importantly, Whitson combines his discussion of gentrification with what he calls 'sportification' of many outdoor activities. For example, cross-country skiing, mountain biking and rock climbing have spawned entire leisure industries and are increasingly claiming places as their own. Moreover, Whitson (2001: 148–149) notes that these developments carry the forces of change into many small Canadian communities because:

... affluent lifestyles were quickly transforming into images of popular aspiration in an upwardly mobile society; and as golf and skiing, in particular, became part of the cultural capital of the business and professional classes, interest in these sports would start to change the face of many rural areas. This is because each of these sports requires significant land assembly, extensive transformation and contouring of that land, and increasingly heavy capital expenditure.

Much like the previous discussions of gentrification, theming and branding, when places are constructed as familiar and play spaces for outsiders, the delicate dialectic of public memory and sense of place (following Hoelscher, 1998) is out of balance and the communities become other-directed. As is the case with Vulcan in particular, when this imbalance begins to have an impact on everyday life in the community, or the experience of community events more specifically, resistance is inevitable. Unfortunately, authors such as Whitson (2001) would go even farther to argue that we must take into account the fact that these new tourism-related developments push out rural working classes both physically by taking the nature-based sites and making them private, corporatized spaces, and financially, by driving up the costs of land, real estate and resources for everyday life. Whitson's call echoes Hall's suggestion that the phrase cultural change is a 'polite euphemism for the processes by which some cultures, and the people who live in them, are actively pushed aside so that others can take their place' (Hall, 1981 in Whiston, 2001: 161). Further, it is important not to lose sight of this development as 'places ... with the right kinds of recreational resources have become playgrounds for urban (and increasingly global) money, workers have too often found themselves pushed aside, either to the fringes of their own communities or to the margins of the cities that ex-urbanites have chosen to leave behind' (Whitson, 2001: 161). Next, we look briefly at the idea of sense of place and the role that tourism may play in its construction.

Sense of place

Conceptually, we use the term sense of place to convey the extent to which an individual feels an attachment to a particular setting based upon a combination of use, attentiveness and emotion (Stokowski, 2002: 368). But, as geographers and others are beginning to make clear, how a sense of place is created and even manipulated speaks more to the social construction of place and the power relations that are part of this construction than any physical definition. For example, Stokowski (2002: 371) asks:

- What circumstances lead to the social creation of places?
- What are the symbolic values of places, and how are these meanings incorporated into management decisions?
- How do groups and communities of people come to share meanings about place?
- How is place represented and produced across a society (and how might it differ across groups and societies)?
- What are the social and political consequences of different versions of place realities?

- Which spokespersons are allowed to define place boundaries, or tell the histories of place, or interpret the meanings of place?
- How do different conceptions of place exert influence on people and groups?
- How is place manipulated for social good or evil?

While it is worth noting that places are constructed by individuals who have the power to do so, there are also broader contextual elements at work here. Globalization, and particularly neoliberalism through restructuring and economic uncertainty, creates conditions that can change how we feel about places. Williams (2002) argues that while globalization is often seen as a homogenizing force, it can also provide opportunities for localities to build upon ideas of difference and distinction. Indeed, the idea of branding is really about setting one place apart from another. However, as Williams argues, tourism is bound up in contradictory tensions and tendencies as it can be a force of preservation and protection in times of change just as it can be a force for change all on its own (p. 357). All communities have many stories and versions of stories, it is important to be aware that these multiplicities of meanings engender difference images of community and are not well-captured by attempts to theme or brand communities.

Conclusion

This chapter sought to set out and discuss in some depth the key factors in the relationship between tourism and the changing rural landscape. More directly, we aim to consider the connections between the forces of gentrification, theming and branding, and broader ideas of political economy. As Shaw and Williams (2004: 261) argue, this has not been well done to date in tourism studies as the transformation of landscapes into 'new playgrounds of consumption' reveals 'the interlinked forces involved in the re-use of industrial spaces, the construction of a heritage industry and the strategies of place promotion'. Further, they follow Gotham (2000; in Shaw & Williams, 2004: 261) and others by arguing that cultural perspectives have failed to:

> ... expose the links between culture and the political economy. In this respect, they have neglected the profit-making role of surrounding the production of new tourism spaces. To this we should add that that this neglect also extends to the role of the state through public-private initiatives.

Thus, in this exploration of the changing rural landscape, one can see the coming together of many themes explored in this book, the forces of restructuring and the role of public–private government relationships (explored in more depth in Chapter 12). As the discussion of the cases made clear, the forces of gentrification as well as the efforts at branding lead to the exclusion and the marginalization of some who do not fit (or cannot afford to fit) into the tourism developments. Shaw and Williams (2004: 267) argue that the only way to prevent or alleviate this exclusion is to understand that these efforts need to be grounded in local social relations. In the next chapter, we move towards a better understanding of these local social relations as we consider the notion of community in more detail.

Chapter 10
Notions of Community

Introduction

The intent of this chapter is to provide the reader with some understanding of the theory and principles of community development practice as it applies to tourism development. Further, it is intended to argue the importance of community control of tourism development given its invasive nature, particularly in rural communities.

This chapter first describes the notion of community. What constitutes community and community development (CD) is examined. The importance of taking a CD approach to tourism planning, particularly in rural communities, is discussed. Reaching the proper balance between individual freedom to act that encourages creativity, and the need for community control of the product is also examined.

Key Theoretical Concepts: Community; Community Development (CD); Tourism Planning

The Idea of Community

Community is often defined as a geographic concept or from a collective interest point of view. The idea of community is contested but simply put, Pedlar (1996: 9) defines community as, 'some sense of place, psychological involvement, social interaction, and feelings of connectedness'. Defining community has been an ongoing quest for theorists and scholars alike. According to Johnston *et al.* (2000), 'community is a social network of interacting individuals, usually concentrated into a defined territory'. Burr (1991) argues that there are four theoretical approaches to understanding community. These four approaches are: the human ecological approach, the social systems approach, the interaction approach and the critical approach. Pearce *et al.* (1996) discuss these approaches.

By taking an ecological approach, the focus is on the community living together and adapting to the setting, a process that produces distinctive community characteristics. The social systems approach emphasizes the roles and institutions that govern society; its focus is on the ordering of social relations and the primacy of group membership. An interactional approach can be seen as the sum of the regular social interactions of individuals. Consistent with this approach, Warren (1978) views community as the sum of the clustered interactions of people and organizations occupying a restricted geographic area. In contrast, a critical approach stresses the opposing forces in groups of people, paying particular attention to the power of key groups in decision-making processes. Generally, though, community is understood to encompass notions of: membership; shared spaces of place and identity; shared interests, customs and modes of thought or expressions; collectivism, human association and social networks (George, 2004).

In rural communities, particularly isolated areas, these concepts of community are highly pronounced, and are depicted through enduring intergenerational and family relationships, community interdependency, trust and respect, kinship and strong social bonding. Rural communities tend to have a strong attachment and rootedness to place. Vitek and Jackson (1996: 3), in *Rooted in the Land*, point out:

> The connection between human communities and place is not unique to rural areas, but here one can be certain that the land is not mere scenery and hiking trail, or resources in need of extraction. Here the land becomes part of people's lives, intermingled with buying and selling, working and playing, living and dying. It is both history and future.

In making this concept operational, some (Etzioni, 1996) would emphasize the communitarian aspects of community, while others (Friedman, 1975) may see it as a necessary but limited part of human existence that only serves to facilitate the creation and maintenance of neoliberal values that enable and give expression to individualism. The attempt to reduce the role of community in society is reflected in Margaret Thatcher's famous comment that 'there is no such thing as society', which undermines the notion that community exists at all. So at best, community can be thought of as a set of the values expressed above by Pedlar (1996) whose strength and combination are contrasted on a continuum. Some among us would be most comfortable to rest their idea of community at the communitarian end of the spectrum, while others may be more content to place emphasis on the facilitation of the individual. So, the operationalization of community is a contested process. Thus, reaching a consensus about what it means is an extremely important first step before planning for development can begin.

To summarize, community can be defined as a geographic location bounded by political boundaries. However, it is also possible that a larger area or region may see itself as a community for tourism development purposes. Some would consider this a community of interest, that is, a group of people or institutions that have a common interest in the same issue or subject. In this example, and to complicate matters, geographic communities share boundaries with neighboring municipalities that also share an interest in tourism development. Often this shared interest is centered on the natural environment, so all concerned are affected by the development of one component in the ecological system.

At its base, community provides the support for individual interaction and safety and yet it also allows individuals to practice individualism. In its simplest form, community provides the opportunity for individuals to act on their initiative and for individual expression and satisfaction to flourish while keeping the interests of the collectivity paramount. Without community and its potential to enforce sanctions that protect the collectivity, individuals may simply engage in unfettered self-advancement at the expense of their fellow human beings as well as the social and ecological environment.

Now that we've discussed notions of community, it is important to note that tourism development in rural communities will have an impact on the lives of all citizens, whether they are beneficiaries or not. Thus, tourism must be planned keeping the communitarian, collective aspects of community in mind and not simply left to the discretion of individually-oriented entrepreneurs. Individual entrepreneurs seeking to start or expand their business opportunity quite rightly are singularly focused on their activity and do not recognize the potential of their activity to both positively and negatively affect those living around them. It could be concluded that they often don't see their activity as a community concern.

Tourism businesses are treated similarly to other commercial endeavors, however, while most economic activity exports goods or services out of the local area for economic inflow, tourism imports people as its export, thereby adding considerable stress to local areas and communities. Some rural communities double or triple their permanent populations with visitors during peak periods, causing great stress to the facilities and services that were designed for a much smaller permanent population. With this fundamental point in mind, the involvement of community members in tourism product development becomes critically important to all those affected as well as to the sustainability of the tourism product over the long term.

Conventional wisdom sees community as a homogeneous entity containing a singular mind. However, it may not be quite as simple as that impression would suggest. Given the variety of interests each of us has, we often find ourselves a member of many different communities at any given time, some of which may be in conflict depending on the issue being addressed, which further complicates the notion. The concept of community may act quite like the individuals that comprise it; complex, conflicted and concerned over the many issues they encounter at any single period in time. Given these complexities, balancing the values of community members in planning for tourism development is critical and is addressed in more depth in Chapter 13.

Further to the idea of community as either a geographic or interest collective, 'there is a strong connection between community and the ethical ideal of a strong, deep democracy' (Kerans & Kearney, 2006: 145). The idea of community is deeply embedded in the concept of democracy. Unlike what some would have us believe, democracy is not simply a well-functioning market system, but democracy consists of active and ongoing discourse among all citizens that is focused on creating and recreating society. Further, democracy demands that individuals act independently and collectively to create a society that responds to the needs and aspirations of all its citizens. Certainly, the implementation of democracy may fall short of this aspiration, but the goal remains steadfast.

Democracy is played out in different ways, according to the prevailing and dominant world view held by society at any given time. Most of the world presently lives within a neoliberal, ideological framework or is headed in that direction, which tends to value individual freedom and initiative over collective and communitarian values. As stated earlier, however, and important to repeat again, the ability to act individually with success and satisfaction depends profoundly on the construction of a solidly functioning society and community. Individualism without society deteriorates into anarchy to the point where individualism cannot be productive or successful. Society and community allows individual initiative to flourish. A strong and well-functioning community produces and supports strong and respectful individual initiative. Neoliberalism provides the ideological foundation for the global, capitalist economic system, and this system often neglects the importance of community. Underscoring the neoliberal philosophy are ideas founded in classical liberal theory. As McPherson (1977: 1) suggests the notion of liberal, 'can mean freedom of the stronger to do down the weaker by following market rules; or it can mean equal effective freedom of all to use and develop their capacities'. If the latter, rather than the former is to occur, then it is desirable for society to create a framework to assist that process. A geographic or community of interest, in most cases, provides just such a framework.

We are not suggesting that Western society needs to adopt a full-blown communitarian social organizing system before or during the development of tourism in rural areas, but perhaps to adopt many of the communitarian values such as increasing democracy through enlarged communitywide discourse and by providing greater access to the decision-makers and the decision-making process. Tourism development in rural areas can create considerable, and sometimes intolerable, impacts on local areas. These impacts not only come in physical terms like increased traffic and congestion, but also in changing, perhaps even undermining local culture as the case study in Lunenburg demonstrates. It appears to us that most forms of tourism decision-making are elitist and inward looking, and do not engage the community in a wide-ranging discussion so vital for fostering democracy. As a society, we have tended to lean more toward the liberal end of the community continuum, to the neglect of some very important democratic principles that give control of development to those living *in situ*. In many cases, the process for decision-making has followed McPherson's idea outlined above where the stronger do down the weaker. In order for tourism to be of benefit to local areas, a more balanced power structure that favors community is required if tourism is to become sustainable over the long term. After all, in rural areas it is the history of community and the reflection on a simpler time period that often provides the focus for the tourism product. To ignore this focus is to damage the tourism product itself.

If the tourism project does not strengthen the general community, but only adds to individual wealth at the expense of the social and ecological environment, its purpose and usefulness need to be questioned. Of course, the criteria on which the measures are undertaken are also a matter of debate, but all too often these criteria speak directly to economic concerns only and leave out some other important variables from the social and ecological arena. While important, economic variables are not the only indicators that need to be addressed. Quality of life variables, which reflect the values of the whole community as well as its ecological foundation, need to be identified collectively by the community. Further, the assessment and monitoring of these variables should be incorporated into an ongoing evaluation process. Chapter 13 sets out some guidelines for this process.

Decisions that affect our individual and collective lives are made on a continual basis and the process through which those decisions are made may be just as important as the decisions themselves. The idea of democracy is one of engagement in setting out visions and goals for community issues, including economic development strategies, at some level by all citizens. Community, therefore, must be thought of as not only a collective of citizens, but also as a process for decision-making. Once that process has been agreed to, citizens may choose to be quite active participants on some issues and less so on others. The notion of community then does not indicate that all citizens will be equally engaged in the decision-making process on all issues, but that there are well-established and agreed-to processes that are open to all citizens who wish to be involved.

The Enemies of Community

While the arguments for community involvement in the planning process are evident from the previous discussion, there are forces in society that would limit this involvement and would leave these decisions solely to members of the business sector. Gramsci (1971) introduced the term *hegemony* to describe the ways groups with power (e.g. the ruling class) maintains control over others by means ranging from enacting legislation that serves their interests to outright coercion. Often, tourism entrepreneurs believe that they have a premier position in the decision-making process because of their financial risk in the proposed project. What is not considered is the potential risk to the community's lifestyle that the project also brings. Further, the idea that those who risk capital should have a dominant position in the decision-making process seems to be accepted as the norm in tourism planning and development. However, recently there has been much debate about other forms of risk as well as capital. The issue of assessing risks of tourism to lifestyle and community integrity is gaining legitimacy and may be seen as a legitimate risk factor – much like capital risk for the entrepreneur. All risks need to be recognized and those who are subjected to them need to have voice in the decision-making process that leads to an acceptable project.

There is much discussion today about the advancement and supremacy of individualism over thinking and acting collectively. While the elites and most powerful in society might argue that thinking and acting collectively is not in our best interest, we argue that acting only as individuals, in fact, works against our welfare and freedom. Others

(Etzioni, 1996) argue that only through collective action and by the creation of such fundamental instruments as legislation, can we act independently. The issue for many of us is not whether we act as individuals or in collectives, but the balance between the two. Given that much tourism development is entrepreneurially driven, citizen participation in many of these developments has been approached from the individual end of the community continuum. This approach is based on the idea that those who are risking the most should have the most power in decision-making. That said, it is important to determine on what basis risk is assessed. As noted above, common wisdom would suggest that financial risk is paramount in the process, and yet, the risk of loss of community integrity and environmental sustainability must also rate high on the risk assessment scale. Determining the balance between the interests of the individual and the collective is necessary at the initial stage of project development. Ascertaining this balance is a collective affair, and the size and potential impact of the project is likely to be the determining factor. What is often hidden at the project initiation stage of development is the potential size of the final outcome. Because tourism is an additive activity, that is, one business feeds off others, tourism tends to grow through inertia rather than planning. It is extremely opportunistic, so communities need to be vigilant about how tourism is growing over time in their area and markers need to be determined in advance that will alert the community to threats and overdevelopment.

Finally, mention should be made of the power of the economic imperative as a major risk to society generally and the environment specifically. Tourism has long been considered a benign human activity. We are coming to the conclusion, however, that travel, particularly airline travel, is one of the most damaging environmental practices in society. In addition, the exhaust from buses, has had a major effect on many of the treasured Mayan ruins in Mexico and other parts of South America. As a consequence of the economic imperative, many tourism sites have been overbuilt, leading to exhaustion and decline. While this is tragic to communities that have come to depend on tourism for their livelihood, many business owners are not local residents so they can pick up and move on to new locations until they too become spoiled. This type of 'throw away tourism' is no longer acceptable in the face of increasing concerns for sustainability. Balance in development and economic gain once again becomes a principle on which tourism development must proceed.

Community Development and Cultural Commodification in Rural Tourism Planning

As noted earlier and made clear in the case studies, much of the attraction in rural communities for tourism development lies in their culture and heritage, whether real or contrived. The consumption of community and its culture is denoted by the logic and rationality of commodity production, and has become deeply embedded within the sphere of tourism. It is the increasing commodification and consumption of idyllic rural countryside, local cultures and leisure experiences, where local images, symbolic artifacts and expressions, and other intangibles have been reclaimed, reconstructed and revalued for the marketplace. The creation and marketing of novel and alternative cultural goods and experiences, as demonstrated in Lunenburg in Chapter 3 in this volume, is a prime example of capital accumulation through tourism. Ray (1998) refers to this commodification of culture as a *culture economy*, a notion that consists of strategies to transform local knowledge into resources available for the local territory.

Relative to this notion of community, heritage (cultural) tourism, according to the literature, is increasingly taking its place as the *new* phenomenon in contemporary tourism development. This notion is very evident in Lunenburg, where heritage assets, particularly architectural heritage, provide a major component in the community's tourism offering. According to Nuryanti (1996: 249), 'heritage' in its broader meaning, implies 'something transferred from one generation to another; as a carrier of the past, it is viewed as part of the cultural tradition of a society'. In contrast, he continues, 'The concept of tourism is really a form of modern consciousness'. Thus, we have what appears to be a dichotomous arrangement; their interconnections and relationships may 'parallel the debate that takes place within a society's culture between tradition and modernity' (p. 249).

Today, tourism is often conceptualized by *complexity*, as a highly complex series of production-related activities (Boyne & Rattansi, 1990; Cohen, 1995; Munt, 1994; Pretes, 1995; Nuryanti, 1996). In support of this view, Nuryanti (1996) claims certain characteristics of tourism are evident in postmodernity; rapid movements occur through areas that are segmented into national and regional cultures and traditions, creating an international identity. In the world of tourism, fantasy and reality are interwoven and time and space are collapsing; travel is attainable for many in contemporary society. Tourists are searching for novel ways to identify with the past. New forms of 'reproduction of the past,' and associated consumption patterns, are being reflected in the choices of travelers. This is evidenced in Lunenburg; for example, in 2003, it received a contingent of tourists who were descendents of the Swiss Foreign Protestants to attend an event that was marketed as a *special* reunion, and to erect a large granite memorial in tribute to the early founding settlers. There is also a movement afoot towards rediscovering one's roots and a growing appreciation of tradition that relates to one's total environment. This notion may explain why many tourists visit Lunenburg's genealogy center, located in the Fisheries Museum, which contains a large archive of resources of particular interest to the descendents of the early settlers in the community. As outlined in the Lunenburg case, George's research suggests that the above notions and trends are manifested within both the supply and demand dimensions of Lunenburg's tourism development. Nuryanti (1996) states,

> Heritage tourism offers opportunities to portray the past in the present. Postmodern tourists use the power of their intellect and imagination to receive and communicate messages, constructing their own sense of historic places to create their individual journeys of self-discovery.

New approaches to tourism appear deeply rooted in the cultural. It was Adorno (1991), as part of a larger Marxist discourse on capitalism, who critiqued the ways in which cultural artifacts and experiences have been commodified by being easily reproduced in mechanical form and therefore debased (Hannauss, 1999). In the commodification of culture, 'the past has been made to live and has become a commodity with a large economic industry [tourism] riding on its back', as evidenced in Lunenburg.

The next section sets the stage to discuss one of the main themes in this book: participation in tourism development and planning. In short, we argue that one of the ways to stem the tide of commodification in rural communities is to ensure that tourism development and planning embraces the needs, wants and values of all community members.

What are Community Development (CD) and Citizen Participation?

Integral to the placement of community as a guiding force in the tourism development process are the ideas of CD and citizen participation. CD is often associated with the notion of 'alternative development'. Friedmann (1995: 31) suggests that alternative development:

... involves a process of social and political empowerment whose long-term objective is to rebalance the structure of power in society by making state action more accountable, strengthening the powers of civil society in the management of its own affairs ...

The concept of development in the CD model views human activity in a larger perspective than simply in terms of economic growth. CD is concerned with process rather than focusing solely on outcomes of development. CD is used as a verb in this volume rather than as a noun as it has come to be regarded. Reid and van Dreunen (1996: 49) summarize the concept of CD as follows:

CD is broadly defined here as a process for empowerment and transformation. The focus on CD is to identify and resolve problems of a social, physical, or political nature that exist in a community in such a way that these conditions are changed or improved from the perspective of the community members. The goals of CD are self-help, community capacity building, and integration.

CD views development as human development and, as a result, focuses on individual learning and collective capacity building in addition to economic growth. It takes as a guiding principle the idea that involvement in community decision-making contributes to individual learning that enhances the perspective of the individual involved, which, in turn, provides greater resources to the community for potential future endeavors. The intent of CD is cumulative in that the goal is to continue to develop the capabilities of community members thereby adding to the competence of the community in decision-making and its ability to develop future projects. While there are many definitions, there are common elements to most of them. These elements can be synthesized to include a focus on change, indigenous problem identification, self-help, open participation of all community members in the decision-making processes (if they so desire), and community control of the development process and outcome. CD stresses process over product. As Ross (1967: 15) points out when speaking of CD, 'development of a specific project (such as an industry or school) is less important than development of the capacity of people to establish that project'.

More specifically, CD comes in different forms and intensities. Sanders (1970) has provided the most complete delineation of approaches to CD. He suggests that it can take the form of a *method*, a *movement*, a *program* or a *process*. As a *movement*, it is expected to lead to the empowerment of those involved in the process, as one might expect from the foregoing discussion in this section. CD as a movement sees CD in its purest form. It assigns the problem identification to the community rather than to some elite group of individuals. Seeing it as a *method* requires those leading the process to place great emphasis on citizen participation in moving to some desired state however, the problem may be identified *a priori* by those in power in this rubric, which is not the case in either the definition of CD as a movement or a process. Seeing CD as a movement stresses that the community defines the problem collectively, whereas using CD as a method focuses on determining what actions to take on a problem that has already been defined by another (elite) group.

Viewing CD as a *process*, places paramount emphasis on the learning experience of those involved, but not necessarily on outcome or community control. Identifying CD as a *program* limits both the problem to be solved and the method used in its resolution. Community economic development initiatives are usually considered by us to be in the program mode of CD. It strives to involve most citizens in solving the economic concerns of the community, but it identifies the problem as an economic one *a priori* and reduces the methods of solving those issues to a well-identified repertoire reducing creativity.

Selecting one of the approaches identified above to problem solving and decision-making enhances and/or limits the potential to reach certain objectives. While CD is often talked about as a singular notion, Sanders views it as a multiple concept, so a community must decide what form of CD best suits its needs when planning tourism. Given our experience in using CD as an approach to tourism development, we urge the adoption of the *movement* and *process* end of the continuum be implemented by community tourism planners as the preferred process of development. It is a powerful approach to development, one that not only aids community capacity building, but also the sustainability of the product for the developer as well.

CD and capacity building are fundamental ingredients in enhancing democracy generally. While many observers suggest that the market mechanism is a major (some would say primary) ingredient in democracy, we argue that generating community capacity through CD initiatives is not only fundamental to democracy, but also an important foundation mechanism for market development as well.

In an earlier volume, Reid (2003) suggested that *community awareness raising* and *community organizing* were two important development processes that were largely overlooked by many rural communities when they launched a tourism development project or product. The overlooking of these two extremely important process activities often led to the breakdown of the project as implementation proceeded. Planners are in the habit of developing project plans and then introducing those plans to the public once they are established. The problem often arises that while the plan may speak to the needs and aspirations of the development proponent, they neither speak to the needs and aspirations of the public nor to the sustainability of the community where the plans are to be implemented.

Communities members may organize themselves in opposition to development if it has become too large or antithetical to their lifestyle and tastes. Many of the problems that lead to this type of oppositional movement could be avoided if greater care was taken to involve the public earlier in the process and in a much more meaningful way than is often the case. We recommend that community citizens be invited to participate right at the visioning stage of the development process rather than waiting until the draft plan has been developed. This would provide valuable input to the planner in the design process at no additional cost to the developer. A process that would accomplish this principle is outlined in Chapter 12 of this volume. Not only does CD, including participation in project design and decision-making, provide a more sustainable project, it also leads to greater democracy.

Integral to the implementation of the CD approach to tourism development, whether it is in the form of a movement, method, process or program as outlined earlier in this chapter, is the leadership function. Leadership, as discussed elsewhere (Reid, 2003), is critical to the CD process, or to any process, for that matter. The CD approach requires a facilitative leadership style that is focused on the process of development rather than on the product. Business people and entrepreneurs cannot give appropriate leadership to a tourism project that is attentive to CD if they are single-mindedly focused on a preconceived product. This type of leadership is bound to be combative when their ideas about the outcome do not match up directly with those of the community. Leaders using the CD approach to development will focus their attention on gaining agreement to the overall vision and goals of the community, which will set the framework for the development project. So, the vision, goals and objectives of the community set the stage in which tourism development unfolds. Attaining the community vision becomes the goal of the project, and tourism development becomes one vehicle in achieving that goal.

The Importance of Involvement of Community in Tourism Development

Involving community in the tourism development process is often talked about but little understood. In fact, community involvement in the tourism planning and development process is often nothing more than window dressing designed to sell an already developed concept to the public. In many jurisdictions, the citizen participation process is legislated so planners and developers have no choice but to take developed plans to the public for discussion. While legislation of this type is well intentioned, it does not provide for sound and meaningful participation on the part of the public, but helps to establish the proponent/opponent adversary process.

There are essentially two types of community involvement. The first type is often described as negative and the second is referred to as positive. Negative involvement occurs when community groups form to oppose some type of proposed development. It may rise up in reaction to an existing product that has grown to the point where it has become extremely intrusive in the lives of community members, or it may be a reaction through fear for a proposed project because of a flawed process that introduced the project to the public initially. Often proponents of a plan fail to view their project from the eyes of those who are not involved with it other than having to live with it on a day-to-day basis. There are numerous examples where community citizens choose to shop outside their community because of the congestion in their own shopping areas produced by an overabundance of tourists. Also, the growth of visitors to the area frequently produces noise as well as garbage pollution, which acts as a catalyst for groups to form with the sole intention of opposing additional growth. However, community groups might also form in advance of, or in tandem with, tourism proposals in order to consider them in the larger context and with regard to the project's value in contributing to the community's overall vision. This is said to be positive in that it is not a reaction against some existing entity but, rather, is initiated to advance the common good as development occurs. Tourism planners must become more schooled in the nuances of CD and organizing, in order to develop projects that advance community goals as well as their own.

Perhaps 'true' community involvement rests on a major underlying ingredient. That principle is what Pedlar (2006: 428) has identified as 'openness to all':

Of particular relevance to CD is the openness of community; I see openness and the option of belonging as key to a healthy community; one cannot belong if the community is closed, and further, without belonging there can be no expression of citizenship. This communitarian perspective sees openness as critical to the possibility of congruence and compatibility between diversity and individual flourishing. While there are many strands of communitarianism with differing tenets and perspectives, virtually all suggest openness is a potent vehicle for the development of not just a community, but more importantly, a healthy community.

Rural areas are in great flux throughout the world. One major shift that is occurring at the local level is the community's transition from a traditional production-based industrial economy, where goods were processed, manufactured and packaged for outside markets, to the current economic situation, which is chiefly built on supplying services and cultural goods, experiences and intangibles, for consumption by tourists. In contrast to the *old* economy, the simultaneous production and consumption of services and experiences for tourism takes place within the community landscape. The old ideology was built within a setting where the workspace (i.e. vessels, fishing industry, waterfront, farm, forest or mine) was clearly separate from leisure and social activities, generally. With tourism, tourists often fail to recognize or respect the difference between local workplaces and social spaces for tourism activity, e.g. tourists wandering around the restricted areas, because the community as a whole, generally, is perceived as a *tourist zone*.

Under tourism, there is also a difference in goals and objectives between the community and the tourist; while the host (community) engages in the activity as work, the consumer (tourists) engages in it as leisure. In the new ideology, many of the leisure activities of the tourists are based on the cultural aspects outlined in Schein's model (1985), aspects that still hold personal meaning for many and which once belonged specifically to community. As the case study illustrated, in Lunenburg, where many of its cultural aspects – artifacts, crafts, architecture and historic sites, and experiences, such as fishing demonstrations, storytelling, historical reenactments, and visits to graveyards, are used now as leisure commodities strictly for the benefit of tourists and to generate income flows.

Given that the tourism product in rural areas is usually a commodification of the local history or culture, or the natural environment for outdoor recreation pursuits, those whose lifestyle will be directly affected by that commodification are the local residents. This interruption in the normal course of local citizens' lives necessitates that they have a large degree of control in the tourism decision-making process. This can only happen through a well-designed process that begins with the creation of a community vision, (not to be confused with developing a vision for the product) goal and objective setting and, once the product is designed and implemented, ongoing evaluation and monitoring to determine the changes in the community that are caused by the introduction of the tourism product in the system. This suggests the need for the gathering and establishment of baseline data against which changes in the system can be compared. All too often, tourism planners and developers neglect this important step and are then left without a record of the initial conditions of the social and ecological environments, against which future conditions produced by development can be measured. Chapter 13 of this volume provides greater detail on the actual steps for planning tourism at the community level.

Community Development is not a Panacea

A number of rural communities are suffering the collapse of their original economies, which are often based on extractive industries. Certainly, the case studies of Lunenburg and Canso, presented earlier in this volume, are good examples of difficulty. In this type of crisis situation, tourism is often turned to as a savior of the local community. While the effort to take a quick fix approach to an immediate problem is noble and probably necessary, communities should approach this type of problem from both a short- and long-term perspective.

There are inherent difficulties and problems with turning communities that have existed for centuries on manipulating or extracting resources from the land or the sea into relying on service-based industries like tourism. Workers in resource-based industries do not automatically possess skills that will allow them to be successful in the service industries like tourism and hospitality. At the very least, a great amount of training of personnel is required to accommodate this change if it can be accommodated successfully at all. In many instances, communities embarking on this path find that, over a generation, the composition of the community changes and a whole new set of entrepreneurially and service-oriented people move in, while the former residents move out. Rising housing costs can make it extremely difficult for the offspring of long-term local residents to stay in the community.

This may be happening in the case of Lunenburg presented earlier in this book.

When rural resource- and commodity-based communities are transitioning to tourism, many families think about turning their homes into bed and breakfasts or some other type of tourist accommodation. While this can provide additional income to a farming family or a family that may depend on some other type of extractive industry like fishing, it also takes considerable renovation and change to the household in order to make it operational. In the developed world, bed and breakfasts and small inns are subject to considerable health and safety regulations that can be costly and difficult to implement. So, the conversion of a family home into tourism accommodation requires a long-term commitment and a business plan that will demonstrate profitability at some specified future date. The urge to introduce the family home into the tourism system on a short-term basis, or until the resource on which the family has depended for their living recovers, should be resisted. The tourism market is now much too sophisticated for this type of short-term temporary approach.

Cultural conflict is also a phenomenon that needs to be considered. Rural communities have a cultural character that is different from urban communities, even within the same general geographic region. This difference is intensified in cross-cultural settings. However, most tourists to rural areas come from urban environments and, therefore, from different cultures. In addition to the country smells that are foreign and may even be insufferable to the city dweller, there are more subtle cross-cultural differences that may be problematic. For example, many cultures teach their young through demonstration rather than by verbal acuity. When the tourist asks a question but does not get a verbal answer, they may miss the intended answer because it was given through demonstration. What is not seen as a suitable answer to the simple question by the visitor is often interpreted as antisocial behavior. While this is only a small illustration, examples of this nature that cause confusion at best or hostility at worst, abound and affect the tourism enterprise considerably.

Developmental Intent of Citizen Involvement in the Tourism Planning Process

Citizen participation in tourism decision-making and development is intended to accomplish more than to simply reach appropriate decisions on tourism plans and products. In addition to the product formation aspects of citizen participation, and perhaps even more paramount from

the developmental point of view, is the human expansion and development aspect of the process. Further, providing the opportunity to develop
individual skills, which are certainly always an outcome of the
participation effort, collective capacities are fostered that will have
carryover value for participants and their community. Some (Putnam,
1993) have termed this phenomenon 'social capital' accumulation.
Putnam (1993) argues that civil society rests on the ongoing development
and accumulation of social capital in the community. While from our
point of view, the use of the word 'capital' is unfortunate because of its
economic connotations, it does nevertheless provide for CD as well as for
the benefit of the economic sector and the individual entrepreneur. In
spite of the semantic argument, it is a useful concept in that it adds a
collective networking component to what is generally considered simply
a product-oriented event. It is through the meaningful participation of
citizens in the planning and execution of economic efforts like tourism
development projects and programs, as well as other social development
initiatives, that leads to the accomplishment of the collective community
vision that widens social capital development and the expansion of civil
society generally.

Development is not only defined through economic growth, but also
by the development of human and community capacities. As Hettne
(1995: 15) reminds us, 'development involves structural transformation
which implies cultural, political, social and economic changes'. Essentially, development transcends the singular notion of economic growth
and involves all aspects of increased human welfare. What's more,
development through active participation in community events and
projects can help to identify the skills and talents of individual
community members that, after being identified, can be upgraded and
put to ongoing use in a variety of projects, economic or otherwise, in
addition to the project that formed the focus of the involvement
originally.

Community and national leaders have often found their talent for
public leadership through volunteering in community events and being
involved in some type of citizen participation process. Some have been
tourism projects. This type of informal education gained through 'on the
ground' community participation is vital for the development of a
healthy democracy. Not only is citizen participation necessary for
appropriate advancement of the project under focus, but also for the
continued development of civil society and ultimately democracy itself.

In addition to the focus of citizen participation in protecting the rights
of the larger collective against exploitation, involvement in community

activism may also lead to citizens becoming entrepreneurs themselves. It is quite possible that citizen participation in a tourism project leads to synergy that encourages others in the community to view the original project as an anchor enterprise and capitalize on this occasion through creating secondary businesses that profit from the original scheme. This type of expansion can add to the facilities and services of the tourism system that, in turn, can provide great benefit to the whole citizenry if it is accomplished in a responsive manner that speaks to the needs of local citizens as well as to the potential tourist.

The preceding paragraph introduces the notion that quite often the most sustainable tourism events are those that are first established as leisure events for local citizens and are eventually shared with the outside world. Of course, this becomes a matter of limiting the size of the event, and as we have seen in some of the cases presented earlier in this volume, the tourism imperative often overtakes the local recreational aspects of the initiative. This type of degradation of the project can be observed through Butler's life cycle model that was explained earlier in this text. Tourism has had a history of overexploiting community leisure events to everyone's dissatisfaction, so it is important for communities to view such activities as primarily for local residents that have additional appeal to visitors. This may ultimately define what is often sought in the form of community sustainable tourism.

Chapter 11

Rural Community Sustainability and Sustainable Rural Tourism

Introduction

As noted throughout this text, tourism has become a significant economic generator for Canadian communities attempting to achieve sustainability and reduce dependency on traditional and declining forms of industry, such as fishing, farming and other resource-based industries. In this chapter, we briefly discuss some of the key ideas related to the concept of sustainability and consider how it applies to rural communities. For rural communities, achieving sustainability in the 21st century means protecting their resources and building community capacity. Furthermore, tourism policy, at all levels, must take this into account. According to Edgell (1999: 1), '... the highest purpose of tourism policy is to integrate the economic, political, cultural, intellectual and environmental benefits of tourism cohesively with people, destinations and countries in order to improve the global quality of life and provide a foundation for peace and prosperity'.

Key Theoretical Concepts: Sustainable Development; Sustainable Tourism; Cultural Capital

Sustainability (Sustainable Development)

As defined in the *Bruntland Report* (WCED, 1987),[1] sustainable development is development that 'meets the needs of the present without compromising the ability of future generations to meet their own needs'. It is a process of continual and ongoing planning, monitoring and controlling (Nelson *et al.*, 1993). Until recently, sustainable development has been framed largely in terms of global environmental concerns, and the local perspective is frequently seen as subordinate to the global (Overton & Scheyvens, 1999). Others contend that the spatial dimension is also conspicuously absent in many definitions of sustainable development (Kreutzwiser, 1993). Ecological and economic constraints are considered the key factors in guiding any

177

effort toward sustainability (Prugh *et al.*, 2000; Bryden, 1994), which explains, generally, why ecological and economic perspectives have dominated the literature (Overton & Scheyvens, 1999). Social and cultural perspectives have tended to be bypassed in the research.

The notion of economic sustainability is based on conventional models of economic development of industrialization, resource extraction and sustained growth in material consumption, as a means to improve the wellbeing of society and sustainable livelihoods. This perspective places economic analyses at the center of the sustainability equation. Proponents of this view either do not recognize the environment as a factor or they believe that it can be turned into a tradable product or a commodity. Such a perspective is considered paradoxical as such models are seen 'to impose severe pressures on the environment through resource depletion, waste disposal or disturbance of natural ecosystems' (Redclift, 1984: 56). The search for sustainable development from the environmental, or ecological, perspective puts emphasis on the natural environment and ecosystems and 'seeks to minimize growth, preserve the natural environment and seek stability' (Adams, 1995: 94). This perspective sees 'current patterns of human activity and resource use as inherently unsustainable and points to the ways humans are rapidly destroying key ecosystems and species' (Overton & Scheyvens, 1999: 7). It places the environment at the center of the sustainability debate.

Sustainable tourism

While 'sustainable tourism' may be considered an offshoot of 'sustainable development', there have been debates about the concepts, definition, validity and operationalization. Hardy and Beeton (2001) point out that the term lacks integrity, and may be no more than a 'buzz word' or marketing gimmick. Hardy and Beeton argue that sustainable tourism emphasizes the development aspect of sustainable development. It focuses on business viability and customer satisfaction rather than the traditional notion of environmental ethics, quality of life and cultural integrity with ideas about achieving growth and progress. Sustainable tourism is able to deal with short- and long-term impacts with respect to stakeholders who have a sense of ownership. Therefore, it is important to understand how stakeholders who live in, use and manage the resource, perceive tourism. Sustainable tourism development requires the informed participation of all relevant stakeholders, as well as strong political leadership to ensure wide participation and consensus building (WTO, 2004). When the needs and requirements of the stakeholders are not identified and/or respected, and the status quo is maintained in response to short-term trends and impacts, sustainable tourism is replaced by *maintainable tourism*. In the long term, inappropriate management will lead to detrimental environmental, social and cultural impacts. The natural, human-built and sociocultural environment need to be managed, not merely maintained, in the name of tourism.

UNWTO/UNEP global goals for sustainable tourism

The United Nations Environmental Programme (UNEP) was appointed by the Commission on Sustainable Development (CSD) as the lead agency responsible for the implementation of the Agenda 21 program as it relates to tourism. In concert with the World Tourism Organization (WTO/OMT), UNEP (Tourism Programme) has become the main reference point on sustainable tourism for CSD. In 2004, WTO (now known as UNWTO) put forward a conceptual definition for sustainable tourism that has been adopted by UNEP and is now being widely embraced:

> Sustainable tourism development guidelines and management practices are applicable to all forms of tourism in all types of destinations, including mass tourism and the various niche tourism segments. Sustainability principles refer to the environmental, economic, and socio-cultural aspects of tourism development, and a suitable balance must be established between these three dimensions to guarantee its long-term sustainability. (UNEP: Sustainable Development of Tourism, Web site, para 2)

UNWTO (UNEP website, 2007) contends sustainable tourism must: (1) make optimal use of environmental resources that constitute a key element in tourism development, maintaining essential ecological processes and helping to conserve natural heritage and biodiversity; (2) respect the sociocultural authenticity of host communities, conserve their built and living cultural heritage and traditional values, and contribute to intercultural understanding and tolerance; (3) ensure viable, long-term economic operations, providing socioeconomic benefits to all stakeholders that are fairly distributed, including stable employment and income-earning opportunities and social services to host communities, and contributing to poverty alleviation. Further,

> Achieving sustainable tourism is a continuous process and it requires constant monitoring of impacts, introducing the necessary preventive and/or corrective measures whenever necessary ... should also

maintain a high level of tourist satisfaction and ensure a meaningful experience to the tourists, raising their awareness about sustainability issues and promoting sustainable tourism practices amongst them. (UNEP: Sustainable Development of Tourism, website, para 6)

Sustainable tourism in Canada

The Tourism Industry Association of Canada (TIAC) represents the voice of the tourism industry at the national level. In 1930, the organization was founded to encourage the development of tourism in Canada and today serves as the national private-sector advocate for this $66.9 billion industry, representing the interests of the tourism business community nationwide. TIAC has successfully influenced government thinking and action on behalf of Canadian tourism businesses, promoting positive measures that help the industry grow and prosper. To do this, TIAC has sought to ensure that the government agenda is conducive to a growing and sustainable tourism industry (TIAC Website: About Us, 2007). The membership of TIAC 'reflects partnerships among all sectors of the industry, and provincial, territorial and regional tourism associations, enabling the association to address a full range of issues facing Canadian tourism—forcefully and effectively. Its activities focus on legislative and regulatory barriers to the growth of Canadian tourism' (TIAC Website, 2007).

In the early 1990s, TIAC developed an industry code of ethics for sustainable tourism in collaboration with key partners in the public and private sectors (see Table 11.1). Supported by a set of recommended guidelines, this provided a framework for the signing of the TIAC-Parks Canada Accord for Sustainable Tourism. With extensive growth and diversification of tourism in Canada, TIAC updated its Code of Ethics and Guidelines for Sustainable Tourism in 2005 to provide a common basis and framework for all sectors of the industry in order to move forward effectively in support of a shared responsibility for sustainable tourism. The aim was to enhance the quality and sustainability of natural and cultural heritage-based experiences.

TIAC has since communicated and promoted Canada's Code of Ethics and Guidelines for Sustainable Tourism to stakeholders across the country, including tourism industry associations, destination marketing organizations, provincial marketing organizations, convention and visitor bureaus, tourism businesses, and universities and colleges that have tourism programs, in order to develop a tourism industry that is

Table 11.1 TIAC code of ethics and guidelines for sustainable tourism

1. Protect natural and cultural heritage resources
Support and contribute to the protection, enhancement and restoration of the integrity of natural and cultural heritage resources and places; encourage the establishment of parks, sites and reserves; support legislation to ensure protection of historic places and resources; condemn willful destruction of heritage resources; and work to enhance public awareness and involvement in the protection of heritage.
2. Promote appreciation and enjoyment
Enrich travel experiences, understanding and enjoyment by providing accurate information, engaging presentations and opportunities to connect with Canada's natural and cultural heritage; and foster support for the protection and sensitive use of heritage resources and places.
3. Respect and involve host communities
Respect the rights and values of host and local communities, property owners and Aboriginal peoples; educate communities about the importance of tourism and provide them with a meaningful role in planning and decision-making for the design, development and delivery of tourism programs and services; and optimize the long-term economic, social, cultural and environmental benefits to the community.
4. Influence expectations and use
Influence traveler expectations through marketing, trip-planning materials and tourism activities which foster responsible use and enjoyment of our nature, culture and communities; and support leading-edge services and facilities that respect heritage resources and places while achieving economic goals.
5. Minimize impacts
Limit the negative impacts of tourism on the natural and cultural environment through the responsible use of resources, effective waste management and minimizing of pollution; limit activities, services and facilities to levels that do not threaten the integrity of heritage resources or systems while continuing to support economic goals and traveler access; and seek innovative solutions to mitigate or avoid undesirable environmental, social and cultural impacts.
6. Raise awareness
Conduct research to expand the knowledge base upon which sound sustainable tourism decisions depend; share the knowledge through education programs, staff training and scholarships; and recognize excellence and best practices through awards and accreditation programs.

Table 11.1 (*Continued*)
7. Work together
Advance sustainable tourism by working with governments, communities, stakeholders, travelers and other industries to agree upon common goals, contribute to coordinated and cooperative actions, exchange information, technologies and solutions, and develop shared plans.
8. Contribute globally
Show leadership in sustainable tourism by honoring international commitments; participate in international policy development and initiatives; contribute to the building of capability on a world scale; and share best practices and technologies with other countries.

committed to sustainable business practices (TIAC website, 2007). The association's key objectives have been to:

- educate the tourism industry about the importance of adopting sustainable tourism practices;
- encourage the tourism industry to support and sponsor the principles of sustainable tourism;
- develop options for implementing the eight guidelines and encourage tourism businesses to share best-practice examples.

Rural Communities and Sustainability

Traditionally, the application of concepts of sustainability to rural areas has focused on agriculture and on 'individual components of rurality, e.g. attempts at developing agriculture rather than a comprehensive approach to integrate the socio-cultural, economic and environmental components of both sustainability and rurality' (Butler & Hall, 1998: 251). Along with the restructuring of the agricultural industry and the decline of other primary resource industries that have long dominated rural economies, there has been an increasing adoption of tourism development, a service-dominated industry, as a diversification strategy. This has required a shift in thinking of what constitutes rural community sustainability. Blake (1996: 211) points out that 'rurality is no longer dominated by concepts of food production and notes that new uses of the countryside are redefining the idea of what constitutes the rural landscape'. When a community adopts tourism, in many instances, it does not manifest as a diversification strategy, but rather it replaces a former industry and dominates its economy. This presents a whole new set of challenges for a community's sustainability, e.g. restructuring of community resources for new forms of consumption.

Community Capacity and Sustainability

All communities have multiple resources that can be consumed and are, therefore, not available to current or future generations (Flora, 2001), or are stored for future but not for the current generation, or are invested for the present and future needs of all generations (World Commission on Environment and Development, 1987). When resources are used to create new resources, they are called capital. DeGroot (1994) and Berkes (1998) in Flora (2001) define capital as 'a stock of resources with value embedded in its ability to produce a flow of benefits'. The business sector refers to capital as money. Flora (1998, 2001) notes that sociologists distinguish between different forms of capital – human, social, financial/ built and natural. She further refers to the notion of sustainability as investing in forms of capital that do not deplete other forms (Flora, 1998, 2001).

Following this sociological perspective, Flora argues that, to achieve sustainability, communities must have a balance of four forms of capital. These are outlined in Figure 11.1, which depicts a model for rural community sustainability adapted from Pretty's asset-based model (2001), which was designed to analyze the interaction of people with the agroecosystem (Flora, 2001).[2] Flora states that healthy agroecosystems with multiple community benefits are more likely to be sustainable than those that enhance only one of the capitals. Based on the assumption that agroecosystems (see Endnote 2) are rural communities, it follows that healthy rural communities with multiple community benefits are more likely to be sustainable than those that enhance only one of the capitals (George, 2004). The following discussion explains and critically assesses Flora's adapted version of Pretty's model (Figure 11.1) as a framework to examine sustainable rural communities.

Flora's model shows four community capitals, in clockwise order, that, in her view, best address community development: *human, social, natural* and *financial/built*. The concept of capital is an extension of the traditional economic notion of capital, defined as the manufactured means of production (Prugh, 1995). Folke and Berkes (1998) in Flora (2001) are more explicit, defining capital as 'a stock of resources with value embedded in its ability to produce a flow of benefits'.

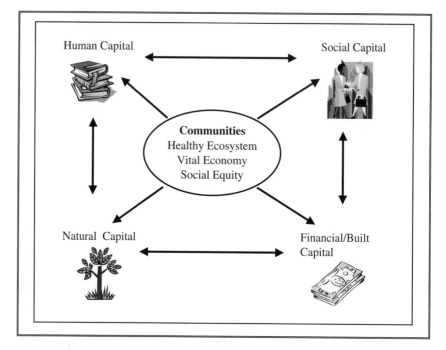

Figure 11.1 Community capitals and system sustainability (adapted by Flora, 2001)

Flora (2001) argues that one must deal with people first (human capital) and relationships (social capital) before efforts are made to enhance the other capitals. Her preposition supports the notion that a community's people and their relationships must be the key variables in any model for sustainability. There is a burgeoning literature on social capital (OECD, 2001; Lin *et al.*, 2001; Baron *et al.*, 2000; Cohen & Prusak, 2001; Coleman, 1988; Wall, 1996) and human capital (OECD, 2001; Seltzer, 1999; Ferlenger & Mandle, 2000; Fukuyama, 1995; Mincer, 1993; Mankiew *et al.*, 1992; Keohane *et al.*, 1999).

Human, social, natural and finance/built capital

According to the Organization of Economic Co-operation and Development (OECD, 2001), *human capital* is 'embodied in individuals; it grows though use and experience, both inside and outside employment, as well as through informal and formal learning, but it tends to depreciate through lack of use and with age'. The concept of human capital encompasses the knowledge, skills, competencies and attributes embodied in individuals that facilitate the creation of personal, social and economic wellbeing. Skills and competencies are largely acquired through learning and experience, but may also reflect innate capacities (OECD, 2001). Hancock (1999) refers to human capital as consisting of healthy, well-educated, skilled, innovative and creative people who are engaged in their communities and participate in governance.

Social capital is a relatively new term and its meaning is not universally agreed upon or accepted. Some describe it as 'the social networks that constitute our civic society' (Putnam, 1993; Campbell & Kelly, 1999). However, it is well-understood that social capital resides in social relationships and as a capital, may be conceived as a resource in which we invest to provide a stream of benefits (OECD, 2001). Social capital is also the product of inherited culture and norms of behavior. It is perceived to be different from human and physical capital in three ways because it: (1) is relational rather than being the exclusive property of an individual; (2) is a public good shared by a group; (3) is produced by societal investments of time and effort. Thus, one might argue that an active volunteer network in a community is a form of social capital.

Natural capital can be divided into two major categories and one hybrid: renewable natural capital, non-renewable natural capital and cultivated natural capital (Prugh *et al.*, 1995). Prugh *et al.* define renewable natural capital as living and active, such as forests, flora and fauna and fish, and so on, which can be destroyed or its ability to regenerate can be impaired by overuse and other factors. Ecosystems consist largely of renewable natural capital (Prugh *et al.*, 1995). Non-renewable natural capital, such as fossil fuels and mineral deposits, are passive and such stocks are finite. Cultivated natural capital include agricultural and aquacultural systems, such as tree farms, sod farms, fish ponds and greenhouse nurseries, where some of the components are not manufactured by humans, but are not entirely natural either (Prugh *et al.*, 1995).

Finance/built capital refers to financial investment, cash, buildings and other assets, used to create new resources and generate new wealth (Gunn & Gunn, 1991). Flora (2001) argues that for a community to be sustainable there must be a stable balance between these capitals. Finding the common ground among people who have emotional, symbolic or economic identification with a place, whether they live there or not, is essential to making decisions about development and resource use that will enable communities and their resource base to survive and thrive (Flora, 2001). Privileging one form of capital over another can destroy rural communities and agroecosystems (Flora, 2001).

While Flora's model depicts four capitals and interrelationships between them in a framework for assessing sustainability in rural communities, it does evoke several concerns as to its effectiveness in assessing rural communities. First, a process of giving heavier weightings to formal education and skills versus informal education and skills may skew the assessment of human capital in rural communities. Bourdieu (1986) questions what constitutes knowledge, how knowledge is to be achieved and how knowledge is validated. He argues that *educational* capital is created and transmitted primarily through post-primary institutional education and in such a way as to maintain a particular desired social structure (Bourdieu, 1973).

While not supported here, there is often a common perception that levels of formal education (i.e. post-secondary education) and various skills are of a lower standard in rural areas. As George (2004) points out, it is important to value knowledge gained through informal education and practical skills, which may be higher (i.e. farming, fishing, etc.) in rural areas. How value is allocated to formal/informal education and skills remains questionable. Assuming that people in rural communities do have less so-called *formal* education and skills training, does this infer they have lower levels of human capital? In addition, as rural communities increase efforts to build human capital (through higher education for residents and their children), locals often become overeducated and overskilled for community needs, and relocate to urban centers where they can apply this knowledge and maximize utility. While the idea of valuing knowledge is very abstract and contested, it is certainly a key component for measuring human capital. Moreover, social scientists argue that knowledge has become the most important factor in wealth creation.

The challenge faced by a rural community in generating local wealth, is very often related to its ability to hold on to its residents, particularly, its youth. This problem may generally be symptomatic of the current rural situation, exacerbating an already existing isolation from the larger global economic and social systems in which rural communities are struggling to survive. The outmigration from some rural regions (Atlantic Canada) is staggering (Statistics Canada, 2001). Thus, in rural areas, knowledge acquired through formal institutional systems is likely to be exported while *knowledge* wealth acquired through informal mechanisms is more inclined to stay in the community. Further, much of the knowledge built in rural areas is culturally-bound and relevant to cultures that have been spawned by a particular community's way of life (e.g. fishing, farming, or mining). Hence, George (2004) argues that

Flora's adapted model (2001) is flawed if it does not include a cultural capital component. Given that cultural capital, and its many expressive forms, is a proven and promising asset for tourism, it should be included in the community capitals model (George, 2004). The notion of cultural capital will be described in more depth further in the chapter.

Social cohesion, social relations and social sustainability

Assuming the four capitals discussed above are considered central and essential to the wellbeing and sustainability of healthy communities, it seems logical to assume that all community capitals must be sustained; that is, economic (financial) sustainability, human sustainability, ecological (natural) sustainability and social sustainability should equally be considered imperatives. While both Flora (2001) and Littig and Griessler (2005) allude to the idea that these capitals/dimensions of sustainability are interdependent and one cannot be sacrificed for the sake of the other, it is the social dimension that will be emphasized in the following paragraphs.

Chambers (1986: 10) purports that social sustainability, or the social approach to sustainable development, places poor people and their basic human needs at the center of sustainability. Those supporting this perspective believe that 'development must be framed in a way that focuses on meeting people's basic needs rather than concentrating on aggregate economic growth' (Overton & Scheyvens, 1999: 7). It is locally based and mostly small scale, allowing for forms of development that do not compromise the environment, and which use and modify ecosystems (without harming them) to improve economic and social well-being (Overton & Scheyvens, 1999). In this perspective, the emphasis is also placed on social equity, justice and liberation given that 'unjust societies are not sustainable societies because they are subject to exploitation and subordination' (Overton & Scheyvens, 1999: 7). In contrast, Littig and Griessler (2005: 72) define social sustainability as

... a quality of societies ... signifies the nature-society relationships, mediated by work, as well as relationships within the society ... is given, if work within a society and the related institutional arrangements satisfy an extended set of human needs ... are shaped in a way that nature and its reproductive capabilities are preserved over a long period of time.

Work, including paid and unpaid labour, and care work, as Littig and Griessler (2005) argue, is central to sustainability in order to meet ones' needs. 'One major driving force behind society and societisation seems to be the creation of opportunities to meet one's needs and for this purpose, societies come up with various functional systems and institutions' (Littig & Griessler, 2005: 71). Social coherence, which is both their condition and outcome, is vital for the creation and working of these systems (Littig & Griessler, 2005). According to research by Littig and Griessler (2005: 71)

> The strong emphasis on work in the existing working societies still needs to be taken into account; not just with regard to securing people's incomes, but also with regard to the psycho-social functions of gainful employment (time structure, identity, etc.), citizens' integration (due to the high social status of paid work), and the significance of paid labour for social cohesion. (Senghaas-Knobloch, 1998; Bosch, 1998)

Other concepts related to social cohesion and social relations are social capital and social sustainability. Michael Woolcock (2001: 12) concurs with Flora's (2001) view, as discussed earlier, that social capital resides in social relationships. It is composed of a structure of networks and social relations, which also includes behavioral elements such as trust, reciprocity, honesty and so on. Woolcock (2001: 12) contends

> Social capital is that one's family, friends and associates constitute an important asset, one that can be called upon in a crisis, enjoyed for its own sake, and/or leveraged for material gain. Communities endowed with a rich stock of social networks and civic associations will be in a stronger position to confront poverty and vulnerability, resolve disputes and/or take advantage of new opportunities.

Although social capital refers to the norms and networks that facilitate collective action, it is important to concentrate on its sources rather than consequences; in short, what it is and not what it does (Woolcock, 2001). Woolcock (2001: 13) suggests it is a relational variable that is multi-dimensional in nature; that is, it has not only horizontal dimensions (including family/friend connections and connections between people of similar demographics), but also vertical dimensions (linkages to formal institutions and those in power). Social cohesion, arguably, is those behavior elements mentioned above that provide the 'glue' that binds the other elements of social capital together. Finally, Woolcock suggests that, for countries and communities alike, rich or poor, social capital is an asset that can be leveraged in managing risk, shocks and opportunities and is a key factor in efforts to achieve sustainable economies (Woolcock, 2001: 16). In brief, it bolsters a community's resilience in times of crisis by helping to sustain, strengthen and/or rekindle a community's spirit and identity. Arguably, a community's (place) collective identity is borne out of the strength of its social capital. This was exemplified in the situation of Canso, Nova Scotia, discussed in Chapter 6.

Culture as Capital

Pierre Bourdieu, a French sociologist, first conceptualized the term *cultural capital* in *The Forms of Capital* (1973, 1986). He identified three forms of capital – economic, cultural and social, paying special attention to mechanisms of accumulation and conversion (in Schurgurenshky, 2002). He challenged economic theory for its narrow focus only on economic capital – that which is immediately and directly convertible into money and institutionalized in the form of property rights. Bourdieu (1986) understood capital as power, and along with the economic perspective, this power was also manifested in social and cultural capitals. He saw cultural capital as the habits or cultural practices based on knowledge and demeanors learned through exposure to role models in the family and other environments.

Cultural capital theory attempts to construct explanations for things like differential educational achievement in a way that combines a wide range of differing influences. This allows for an extensive range of views, including support of the culture-based approach to understanding achievement. It also brings into focus the question of cultural values and relations to what constitutes knowledge; how knowledge is to be achieved, and how knowledge is validated (Author unknown, http://www.sociology.org.uk/tece1ef.htm, August, 2003).

According to Bourdieu, the concept of cultural capital includes three states (see Figure 11.2); that which is: (1) embodied in the individual, (2) objectified in cultural goods and (3) institutionalized as academic credentials or diplomas (as described by Schugurenshky, 2002).

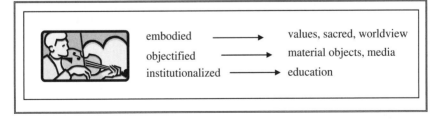

embodied	⟶	values, sacred, worldview
objectified	⟶	material objects, media
institutionalized	⟶	education

Figure 11.2 Cultural capital conceptualized

Ray (2001) contends that cultural capital (material and intangible), as capital must be a function of a process of accumulation. This accumulation refers to the array of unique and enduring material and intangible cultural attributes and expressions that have evolved and been reproduced in a particular community or region over successive generations. For endogenous development (rural region or community development), this accumulation occurs using various sources and techniques, including:

- the private family sphere, which can be mined for memories of traditional knowledge and anecdotal history as well as for artifacts (local traditional recipes);
- the voluntary/community sector, which can also operate as a tool for recovering local knowledge or for the creation of new local cultural objects;
- regional revivalist movements by the fact of their existences;
- information exchange networks between localities can work to supplement local repertoires of cultural identity and assist in valorization of local culture;
- through concepts of reflexive modernity, and economies of signs and space.

In addition to other definitions of cultural resources or cultural capital, (Ray, 2002; Bourdieu, 1986; Schein, 1985; McMercher & du Cros, 2002), Jamieson (1992: 93) has also developed a typology of potential community resources available in small rural communities that would comprise cultural capital; these include: handicrafts, language, traditions, gastronomy, art and music, heritage resources, the nature of the work environment and technology, religion, education and dress. He suggests that this cultural inventory and analysis process for tourism should assess the full range of cultural resources whether they are tangible or intangible. Further, he stresses that this process of identifying cultural capital for tourism must not concentrate exclusively on the buildings of the community, but must also stress the way of life and cultural traditions, which are important in making a community unique. Although not conclusive, Jamieson (1992: 94–96) does provide a list of potential resources that might be included in a community's inventory of cultural capital:

1. Historic resources, e.g. sites, buildings, districts, landscapes ...
2. Tangible and intangible ethnic features, e.g. settlement patterns, languages, lifestyles ...
3. Natural features, e.g. water, vegetation, dominant landforms ...

4. Sequences, e.g. sense of entry, clarity of route, visible approaches to dominant features ...
5. Visibility, e.g. general and targeted views, visual corridor ...
6. Detail and surfaces, e.g. street furniture, floorscape ...
7. Ambient qualities, e.g. wind, temperature, fog, noise, smells ...
8. Visible activities, e.g. people observing people; everyday life and special activities ...
9. Physical factors, e.g. boundaries, housing types and settlement patterns ...
10. Daily environment, e.g. corner stores, open spaces where children play ...
11. Intangibles – conversations, history, traditions, values, sense of community, sense of security, emotions, lifestyles ...

Researchers, generally, have attempted to loosely situate the notion of cultural capital within the contexts of human capital and/or social capital According to OECD (2001), cultural capital is recognized as one dimension of social capital. But Prugh *et al.* (1995) also state that human capital is also sometimes referred to as cultural capital. Indeed, a number of commonalities between cultural capital as described in the literature (Bourdieu, 1986), and physical property, support the claim that it is *capital* in the same sense (Thompson, 1999) as other capital. Similar to much physical property in the capital system, cultural capital (Thompson, 1999: 399) is:

- Appropriated by individuals.
- Used by them as a basis for earning income.
- Accumulated by and in families (Cohen, 1989).
- Passed between generations by inheritance (Cohen, 1989).
- Protected by state mechanisms.

With respect to ownership, commonalities also exist. As it is with much physical property, a great deal of the accumulated knowledge of humankind is common property (Thompson, 1999). As Thompson points out, 'Parks and reserves, heritage sites, and public museums, and so on, preserve communal physical property. Public schools, universities, research institutions and museums preserve communal cultural capital' (p. 399). However, in recent times, what were once considered common properties now face privatization and annexation.

As discussed in Thompson (1999: 396), Gouldner's (1979) concept of cultural capital comes from the conventional economic definition of capital as 'a produced object whose public goal is increased economic productivity'. Gouldner argues that culture, obtained through education, satisfies this definition, because capital has income equivalence, that is, 'anything, including culture, which increases incomes also increase its capital value and those possessing culturally acquired skills [and knowledge] can capitalize on these skills through increased wages, royalties, patents, copyrights or credentializing' (in Thompson, 1999: 396). Cohen (1989) describes how the accumulated wealth of one generation becomes the privilege of the next, and there is an evolutional potential for both cultural and physical capital to accumulate from generation to generation.

Capital is defined and generally understood as 'a stock of resources with value embedded in its ability to produce a flow of benefits' (Flora, 2001). It becomes obvious then, as George (2004) contends, that culture commodified for tourism can clearly be defined as capital. Chambers (1995) finds several definitions of capital in his authoritative writings on accounting, as:

- Owners' of stockholder's equity in business assets.
- A liability.
- Net assets.
- Aggregate assets.

Outside of accounting, notably in economics and sociology, the meaning of capital aligns with the last of the four alternatives – aggregate assets (Thompson, 1999). In this sense, Chambers (1995) agrees that capital is synonymous with wealth, assets, property and resources. Capital can mean resources, property or assets (the common usage) or it can mean claims to resources, property or assets (accounting function). Fisher (1906) asserts that wealth is the concrete thing owned; property is the abstract right of ownership. He suggests these two concepts mutually imply each other (as cited in Thompson, 1999).

In rural communities, cultural capital may be more implicit as it reveals itself through strong traditional ties. It is generally perceived to be a very distinct and integral element in a community's identity. Concepts of cultural and place identity, sense of place and social representation, cultural attachment, symbolic constructions and meanings, and historically layered social relations, are emerging in the literature (Kovac, 2001; McIntosh *et al.*, 2002; Barthel-Bouchier, 2001; Ziff & Pratima, 1997; Schouten, 1996). These form the cultural markers as identified by Ray (2001) in a culture economy, discussed earlier in this text.

Cultural identity is the expression of one's place in the world (Schouten, 1996). Schouten contends, 'cultural identity represents the wish to protect the uniqueness of one's own culture, language and identity, and their attached value systems' (p. 54). He further states, '... cultural identity as a living force will eventually prove itself as a powerful counter-trend against the global cultural domination of the West and the cultural uniformity it brings with it' (p. 54). Cultural identity and place identity lend support to the notion of intangibility, a dominant feature of culture.

Cultural capital and intangibles

Intangible, according to the *Collins Concise Dictionary* (2001), is defined as 'that which is incapable of being perceived by touch; impalpable; imprecise or unclear to the mind; saleable but not possessing intrinsic productive value'. In modern society, many so-called intangibles – goodwill, volunteer work, ideas, space, time and so forth – are given value-added status with monetary values, which are included in the production/consumption calculation. The concept of knowledge as an asset has been used as a corporate business strategy. The concept refers to the art of creating value from an organization's intangible assets (Sveiby, 1998).

Cultural knowledge consists of many intangibles: history and land-scapes, symbolic meanings, rituals, expressions, social customs and processes, unwritten stories, music and art, cultural cuisine, community idiosyncrasies and characteristics, patterns, folklore and myths, community identity and sense of place, hospitality, friendliness and so on. A common assumption about older rural communities is that they are typically laden with such intangibles. Many have strong traditions, customs and heritage, and thus have a richer cultural capital content than newer or urban communities, for instance, a long-established coal-mining community in Cape Breton, Nova Scotia, an aboriginal community in the North or a small fishing community on the West coast.

Generally, such intangibles are exclusive to a particular community, contributing to its uniqueness and identity. Arguably, these intangibles give *value*, as something that is exclusive and distinct to a specific community, particularly as a potential resource for developing its own specialized tourism product. In contemporary society, according to Cloke (1993), the rural is inescapably bound up in very modern image markets, implicated in the *society of the commodity* and *society of the spectacle*, which are social and cultural constructs.

The notion of giving value to intangibles is central to the tourism and service industry. In fact, the bulk of tourism product offerings is comprised of intangible aspects – image, service, goodwill, hospitality, bundling of services with tangible goods and so on. Suppliers of the tourism product use these aspects to add value to their products. Tourism marketers often tend to capitalize on the intangibles of a community's countryside and culture (i.e. bus tour groups viewing local landscapes, flora and fauna), while providing little or no return to the host community (cultural appropriation is discussed in depth in Chapter 8). Thus, such intangibles and other aspects of culture have been converted into commodities to be sold to tourists. Arguably then, culture can be considered a major capital asset in many rural communities (George, 2004).

New Conceptualizations of Community Capital for Sustainability

Drawing on the perspectives of Bourdieu, Jamieson and Ray, discussed above, and Flora's adapted model for community sustainability, we argue that cultural capital, as a dominant attraction for tourism and an economic generator for community, should hold a central position in the model of community capitals and capacity. In point, cultural capital derives and builds most of its asset value from the other capitals. Consequently, the inclusion of cultural capital into the conceptual model results in an alteration of the community asset structure. 'The reconversion of capital held in one form to another, more accessible, more profitable or more legitimate form tends to induce a transformation of asset structure' (Bourdieu, 1984: 131).

Bourdieu, Ray, Gouldner and Cohen all conceive cultural capital (actual or presumed) as knowledge or skills possessed by, or available to, individuals (and communities) and with income-earning potential. Consequently, George (2004) attempts to address the absence of cultural capital in Flora's adapted Model for Community Sustainability (2001), and introduces a new modified version that includes the cultural dimension. This proposed model includes five essential components, or capitals, that must be considered when assessing communities that plan to undertake cultural tourism development as a sustainable development strategy (Figure 11.3).

In this newly modified model, culture becomes positioned at the core and interconnects with all other capitals. When culture becomes commodified for tourism and sustainability, it becomes the central asset, drawing

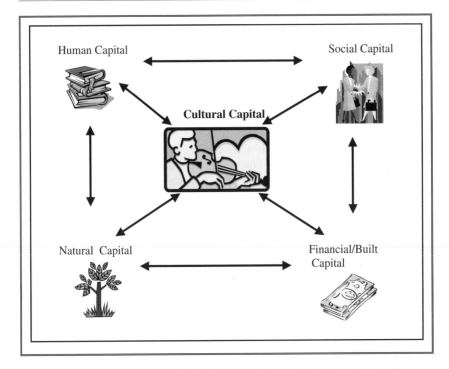

Figure 11.3 Community capitals for sustainability (modified by George, 2004)

much of its value through conversion of other capitals. In this context, cultural capital, as a community asset, constructs itself through appropriating and converting elements of other capital assets. For instance, natural landscapes, built environments, human knowledge and social forms, frequently become reassembled under the notion of 'cultural capital' and marketed and 'sold' for tourism. As discussed in Chapter 3, Lunenburg's built and natural environments – its historic houses, waterfront, schools, churches and historic landscapes– have all become facets of cultural capital and the community's tourism product offering. Further, the skill sets of retired fishermen have been used as part of the tourism appeal and experience; as well, social networks in the community have become centered on tourism development and sustainability of the tourism product, *not on community sustainability.* Flora (2001) calls attention to the point that one capital cannot be profitable and retained at the expense of another. 'Privileging one form of capital over another can destroy rural communities ...' (Flora, 2001). How capitals are balanced and maintained is critical to developing and maintaining a healthy community and sustainable economy (Pretty, 1998, 2001).

The Future: Community Capacity and Rural Sustainability

Wendell Berry (1990) paints a gloomy picture for rural communities:

... Country people more and more live like city people, and so connive in their own ruin ... allow their economic and social standards to be set by television and salesmen and outsider experts. As local community decays along with local economy, a vast amnesia settles over the countryside. As the exposed and disregarded soil departs with the rains, so local knowledge and local memory moves away ... forgotten under the influence of homogenized sales talk, entertainment, and education [and now tourism] ... loss of local culture has been ignored ... written off as one of the cheaper prices of progress, or made the business of folklorists [and now the business of tourism].

Regardless of Berry's pessimism, UNESCO APNIEVE 1998 (UN Educational, Scientific and Cultural Organization Asia Pacific Network for International Education and Values Education) offers new perspectives of sustainability and hope with an encompassing definition that may be more compelling to rural communities that are commodifying local culture as a capital asset for tourism development and goal to achieve sustainability:

*   Ecological sustainability – development that takes into account the maintenance of ecological processes, biological diversity and biological resources. To achieve this, our society needs to recognize that the survival of other species is also important.
*   Economic sustainability – development that is economically efficient and that the benefits of such development are distributed between generations. Economic efficiency means that processes and projects undertaken must give the greatest output per unit of input.
*   Social sustainability – development that improves quality of life of all social groups. It requires development that increases people's control over their lives by giving them opportunity to participate in decision-making.
*   Cultural sustainability – development that requires taking into account the values of the people affected by it. In addition, the

range of cultural groups should be maintained and encouraged, and the value of their heritage and traditions should be recognized.

If we are to keep Canada's rural areas alive, healthy, and viable, we need to apply these same principles to our communities.

Conclusion

For rural communities restructured as tourism economies, the notions of sustainable rural tourism and sustainable rural community become synonymous. Further, Butler and Hall (1998: 254) argue 'true sustainable rural development should include tourism as but one component of the policy mix which government and the private sector formulate with respect to rural development. Tourism needs to be in harmony with the multiplicity of uses, needs and demands which so characterize rural areas in order for it to be deemed as appropriated and potentially sustainable'.

Rural communities provide unique tourism offerings. Rural tourism development draws on five community capitals that must be considered for community sustainability. For rural tourism development, culture becomes an integral capital asset. Thus, when discussing notions of community sustainability, the cultural dimension must be included. 'Any policy response which seeks to use tourism as a mechanism to ameliorate the effects of economic restructuring needs to consider the cultural component of rural change ...' (Butler & Hall, 1998: 255). New research and integrative and flexible approaches that take into consideration this more encompassing perspective of sustainability, may provide rural communities with better options and direction when planning for tourism development and community sustainability. Such approaches may be used to more effectively assess, along with the human, social, natural and financial/built capitals, a community's *cultural capital* and its potential as a valuable resource towards achieving economic sustainability through tourism, and at the same time protect the integrity of the local community and its culture. Moreover, new alternative frameworks, which incorporate interactive and inclusive planning and implementation processes, will give communities the opportunity to reflect, rediscover, recreate and reconstruct a community spirit. In many rural regions, such frameworks could restore a community's sense of ownership, empowerment and sense of local control over shaping its own future. Hence, processes for community tourism planning will be discussed in Chapter 13.

Notes

1. Generally, this definition is accepted as the universal definition, from Bruntland Commission Report, *Our Common Future*, published in 1987.
2. According to Flora (2001), agriculture and forestry represent attempts by which human communities use the perceived potential of a local landscape to extract value and maintain human communities, thus transforming the ecosystem into an 'agroecosystem'. The agroecosystems that emerge are not simply natural outgrowths of humans and landscapes with productive potential, but rather, the product of human communities mediated by culture and technology. Agroecosystems are systems managed for the purpose of producing agricultural goods, including food and fiber (Wall *et al.*, 1998). Based on empirical evidence, such systems are located in rural regions and comprise rural communities. While not all rural communities are agriculture-based, it can be argued that all agroecosystems as we historically have known and understood them, are rural-based (with advancing technology and innovation, this notion may not be so in the future). Therefore, for this chapter, we will transpose the concept of agroecosystems with that of 'rural communities' into my discussion of Flora's adapted model.

Chapter 12

The Role of Public Policy

Introduction

The role of policy is possibly one of the most fundamental aspects of tourism development – and yet it is one of the least discussed. Chapter 2 discussed the evolution of tourism development in the Canadian context and touched on wider issues of development policies. The purpose of this chapter is to consider more fully the role of tourism development policy, as well as in regards to community development more broadly. After first introducing the notion of policy and highlighting its most general understandings, we'll consider the role of policy of tourism development specifically.

Key Theoretical Concepts: Public Policy; Tourism Policy; Social Policy

What is Public Policy?

Hall and Jenkins (2004) note quite rightly that public policy is much more than what governments *do*. They suggest that policy making is political activity, and follow Simeon (1976, in Hall & Jenkins, 2004) in noting that policy is the 'consequence of the political environment, values and ideologies, the distribution of power, institutional frameworks, and of decision-making processes' (p. 527). A policy is a plan of action to guide or influence decisions, actions and other matters. Policies are developed as tools for administrators to reach clearly identified political, management, financial and administrative goals. The term may apply to individuals, groups, private and public sector organizations. The policy process includes the identification of alternatives and choosing which will have the most positive impact. There has been much writing about policies: what they are, how they are formed, how to understand their impact. For instance, Jenkins (1978) stresses that public *policy* is a process, not simply a choice. Birkland (2001: 20) suggests there is a lack of consensus on the definition of *public* policy, but identifies elements common to all definitions:

- The policy is made in the name of the 'public'.
- Policy is generally made or initiated by government.
- Policy is interpreted and implemented by public and private actors.
- Policy is what the government intends to do.
- Policy is what the government chooses *not* to do.

Tourism and Public Policy

Church (2004) argues that there are three main aims of tourism policies (particularly at the local and regional level): economic diversification, economic renewal and (although to a much lesser extent) to address social divides. While tourism garners much attention today as a generator of economic and social opportunities, it took some time before it was taken seriously as a subject for policy development, especially in Canada. Indeed, it wasn't until the 20th century after WWII that policymakers and government leaders identified tourism's role as a tool for economic development and a source of foreign exchange. Thus, for those studying tourism policies, there is a growing need to consider this aspect of development more closely. Hall and Jenkins (1995: 3) suggest that the following topic areas should be included in any meaningful attempt to appreciate the role of government activity in tourism development:

- the political nature of the tourism policy-making process;
- public participation in the tourism planning and policy process;
- the sources of power in tourism policy making;
- the exercise of choice by public servants in complex policy environments;
- perceptions as to the effectiveness of tourism policies.

These same authors argued in a later publication (Hall & Jenkins, 2004) that tourism policy analysis only blossomed in the late 1980s and early 1990s. They write that a few factors gathered enough steam in the public eye to justify taking tourism policy formation and analysis seriously and to understand what they call, 'the regulatory framework for tourism':

> Among other things, interrelated processes in the globalization of economies, internationalization of financial markets, massive growth of multinational corporations, economic restructuring, environmental damage, and most recently, terrorism, have collectively sparked public sector decision and action (or in some cases debate followed

by non-decision and inaction) with respect to tourism. (Hall & Jenkins, 2004: 525)

Lickorish *et al.* (1991, in Hall & Jenkins, 1995) point out that there are primarily two ways that governments can play a role in tourism. First, they take deliberate action that favors the tourism sector. Second, they undertake any other kind of action that has implications for tourism although that is not a direct intention. In addition, and as is described in more depth later, the influence of global restructuring and neoliberal ideology upon rural economic development opportunities means that tourism and place promotion have become a very prominent, and very political aspect of development policies. As discussed in Chapter 2 and as Mair (2006) has outlined elsewhere, it is also important to note the extent to which they have formed the basis of regional development policies, bridging the provincial barriers to work together to attract tourists and money to economically 'weak' areas such as Atlantic Canada. Hall and Jenkins (2004) push this point further and contend that there has been a dramatic shift in the role of government in tourism:

> ... from a traditional public administration model which sought to implement government policy for a perceived public good, to a corporatist model which emphasizes efficiency, investment returns, the role of the market and relations with stakeholders, usually defined as industry.

These authors also trace what they consider to be a corporatization of the approach to tourism evidenced by a move away from tourism planning and policy in the public sector towards a greater emphasis on working closely with the private sector and focusing on marketing and place promotion (discussed in more detail later).

The role of values and ideology

Central to this discussion of policy formation is the point that individuals make policies. Individuals, of course, have values and ideological positions (however latent) that shape their policy decisions. Hall and Jenkins (1995: 35) describe values as 'ends, goals, interests, beliefs, ethics, biases, attitudes, traditions, morals and objectives'; all of which have tremendous impact upon how individuals decide what is important. It is no surprise, then, that we can see the growing influence of neoliberal points of view, as well as that individualism and consumerism are interrelated and make their way into decisions about tourism development. And yet, tourism researchers have not spent much time delving into these questions. As Hall and Jenkins (1995: xi) have argued, 'The role that power, values and interests play in tourism policy and tourism research requires far greater attention than has hitherto been the case'. Later in this chapter, we discuss more about the role of these values and what ideological positions mean for tourism in rural Canada.

Tourism Policy in Practice: A Public-Private Mix

While the above discussion takes us through the extent to which tourism is often discussed by public institutions, it was also noted that there is a growing role for private organizations to influence government policy and also to develop policies in their own organizations. Indeed, many would argue that the role of nonpublic interests and organizations are coming to dominate the tourism policy agenda. Currently, we can see that there are both public and privately created policies regarding tourism at the international, national, provincial and even local levels. These particular contexts of tourism policy are discussed in the next few sections.

The international context

At the international level, one of the first major multistate organizations to discuss tourism was the Organization for Economic Cooperation and Development (OECD). A major international body with 30 member states and on-going relationships with nearly 40 more, the OECD is committed to research-driven policy formation and information sharing with its members and strives to foster the development of 'democracy and the market economy' around the world (OECD, n.d.). This organization takes tourism very seriously, establishing its own department and committee specifically to discuss and formulate tourism policy. The following introduction is taken from the OECD (2007) website.

> Tourism, an important economic activity, is an area of public policy in most OECD countries. The Tourism Committee acts as a forum of exchange for monitoring policies and structural changes affecting the development of international tourism and promotes a sustainable economic growth of tourism.

Introduced briefly in the chapter, the United Nations World Tourism Organization (UNWTO), formerly known and still commonly referred to as the World Tourism Organization, is an agency of the United Nations that works to provide a forum for discussions of tourism and tourism development at the global level (UNWTO, n.d.). With 157 member states, more than 300 affiliated members representing the private sector, tourism associations and educational institutions, this international organization is dominant on the global tourism scene. The World Tourism Organization recently released a 10-point Global Code of Ethics (2001) for tourism (approved by the United Nations General Assembly in 1999). While not a legally binding code, the 10 points were developed as principles, with the goal of ensuring that:

> member countries, tourist destinations and businesses maximize the positive economic, social and cultural effects of tourism and fully reap its benefits, while minimizing its negative social and environmental impacts.

The World Tourism and Travel Council (WTTC) is arguably much more industry or private-sector dominated than other tourism-related organizations operating at this level. A self-described, 'forum for business leaders in the travel and tourism industry', it is committed to:

> Raising awareness of the importance of travel and tourism, promoting synergies between the public and private sector, generating profit as well as protecting natural, social and cultural environments ... (WTTC, n.d.)

As with most international organizations, while the goal of fostering discourse at the global level is admirable, the challenge of enforceability is great. This is especially true when it comes to tourism as most organizations develop policies at this level yet do not have the power or the resources to enforce their decisions or to make their policies effective at a local level. Thus, it is important to look more deeply at the other, lower, levels of policy formation to understand its role in tourism development.

Tourism policy in Canada

The formation of tourism public policy at the national level is under the mandate of Industry Canada with input from, and collaboration with, the Canadian Tourism Commission (see below), Heritage Canada, Parks Canada, as well as regional development agencies such as the Atlantic Canada Opportunities Agency (ACOA). In 2003, the various federal, provincial and territorial ministers responsible for tourism and tourism policy signed 'the Quebec Declaration' and made a commitment to create the National Tourism Strategy. This strategy (2004) was produced through consultation with industry and the provincial and territorial governments. In this document, six 'priorities' are established: border crossings; transportation infrastructure; product development; human resource development; tourism information and statistics; and tourism marketing.

Other areas of government activity, everything from policing, immigration, health and safety, infrastructure maintenance to instituting travel bans, while not directly tourism-related policy issues, are all part of the provision of tourism in this country. Thus, there are very few aspects of domestic and even foreign policy decisions that cannot be seen as influencing tourism in some way. Next, we look at two organizations that deal with tourism from a perspective that mixes public and private interests, but are undoubtedly industry-dominated.

The Tourism Industry Association of Canada (TIAC), discussed in Chapter 11, acts as a national advocate for tourism in Canada, and seeks to play a key role in the development of national tourism policy in Canada. The organization was founded in 1930 to encourage the development of tourism in Canada and today serves as the national private-sector advocate for the Canadian tourism industry, representing the interests of the tourism business community nationwide. TIAC has successfully influenced government thinking and action on behalf of Canadian tourism businesses, promoting measures that help the industry grow and prosper. In its efforts to do this, TIAC has sought to ensure that the government agenda is conducive to a growing and sustainable tourism industry (TIAC, 2007: Online Document). TIAC's policy platform (TIAC, 2007) outlines a number of principles that underlie its:

> ... approach to advocating for, creating and supporting policies and programs that advance a viable, sustainable and profitable Canadian tourism industry.

TIAC's policy platform consists of two types of policy – statements of principle and active policies (TIAC, 2007):

1. Statements of Principle are policy statements broadly based on the big picture (e.g. the value and belief statements of an organization).
2. Active policies that advance the Statements of Principle through advocacy programs and strategies.

The Canadian Tourism Commission (CTC) refers to itself as a national marketing organization with a vision of 'compelling the world to explore Canada' (CTC, n.d.). They conduct travel and tourist studies and act to 'promote product and industry development' by developing and fostering the growth of new areas of tourism such as culinary and spa tourism.

While addressing tourism development at the national level is the subject of some policy formation effort, much tourism policy development occurs at the provincial level, primarily in economic development, recreation and/or culture and heritage departments (e.g. the tourism in Ontario is currently under the mandate of the Ministry of Tourism while in Newfoundland, it is called the Department of Tourism, Culture and Recreation). Many have argued that this is hardly surprising given the increasingly reduced role of national governments in economic development opportunities (Hall & Jenkins, 1995; Mair, 2006). As Church (2004) argues, there is a clear hierarchy at work in terms of planning and policy development:

> In many countries the key concerns carried through from national to regional level tourism planning are generating regional economic growth and identifying key tourism locations through spatial planning, marketing and infrastructure provision. Local plans, in turn, carry through the concern for economic impacts and spatial planning by focusing on the key locations for tourism identified at higher scales.

Tourism is, as we have discussed frequently throughout this book, a very attractive option. Indeed, the market-friendly basis of tourism development makes it a *logical* choice for governments and organizations influenced by a neoliberal ideology and value system.

While most provinces will tackle tourism development, there are numerous other types of organizations that work, primarily as marketing originations, from a more regional standpoint; either in terms of bringing two or more provinces together to combine marketing and resources (e.g. the Atlantic Canada Tourism Partnership) or from within a province such as Ontario (e.g. the Southern Ontario Tourism Organization). As Church (2004) makes clear, regional collaborations are increasingly common in tourism development as many locales combine their efforts to generate policies for encouraging and supporting tourism development in their areas. By far the most common task undertaken by any organization (public, private or a mix) is to pull tourists to their location – or to engage in promotion. The next section delves into this complex issue.

Development Policy and Tourism: A Conflict of Values?

Place promotion

An underlying element to all tourism development, and certainly an aspect in each of the four cases we discussed earlier, is the role of place promotion in generating tourism development. While we talk about this in more depth in Chapter 9, it is important to understand that place promotion is also a public policy choice (Gold & Ward, 1994). As was pointed out in the discussion of Vulcan, it is clear that more communities, large and small, are developing place marketing policies and strategies, which may or may not involve branding and theming, to attract tourists, residents and capital investment. Church (2004) highlights the often ad hoc nature of many promotion activities. As this is often a significant part of a community's development strategy, it needs to be discussed in terms of a policy decision. Morgan's writing on place promotion (see especially Morgan & Pritchard, 1998; Morgan, 2004) is very influential and brings to our attention some important points.

Morgan (2004: 173) describes place promotion as a 'complex, culturally contested and ideologically laden act' and that while tourism has only recently been taken seriously within academia (and policy circles), it has become 'arguably the prime determinant of space' (p. 174). Thus, place promotion as a public policy choice is a fundamental part of tourism development. Interestingly, while it might be a public policy choice to engage in place promotion, often power to undertake the actual promotion is awarded to the private sphere. In this way, the creation of place image used in promotion, something that we have seen in our four cases can be a very emotional and political matter to residents of small places, is often done without community input.

While all images convey certain ideological perspectives and privilege some views and voices over others, it is important to realize that the very private nature of their production may seek to limit attention to alternatives even further. While a collaborative approach to tourism development may involve locals in the decision to develop a marketing strategy with the goal of place promotion, it is rare that they would also be asked to participate in the formation of those marketing images. What are the implications of the selection of these marketing images? Female or feminized images, of beaches for instance, as Pritchard and Morgan (2000) have argued, are a manifestation of 'gendered landscapes', as are male or masculinized images of cliffs and rugged parks. These gendered images reinforce cultural stereotypes and do little to challenge the power relationships at work in their creation.

Sustainable Tourism and the Role of Policy

Perhaps the greatest need for tourism-related policies stems from a desire to mitigate the negative impacts of tourism development, (be they social, environmental, economic or political) and to make tourism development more *sustainable*. Timothy (2001: 149, in Church, 2004) argues that even at the level of promotion, there has been a move away from 'narrow concerns with physical planning and blind promotion aimed at the masses towards a more balanced approach that supports the development and promotion of more sustainable forms of tourism'. While discussions of what exactly constitutes sustainability abound, it is important to note that there have been attempts, especially at the international level, to prescribe some policies, at least in principle, that can help encourage sustainable tourism. For instance, The World Summit on Sustainable Development after consultations with industry, government, nongovernmental agencies and other stakeholders, released a tourism sector report prepared in an effort to develop a coordinated approach to the formation of policies that will help to achieve sustainability.

> The challenge is to move from the existing ad hoc approach, to one that can integrate the current social, economic and environmental programmes, funds and initiatives, and evolve new patterns of managing travel and tourism businesses in a more systematic and dynamic way. The inevitable transition to sustainable development strategies gives the travel and tourism industry an opportunity to confirm itself as a solution, rather than a contributor to the economical, social and environmental challenges facing the future. (WSSD, 2002: 7)

In addition, the United Nations Environment Program (UNEP), working with the World Tourism Organization (WTO or UNWTO), created a list of principles that can be used to guide policy formation while bringing together the challenge of tourism development and the broader goals of sustainability. The principles were discussed in depth in Chapter 11 and won't be reproduced here.

As Edgell (1999: 50) argues:

> Managing sustainable tourism in the next (this) millennium is dependent on futuristic policies and sound management philosophies including a harmonious relationship among local communities, the private sector, and governments in development practices that protect natural, built, and cultural environments compatible with economic growth.

Williams and Montanari (1999) argued that the sustainable tourism literature has been 'long on morality, advocacy, and prescription, but weak in analyzing the structures and relationships inherent in tourism production and distribution' (cited in Williams, 2004: 61). A tall order, no doubt. And of course, the big, unspoken question is how might we even begin to meet this goal? In Chapter 13, we set out some steps for a process that we think can take us closer to this goal than most tourism planning and development approaches.

Aside from Williams and Montanari (1999), others have argued that policies put in place to move the sustainable development agenda forward appear promising. From a global perspective, Agenda 21 is an international blueprint that outlines actions that governments, international organizations, industries and the community can take to achieve sustainability. The objective of Agenda 21 is the alleviation of poverty, hunger, sickness and illiteracy worldwide while halting the deterioration of ecosystems which sustain life. It was adopted at the UNCED Earth Summit meeting on 14 June 1992. Since its adoption, initiatives and guidelines have not only been developed at the international level, but there has been a focus on local action, i.e. Local Agenda 21, since 'the true proof of "sustainable tourism" will be the sustainable development of local communities that serve as tourism destination' (UNEP: Tourism and Local Agenda 21, 2003: 7).

While tourism development, traditionally, has been dependent on initiatives taken by the private sector, Local Agenda 21 focuses on the role of local authorities in sustainable tourism development as:

> Local authorities are often the best placed organizations for establishing a sustainable approach to tourism in destinations, setting a strategy and balancing the interests of tourism enterprises, tourists and local residents. Their ability to manage tourism sustainability is related to: their democratic legitimacy; their relative permanence and ability to take a long term view; and their responsibility for a range of functions that can influence tourism development, including spatial planning, development control, environmental management and community services. (UNEP: Tourism and Local Agenda 21, 2003: 8)

Following the Local Agenda 21 approach, a local community creates a sustainable development strategy and develops an action programme to implement it. A local authority initiates the approach and provides leadership for the process. Its success depends on close cooperation between all the stakeholders. This approach has been adopted by many communities around the globe. '[T]he International Council on Local Environmental Initiatives (ICLEI) estimates that more than three and a half thousand local communities worldwide are now establishing Local

Agendas 21 UNEP document' (2003: 9). The Local Agenda 21 approach ties local goals and objectives to the larger global commitments of sustainable tourism development.

Public-Private Partnership Policy Initiatives

In 2002, KPMG Canada, a private consulting firm, prepared a report, *Co-operation and Partnerships in Tourism: A Global Perspective*, for a partnership comprised of the World Tourism Organization, the Canadian Tourism Commission and the World Tourism Organization Business Council. The goal of the partnership was to 'examine international best practices in co-operation and partnership within the tourism sector ... recognizing that public-private sector co-operation and partnership among private companies constitute a rising trend in competitiveness, especially for the tourism sector' (Bund, 2003: i). For this study, the partnering group identified 18 case studies that covered 5 world regions, which were chosen based on their abilities to illustrate the variety of partnerships formed to address key themes in the tourism industry (p. 4). Bund (2003: 8) argues the merits of and opportunities from public-private initiatives:

> Public-private partnerships have become popular vehicles for creating investment in tourism development ... as a rule of thumb, the public sector will likely have a higher propensity to invest when the dispersion of benefits to the public is high and the return on investment is stretched over a long period of time ...

> Each partner brings unique assets and capabilities ... the public sector may be able to offer assets that are underutilized or soft assets, such as reputation or an existing customer base ... the private sector can often bring a business focus and may also be able to bring international operational and marketing experience.

Bund argues that because the tourism sector is under great pressure, it becomes necessary to consider innovative approaches to maximize benefits for all tourism stakeholders. While tourism is an industry that can be creative and resilient, she contends, 'If they are to be successful, tourism operations must master partnering to sustain and grow this important sector' (Bund, 2003: 10). Economic sustainability is the dominant factor in achieving successful tourism.

Many of these initiatives are well intended and are certainly necessary; and yet one can't help but question the extent to which they are really going to make a difference in the way development takes place, especially tourism development. Like all major agreements to take particular directions in regard to policy formation, which are undertaken at the international level in regards to sustainability or even social issues such as equality and freedom, without a strategy for implementation (including resources therefore) no difference will be made.

New Directions: A Role for Social Policy in Tourism Planning?

At first glance, it may seem surprising that social policy has a role to play in this discussion of tourism development. However, as the discussion of community and community development in Chapter 10 made clear, successful tourism development means thinking much more broadly than we have previously. To this end, it makes sense to consider the role of more socially-oriented approaches to public policy development, even in the realm of tourism planning. As has been noted throughout the book, the political economic context of all aspects of development has changed over time. A new era of neoliberalism means that government responsibility and public accountability have shifted and many policy decisions are made not from a universal perspective, but from an increasingly private-sector dominated (or public–private partnership) approach. By discussing both public and social policy, in this chapter, we are aiming to link social issues with development issues and to reframe the discussion of tourism and government responsibility for social and community welfare. Gilbert (2002) calls this a shift from public welfare to the enabling state.

Gilbert (2002: 44) contrasts the traditional, public welfare state to the enabling state in the following way. Social provisions under the welfare state included support for labor, universal entitlement for health and social supports and a focus on direct expenditures to support the delivery of social services. Under the 'enabling state', by contrast, social expenditures are much more indirect (i.e. in the form of transfers and incentives) and include a push to promote employment as the way to support social equity. Given the employment and private-sector-led assumptions that underscore much support for tourism development, it is clear how tourism connects with this enabling state. Harvey (1989) would go even further to describe the new form of government activity as 'the entrepreneurial' state, where entrepreneurialism is fostered and encouraged as a means for stimulating private-sector-led growth.

In short, social policy is concerned with social provision in the public, private, occupational, voluntary and informal sector (Lavalette & Pratt, 2001: 6). Titmuss (1974: 131) defines social policy in the following way:

Social policy is all about social purposes and choice between them ... by acting or not acting, by opting in or contracting out, we can influence the direction in which choices are made.

Gilbert (2002: 62) points out that the challenge of social planning is to determine 'the appropriate mix of public investments, economic sanctions and social incentives to create the social environment desired'. Where does tourism development policy fit into this mix? The danger is that we often don't think of these connections and this means that tourism instead becomes a way of bolstering the entrepreneurial argument instead of becoming a platform for more government-led development activities. At best, social policy and public policy can merge in the realm of tourism development and planning by ensuring that the processes are participatory or at least not exclusionary, communities have control over unwanted and unsupported developments, and environmental protection and conservation are strengthened and held up with strong regulation. In the next section, we consider some opportunities to bring a more deliberate approach to tourism policy development – a conscious effort to counter the previous approaches where tourism has merely been an 'add-on' or an afterthought.

What Constitutes Sound National and Regional Community Development Policy in Rural Areas?

Most government policy with respect to Canada's rural areas dwells on issues of commodity regulation and economic sector development. In Canada as elsewhere, there is no such thing as a comprehensive rural policy that sets out what a government sees as the totality of rural community life and future aspirations for that sector of society. Policy addressing the rural realm is usually reactive in that it attempts to grapple with a profound problem of some description that is affecting a specific area of the country. For example, it may be a crisis in fishing as it was in Canada in the 1980s or in agriculture as it continually seems to be under pressure throughout the world. At present in North America, rural policy has been focused on ethanol production from agriculture produce to offset dependence on imported oil. In effect, however, the ethanol focus is really urban policy because the goal is to clean the urban environment and become secure in energy not because it is seen as good for rural areas. In fact, the pressure to produce ethanol from corn and other agriculture materials has caused the price of food to increase dramatically for many of the rural poor in developing countries. This is one dramatic example of rural policy built for an urban population with little regard for the consequences for rural dwellers. Policy formation and implementation, therefore, has been mostly problem-centered and usually with an eye to solving urban problems rather than forward-looking and working to set out a specific vision for rural areas.

As with the lack of development of a comprehensive rural policy, policy devoted to community development has been mostly reactionary and a patchwork of programs begrudgingly created and implemented by senior levels of government in the absence of a clear comprehensive strategy for both social and economic development. Community development policy has mainly centered on allowing the public to react to government programs and regulation rather than an *a priori* strategy designed to transfer control from senior levels of government to communities and those most affected by the issues. This, in turn, restrains the potential to develop approaches, policies, and even programs for rural development that offer specific answers for local concerns and needs.

It is not our intention to suggest that rural areas should be sovereign or that they be the sole contributors to the design and control of development and policy formation. What is being suggested is that local people understand their situation and aspirations best and, therefore, should be engaged as equal partners in the planning and development policies that will affect their lives directly. Rather than simply being recipients of senior government strategies designed from afar, rural residents should be engaged in the design of rural policies. The process at the local level needs to start with vision creation; not merely having local residents react to draft plans developed in their absence and/or in advance of their input. Citizen input after the fact simply becomes a public relations 'sales job' by the proponents of the plan and not a meaningful exercise of involvement and control. This after-the-fact approach usually fosters resistance and intense reaction against development, hardly a satisfying or positive experience for the developer, local governments or the residents. In Chapter 13, we set out a process that is based upon this fundamental principle.

Conclusion

Rural policy must be comprehensive in its outlook and not simply established to deal with commodity issues like agriculture or mining, or tourism for that matter. Rural policy is obliged to examine rural life in general and take into account the complex and diverse nature of the rural community and its often fragile cultural structure and physical ecology.

Issues of environmental conservation, social development and infrastructure requirements, in addition to the usual economic issues, need to be addressed. It should also make clear the place and role of rural areas in the broader social order.

Many of our history museums are quite good at portraying the role of rural areas in earlier times or during the settlement of this country, but we have not carried that tradition forward through developing rural policy that deals with the present and gives a special role to rural areas for future social and economic development. Too often, rural areas in the modern era are relegated to a nostalgic past and not viewed as a necessary contributing part of a modern society. This portrayal, however, could not be farther from the truth. Rural areas are a necessary component of a modern society, one that not only furnishes many commodities and goods to the urban areas, but provides for the regeneration of the basic ingredients of life. Rural areas provide our food, clean our air and are the sources of much of our drinking water. At present, most Canadians view rural areas as nothing more than repositories for commodities that are meant for the support of urban life and nice places to visit while on vacation. A rural policy that addresses not only the commodity and ecological issues in rural areas, but also the recreational needs of urbanites as well as rural dwellers in the form of tourism policy is vital.

While we as a society view urban centers as complex self-contained entities and treat them comprehensively through policy development and planning, we tend to see rural areas as unique and homogenous resource-based economies rather than as integrated living spaces in the larger society. As a result, policy at the rural area concentrates on the conservation and regulation of economic activity in those spaces rather than developing truly comprehensive rural policy devoted to addressing the needs of that sector of society and their aspirations for the future. And what's more discouraging, these areas are often viewed as simply peripheral lands that are simply there to support the urban environments and not as important independent political areas in their own right. They are viewed as natural capital and not given credit for their value as living spaces and as areas that absorb carbon and important aquifers for cleaning water so vital to life itself. Rural areas are absolutely necessary for the continuance of life yet their function is often minimized to a primary economic function.

In short, we are calling for much more than the creation of rural tourism policies geared only toward economic development. What we need is a comprehensive, national, rural policy addressing all aspects of rural life and embedding tourism policy therein. Tourism policy must be part of a larger construct that addresses the needs of rural areas so that all policies can be seen as wholly-integrated rather than isolated events. This approach to tourism policy creation and development reflects the conditions outlined above that stresses community control of development and life at the local level.

Chapter 13

Presenting a Process for Tourism Planning that Engages Community

Introduction

The aim of this chapter is to present the important concepts and practices that constitute planning for rural tourism development. One of the themes emerging from the analysis of the case studies was the consistent implementation of ad hoc or 'knee jerk' tourism development that often occurs as a response to some critical event faced by a community, and the abdication of formal or even informal planning activities that could otherwise place tourism on a more sound footing early in the process of development. When communities, move ahead with tourism development without taking the time to develop a community tourism plan prior to project initiation, the value of planning becomes clear as negativities mount up in the system and become evident over time. This chapter then is devoted to a discussion of the need for planning and the implementation of those processes either prior to, or in tandem with, tourism development.

Key Theoretical Concepts: Community Tourism Planning Process; Community Engagement

Tourism is often seen as a benign industry without pollution or the potential to produce negative environmental side effects. However, many communities that have gone down the tourism development path have, in addition to experiencing some payoffs, experienced negative externalities and, consequently, have spent great amounts of energy and time trying to mitigate those consequences after the fact. While wide citizen involvement can often mean more uncertainty and adds additional time to the process, it is more likely to produce a product with which all can be reasonably satisfied. Consequently, this will also reduce the time and antagonism that ill-considered projects engender after the development occurs. All too often, tourism growth has been unplanned and without proper preparatory work, including social and environmental impact assessments.

This need not be the case. By making a small number of fundamental issues the focus of a planning process, potentially undesirable effects can be mitigated prior to development. These fundamental issues are discussed below.

Challenging The Prerogative of Economics and Business in the Tourism Planning Process

Because business is thought to take much, if not all, of the financial risk associated with tourism development, business issues and criteria have been the nucleus for much of the tourism planning and assessment processes to date. What is often neglected, however, is the risk assumed by the local inhabitants of the destination site. The risk to them is a severely altered lifestyle because of overcrowding, inflated prices including land and buildings, displacement, noise and other forms of pollution. Traditionally, these issues, if given any attention in the development process at all, are usually subservient to assessments that describe demand for the destination and marketing research. Business is particularly interested in issues of supply and demand as the parameters for decision-making. What are often lost in these equations are issues of production and impact assessments. For instance, major developments such as hotels in rural and remote areas are not the main attraction but instead provide the infrastructure that allows for visitor travel and recreation experiences. It is often a unique environment or culture that is the attraction sought by the tourist, therefore, the local community and environment is naturally the producer of the attraction. Thus, members of the local community should be part of the assessment and decision-making process from the beginning of the project and not an afterthought. Moreover, some authors would argue, and we'd agree, that the local community needs to be in control of any and all tourism development. It is important to note that developers and investors outside the community will be instrumental in producing the infrastructure that gives shape to the final product. However, it is the local area and the environment that are critical to making it all work. They provide the opportunity for the infrastructure to exist. They will also be the people who will have to live on a day-to-day basis with whatever is developed and implemented.

For planning and regulation purposes, tourism is not viewed as a distinct planning category by government regulators, but is usually handled in the planning process like any other type of business. However, and as noted earlier, tourism essentially turns import-export theory on its end. Most businesses in nontourism sectors export a product outside their boundaries and to other geographic locations and receive payment for those exports in return. In the case of tourism, however, the export is an importation of people and their receipts, and usually a large number of them producing significant impact in the local area. It is important for governments to deal with these nuances and to institute a separate planning designation in order to more closely monitor and regulate tourism development so that it becomes more harmonious with the environmental and social setting in which it is located.

Community Visioning Sets the Framework and Controls for Tourism Development

It is our fundamental position that the community must be made paramount in the tourism development process. This involvement is not necessarily in the form of financial investment, (although that may happen, especially when it comes to nature-based recreation development or other anchor facilities like museums etc.) but is a sort of social and psychological investment. Tourism projects are often quite intrusive in community life, therefore citizens invest much of their social and psychological wellbeing in tourism initiatives. As a result, tourism planning must start by having those living in the community create a vision for the development of their community over the long term. This vision will be the touchstone against which all proposals will be assessed.

The community visioning exercise is the central ingredient to community development (CD) and the planning approach being advocated here, which must drive tourism development. It is important that community members come together and develop a basic concept of what type of development they think is compatible for the area in the future and that will respond to their value system and needs for development. Values that can be shared with the outside world as well as those which should remain off limits to visitors are identified in this process. This values identification exercise can be accomplished by organizing human-made and natural features in terms of the following categories: features that can be changed; features that should remain untouched or protected; and features that can be built upon. Features in this example may be cultural as well as built or natural areas. Critical to this assessment is the exploration and critique of the state of tourism in the community and the community's ability to organize and manage development over the long term. This is particularly important for rural and marginalized communities, not because they may not possess the necessary skills in the community to undertake this function, but simply because the pool of skilled people may not be as large as it is in more highly populated centers, resulting in greater demand on what is there. In rural areas, the smaller pool of skilled people is often overworked so the community needs to be prudent when developing and organizing its overall agenda.

In order to assist communities to come to terms with these issues, Reid *et al.* (2001) developed a set of self-assessment statements, which communities can use to focus their discussion and to provide a comprehensive assessment of their present state of preparedness for tourism development planning. These statements are listed below:

- There is a person or small group of people in the community readily identifiable who can give leadership to the tourism and community planning process.
- Tourism plays a predominant role in the economic life of the community.
- There is need for the community to be better organized to meet any tourism development needs that may arise.
- Tourism is a well-developed industry with a long but rocky history in our community.
- We do not have a clear process for solving problems as they arise.
- Tourism development is out of control and is too dominant an industry in our community.
- The residents do not want to see any more tourism development in the community.
- The residents and business community are not in agreement on how tourism should develop in the future.
- Everyone in the community needs to be involved in tourism development and not just leave it to the business community.
- Most residents would be willing to attend a community meeting to discuss an important tourism issue.
- If certain tourism proposals are developed by certain people in the community, they are automatically opposed by others.
- Everyone is willing to pitch in and help when we have a tourism event.

A community discussion with members of communities seeking tourism development, through the implementation of a self-assessment instrument comprised of items from the list above will cause them to critically examine their readiness for tourism planning and development. Depending on the responses to the self-assessment statements, it may quickly become apparent that the community needs to do some 'soul' searching with regard to its philosophical and organizational ability to jump right into tourism matters. In some cases, community leaders may need to address some fundamental governance issues before work on something as controversial as tourism development, or even planning for it, can proceed. Building the groundwork for communication and decision-making, including building trust among the many factions of a community, is critical to undertaking a planning exercise of this magnitude. Then, tourism will rightfully become viewed as one part of a larger system subject to constraints, resource needs, and different values. The discussion based on the self-assessment statements above often leads to a more comprehensive and coordinated community planning and decision-making exercise than the piecemeal approach that frequently transpires when tourism is the sole focus of the initial discussion. Thus, the discussion leads members of the community to recognize their strengths and weaknesses. It also provides them with the opportunity to address weaknesses before planning for tourism goes any further.

Communities that have the greatest probability for success in development generally are those that are experienced in bringing people together to discuss community issues. If there is experience with this type of process in the community, trust is generated and people generally feel comfortable that their positions will be heard and taken seriously by decision-makers. This type of discussion does not happen in a vacuum or as a one-time event. All too often planners, be it in tourism or otherwise, are too prone to call public meetings to discuss a contentious issue, but not complete the necessary community preparation that can then result in a dynamic and highly satisfying process. What often transpires is a truncated, poorly attended public event, which does not deal with anything but the most superficial aspects of the issue in question. More often than not, these types of proceedings become adversarial events, where officials and participants talk past each other, resulting in a highly unsatisfying and stressful encounter. Citizen participation must be viewed as a process that unfolds over time and through positive experiences – not simply as a one-off event.

Unfortunately, tourism development is too often anti-community in its structure and processes. A single person or company usually starts the ball rolling by suggesting a tourism event or enterprise that makes sense from a purely business point of view. This event championing was very evident in the Canso case. This person or group acts like an initial catalyst for the idea and engages people of like minds, which Reid has called the development group (Reid, 2003). It is at this stage of the process that a full-blown community consultation, focusing on community values and organization, is needed. Normally, however, the development group begins to focus on the physicality of the project, bypassing community consultation and the clarification of community values and moving directly to developing full-blown product plans for implementation. Once these plans are prepared and agreed upon by the development group, the job of selling the idea and its manifestations becomes identified as the public consultation process. This process usually focuses on the tourism product and nothing else. In fact, the kind of discussion that usually ensues merely considers what type of product there should be - not whether tourism is an appropriate approach to development in the first place. This type of public consultation usually satisfies the legislated rules for development, if such legislation exists, but is often highly unsatisfactory from the public's point of view. What the public is being asked to comment on is a noncontextual proposition.

The larger issues of community and environmental health and long-term systems planning are not part of the decision-making process. As a result, people who might not object to the proposal if it were presented as part of an overall development plan, addressing all aspects of community life in a comprehensive fashion, oppose it simply because of its failure to address aspects critical to community life beyond tourism. It is at the beginning stage in the overall planning process where the identification of those community features which need to be protected from development, those which could be enhanced by development and those that can be redeveloped if identified by the community can be addressed adequately. The community in this instance includes the general citizenry as well as the other stakeholders in the process including tourism entrepreneurs.

Once the initial *vision* is set by all sectors of the community, other stages in the planning process can be engaged. We say initial vision because visions for communities change as new ideas and needs are identified. Visioning should be considered as a continuing process, one that becomes a forum for ongoing community consultation and debate regarding development and other community issues. That said, the planning process must continue until decisions are made and projects are established. Figure 13.1 sets out a typical rational planning process in the middle column. While the categories in this rendition of the planning process will be alluded to in some detail later in this chapter, the stages in the process are: (1) visioning, (2) goals and objective setting, (3) program and product development to meet those objectives, (4) feasibility assessment of the proposed products, (5) refinement of the proposal based on the feasibility assessment and finally (6) implementation and continued monitoring and evaluation of the development. The two

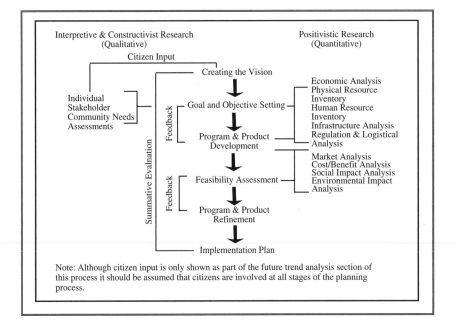

Figure 13.1 Planning for tourism development in marginalized and other types of communities

outside columns in Figure 13.1 display the types of knowledge that can be collected and analyzed to support the planning and decision-making process.

Tourism planning, like all other forms of planning, is informed by information, analysis and the interpretation of what that data means to the system being planned. Historically, tourism planning has relied heavily on technical knowledge (right-hand column in Figure 13.1) that attempts to explain the world around us from a particular point of view. In the case of tourism, given that it is often the entrepreneur or corporation that has initiated the project, data most pertinent to those actors in the system would likely be issues of supply and demand, and marketing. The gathering and analysis of this type of data is basically quantitative in nature. In addition, practical knowledge, that is, knowledge that integrates the results of technical knowledge with the goals of all the actors in the system, is also of paramount importance to those promoting or managing the tourism development project. This type of knowledge usually involves understanding the thoughts and feelings of others on the issue and manipulating the system to the advantage of the supplier (in this situation, the community) and those who will be directly affected by the project.

What is important is that both of these types of knowledge are recognized as legitimate forms of knowing and are integrated into the decision-making process at the right time and with the appropriate amount of influence. Each of the subsets of data and analysis is considered as information that supports various parts of the planning process. The left-hand column represents what we consider to be interpretive knowledge (often qualitative data). This type of knowledge is formed by individual values and aspirations for the future development of the community. It is based on how one interprets their surroundings and the world. This knowledge is usually formed through the interpretation of what the technical knowledge means in light of the values and aspirations of those making the decisions. The major criteria for judgment of its value and worth is whether or not the discourse is truly free from coercion and whether or not appropriate weight is given to all ideas and sentiments in the dialogue.

It should be pointed out that the technical knowledge that is generated on the right side of the diagram is legitimate input for informing the dialogue represented on the left side of Figure 13.1. However, the interpretation of that information and what it means to the issues at hand is the sole prerogative of those engaged in the process and not the researchers, planners or technicians who developed and amassed these data in the first instance. It is not meant to dictate decisions, but to inform those who are engaged in decision-making. Community citizens must be seen as responsible for, and in control of, the decision-making process and not simply recipients of it. Interpretive knowledge, therefore, must also be seen as instrumental in constructing the vision on which the rest of the plan unfolds. Needless to say, this dialogue is not linear but continuous, changing the system through time. This necessitates a well-organized community and one that values the dialogue as a way of creating a satisfying community and lifestyle.

In addition to the planning process outlined in Figure 13.1 and the descriptions of the types of knowledge and their role in decision-making, the diagram suggests feedback loops which recommends that tourism planning is not a one shot linear event but is a cyclical process designed to stimulate social learning (Friedmann, 1987) and not simply a product (plan)-centered exercise. Tourism planners and developers must see tourism planning as an ongoing dialogue with the community based upon the goal of enhancing the community and the lives of those who choose to live there.

Setting the Stage for Planning the Tourism Product

The first collective activity in the tourism planning process might be getting community members to answer the question: What do we want our community to look like in the future? The *vision* that is created through answering this question provides the starting point from which all the other activities in the planning process spring. Following from the vision, *goals* and *objectives* to reach that end state are created. Goals indicate direction and objectives are measurable achievements. These three fundamental pieces of the planning process lay out the basis on which all subsequent activity and output that constitute the body of the plan are judged. All subsequent activity must be devoted to achieving the vision, goals and objectives.

One of the important activities in the planning process is the determination of the strengths and weaknesses of the existing tourism product, if one exists. The features and themes that give strength to the tourism product in the community need to be identified. These features and themes are those things the community wishes to preserve or enhance through tourism development. On the other side of the equation, the community needs to identify the weaknesses in the product that need attention or elimination.

The planning process also turns its attention to some very practical aspects of tourism development. It is important to list and describe the major attributes in the community that will be incorporated into the tourism product. Both human and physical features are identified. Because tourism is often dependent on volunteer activity for its success, human resources are very important to rural tourism development. Volunteering in community festivals and other events that often make up or contribute to the tourism product are often viewed by participants as leisure activities. Motivation for volunteering is varied, so great attention needs to be paid to this part of the tourism development project and great care must be given to volunteer management.

Once the vision, goals, objectives and the resources, including human resources, are known then projects, *programs* and *activities* can be developed. Recommendations for action are critical to the completion of the tourism plan. Items that need to be created or completed should be listed here and ranked according to importance. These may range from attracting new businesses to improvement or completion of existing projects. Each community will have different needs and will set out different actions. Nonetheless, the creation of new special events or a town beautification plan, for example, should be outlined in detail. This detail includes not only the activity itself, but also timelines to completion and the identification of those responsible for implementation. In short, this part of the process answers the question: What needs to be done to meet our objectives?

The development of an organizational structure to *implement* the plan and monitor the system over time is critical to the overall success of the planning process. This component should include people who represent all stakeholders, including community and non-business groups as well as tourism operators. The responsibility of this organizational plan is not only to make sure the recommendations of the plan are implemented, but also to establish a sincere and complete *monitoring* and *evaluation* process for the tourism product to be undertaken on an ongoing basis. This organizational structure represents, and is responsible to, the community at large and not just to the financial stakeholders in the project. This component focuses on how the recommendations will be completed. Not only does it establish the implementation procedure, but also the time frame for completion and who will be responsible for the various actions called for in the plan. Also included is a procedure for monitoring progress of implementation as well as changes to the tourism and community environment in general.

A Sample Community Tourism Development Process

In (Reid *et al.*, 2001) we published a document outlining the process a community might use for hosting a visioning conference. A shortened version of that outline for a community visioning conference is produced here because it has been used with great success since it was first developed. Also, it is highly participatory and is devoted to community engagement.

This conference generally involves 25–30 community participants. Communities are not limited to holding only one conference, but are encouraged to hold several or as many as are needed to engage a large number of the public. It is an event that enables a large group to work collectively to create long-term strategic visions, achievable goals and action plans. The model we use here is based on the Search Conference developed by Emery and Purser (1996). The approach is implemented through a series of conferences, not just one, and the numbers of participants is kept small so that all can sufficiently air their views.

There is a wide variety of potential uses and outcomes of this conference including: developing new strategies for growth and renewal, creating coalitions and partnerships for solving complex problems, community mobilization and many others. The two most important elements of this conference are action and involvement and it is because of the success of the search conference method in community and corporate planning that we have chosen it as one of the first stages in the development of a community-based tourism plan.

The approach sketched above looks and feels a lot different than the typical single community meeting convened to sell a plan developed by some faction of the community or outside developer.

Key to the success of any community-based consultation is having a broad representation of all the voices and perspectives in that community. Identifying these stakeholders and bringing them to the planning table is no easy task. Certainly, the people who are invited to participate may be members of clubs or businesses, and these people are important to the process because of their role in the community, not simply the perspectives they represent. It is important, therefore, that those involved have the wider interests of the community at heart and not just a single perspective or sector.

One of the major issues planners will need to address is getting citizens to participate in the process. Citizens have become skeptical of offers to participate in decision-making because it has usually meant being sold a plan that is already fully developed. The idea of citizen participation in these types of events has become one of selling the public on what the planner or developer has in mind and not the mutual exchange of ideas with community members. Regardless of this negative history in the citizen participation experience of most citizens, the process that is being recommended here proceeds on a different basis. Here, the idea is to get participants to events that will ask them to identify not only what they eventually see as acceptable and even desired development concepts, but also asks them to grapple with identifying such abstract goals as to what they think they want their community to be in the distant future.

In order to help foster broader citizen participation, smaller 'kitchen meetings' can be held throughout the community as a way to prepare for, and generate trust in, the larger community-level conferences described above. These meetings are devoted to asking participants to think about their values and what they would want to see their community become in the future. The second benefit of conducting these meetings is to encourage those in attendance to become inspired by this initiative and to invite their friends and acquaintances to participate in future gatherings.

In the first phase of the larger full-blown community conference, participants are asked to draw their images of the community's past, present and future. Those who have attended 'kitchen meetings' should be well prepared to engage in this exercise given their previous participation.

Newcomers to the process that have not had the benefit of the previous kitchen meetings may be reluctant to jump into such an exercise without prior reflection on the task, but our experience is that once a few images are established, participants get caught up in the ideas and jump into the undertaking.

The walls around the room are covered with paper allowing members of the group to move around and write in events along a flexible timeline. Each member contributes by drawing (or writing) their knowledge of important or novel events (milestones, tragedies, achievements, major events) in the community. With the help of a facilitator, the group then discusses these drawings and works to fill in the missing stories represented by the images. This exercise is not only designed to produce knowledge about the past, present, and future aspirations for the community, but it also builds trust and a common understanding and appreciation for the community and the appropriate place for tourism in the area.

Once the drawing and discussion is complete, we use what many in community development circles call a 'dot-mocracy' approach. Each participant is given five large dots of three different colors (for instance, red, blue and green). Each color is selected to represent a response to one of three questions. For example, Blue might represent: What is inviolable in our community (what do we want to keep)? Red would signify: What could we do without in our community (what do we want to drop)? And green indicates: What are we willing to build upon in our community? Participants place their allotted dots next to the images on the wall as they see appropriate. While these dots are not treated as the final vote on what the group will decide, they do provide a very effective visual indication of what people are thinking about and can be excellent fodder for a broader discussion of goals and objectives.

After the voting process, the group collectively works together to create a list of priorities for each of the three questions. The facilitator makes sure that the lists are agreed upon by the group as these will form the basis for the rest of the visioning conference.

After breaking into small groups, participants begin visioning about the probable and the desirable future(s) of tourism in the community. Keeping the results of the voting process in mind, each of the groups works to address the following two scenarios: 'If nothing changes in tourism development in this community from this point on what is the eventual outcome?' and 'If we can dream about the most desirable future for tourism what would it look like?' After a specified time period, the small groups report back to the large group and discussions ensue.

The facilitator works to pull out commonalities among the groups and begins to create a list of possible strategies for the action-planning phase. The purpose of this exercise is to create momentum and energy around common ground and shared directions.

Keeping and displaying all materials produced by the group(s) over the course of the conference helps remind participants of their progress and may also help address any conflicts or misunderstandings that might arise. It's also a good idea to save the results of this process after the conference. All too often, tourism planners and decision-makers focus on the practical tasks of creating a product and do not keep a good record of important events and how decisions were made. Also, if baseline data is not kept on an ongoing basis, it is almost impossible to evaluate change over the long term.

Following the pulling together of a list of possible activities, it is now time for the whole group to review the list of priorities that were identified from the voting as well as to consider some of the strategies that came from the two scenarios and question exercise. Participants are then asked to create a new list of specific strategies and once again break into small task groups formed around each specific strategy. The task groups work to identify opportunities for achieving their desired scenarios and develop strategies for overcoming constraints. It is important to allow participants to put themselves into the strategy group where they feel most comfortable and fits their particular interests. If participants are working where they feel they have interest and skill, this will encourage buy-in and also help later when the work has to be done. Once the groups are finished this exercise, the results are presented to the overall large group and discussion, questions and new ideas are encouraged and recorded. The purpose of engaging in this exercise is to produce strategies for overcoming constraints, leveraging resources and task development. It is important to repeatedly emphasize the linkages between identifying constraints and strategies for overcoming them. Emery and Purser (1996: 189) suggest telling the group(s) to develop a list 'of the most serious obstacles, together with a way of dealing with each of them', as a way to focus on problem solving rather than simply problem identification.

Once a community conference has reached this stage, the group should have a list of issues and concerns about which it can start to collect information. The community may want to begin gathering information about economic, environmental and social impacts of tourism development with a question and answer session. Selected 'experts' may be employed to help with this process, however, it is best to find locals who have the knowledge and skills to impart information about difficult and complex issues; this is meant to be a community-driven process. If the community feels unable to find these individuals locally, it may be necessary to bring in outside help (e.g. someone from a university or a provincial government field officer with experience in CD) who can present this information to the community. Organizers should do their best to ensure that these individuals are able to speak clearly to the community and they must be willing to answer questions and engage in community learning. After the issue presentations, the community may want to organize a discussion with panelists representing stakeholder groups and special interests who are critical of tourism development in the community. The panelists can talk briefly about their viewpoints and concerns and those of the groups they represent. They could then engage participants (and one another) in question and answer sessions in an attempt to resolve differences of opinion or come to a resolution on how to proceed.

The next stage in the conferencing process is for small groups once again to form around strategic goals to develop action plans that are then reported back to the group. These may be new groups or may be the same from the previous exercise. Plans should be developed including milestones, commitments, champions (one or more person(s) who are willing to personally take on commitments), timelines and progress review checkpoints. The small groups report to the whole group and everyone works to accept, reject or modify the action plans.

The 'search/visioning conference' is intended to be fun and useful. A structure such as this helps people think through what is important to them and their life in the community. It does not begin with tourism development, but on fundamental issues of community life. Eventually, tourism is discussed as a vehicle for achieving that larger vision and may only be one part in reaching the vision. After the visioning conference, a community can undertake any number of options for creating a tourism destination.

Key Attributes of this Approach

The CD approach to tourism planning at the local level produces both enhancing and restrictive features that need to be addressed. There are two primary restrictions that often are so powerful they alone dictate a truncated CD process. The first is the amount of time that a full CD process consumes. Tourism businesses are frequently on a tight timeline as they are concerned with preserving the bottom line. More time spent involving the community in the process means more time spent on planning, thereby delaying the completion of the project and postponing income generation. The only response to this unfortunate perception is to point out that the money and time spent dealing with negative issues later (when the project is in full swing) would be better spent laying the fundamental groundwork in the initial stages of the project, thereby reducing the likelihood of those issues coming up after development (at increased cost).

The second issue may arise when the proponents of the tourism project are required, as a result of working with the community, to change their initial conceptions and plans. Obviously, involving more people in the dialogue increases the likelihood that changes will have to be made. This loss of control is not likely to sit well with most entrepreneurs. Some may even threaten to discontinue the project. In our view, this is still preferable to undertaking and completing a project that is not suitable to residents or environmentally sustainable. Many destination sites have been overexploited in the past, leaving locals and the environment more disadvantaged than they were prior to development.

There are positive attributes to the CD approach to tourism planning, which provides capital to the community beyond economic benefits (as meager as some of those often turn out to be). There is an educational value to the CD exercise whether centered on a tourism issue or any other development issue. Citizens learn from each other when engaged in this type of dialogical approach to planning and development. What become important here are the skills people develop from being engaged- as much as developing the physical structure of the project itself. Developing a 'community first' perspective builds confidence, often in communities which have become used to continually being on the losing side of the equation when it comes to advancement, however that term is defined. The CD approach also develops processes and skills that encourage all members of the community, including entrepreneurs, to make decisions and select priorities together. Through this process, the community moves forward as a group practically eliminating the usual winners and losers in the decision-making process. A successful CD process often attracts participants in community affairs who haven't historically been involved, for instance, newcomers to the community. This expands the skill base in the community and develops an expectation of community participation and control that has carryover value to future community projects.

There are some challenges and barriers to implementing such an approach to planning tourism at the community level. Leadership is a key issue. While most communities, including marginalized communities, have an abundance of potential leaders, these individuals may need to be discovered and encouraged. Leadership is a skill that can be taught, therefore, training in this and other important community process functions is critical. The issue of who provides that training is beyond this chapter, however, it is sufficient to suggest that this is a potential role for government, NGOs or private consulting firms with expertise in this area.

In addition, the role of the facilitator in this process is essential. A common assumption is that the conference facilitator should have skills in tourism development. We'd argue that what are really needed are skills that focus on process and community organization. The tourism discussion can come later and experts can be sought who can speak to the specifics of particular tourism projects and developments.

Finally, a major constraint to community control in tourism development and planning is the stereotypical and unfortunate assumption that the skills, expertise or capacity to undertake this kind of activity are missing in small communities. This stereotyping is often the result of the misperception by the proponents of the development as to what is the required expertise. Again, what expertise is needed for the type of process being advocated here is a skill set dominated by process proficiency and not necessarily tourism know-how.

Murphy (1985) argues that by having involvement and some control, a community can shape the type of industry that is most appropriate to its own needs. Indeed, the case studies presented in this text did not demonstrate wide-ranging involvement of the citizenry in community tourism development. For the most part, the tourism product was the prerogative of one person or a small cadre of individuals.

Thus, increasingly, social scientists emphasize the importance of community involvement in tourism planning in rural communities (Reid *et al.*, 2001; Murphy, 1985; Pearce *et al.*, 1996). They argue the imperative of genuine community participation. To this end, Smith (1984) presents four prerequisites for public participation: (1) the legal right and opportunity to participate, (2) access to information, (3) provision of enough resources for people or groups to get involved and (4) genuinely public – broad rather than select involvement.

Pearce *et al.* (1996) also allude to notions of power and influence as dominant considerations in community tourism development. Community participation implies the ability to exercise power, or at least, have some influence over the outcomes of the tourism development. But Painter (1992) carefully distinguishes between *pseudo* or *partial* and *full* participation. *Pseudo* participation 'is said to be restricted to such processes as informing and endorsement which offers a feeling of participation without its substance' (in Pearce *et al.*, 1996: 183). This kind of participation gives the participants some opportunities for exercising influence, but reserves the final power to make decisions to the authority holders (p. 183). In contrast, full participation implies that every participant has equal power to influence outcomes. Unfortunately, *pseudo* participation appears to be a heuristic; it is often interpreted as *community involvement* when applied to community tourism development. Rural communities contemplating or actively engaged in tourism development must move beyond pseudo participation to partial or, preferably, full citizen participation. Pseudo participation is not what we consider to be community engagement.

Tourism planners and other community officials responsible for development have not been well schooled in the nuances of constructing community engagement in the planning process. As noted earlier, public meetings are often seen by planners and developers as an obstacle to be overcome and not as an opportunity to engage the public fully with the eventual goal of sharing authority and ownership.

If tourism development is to be controlled by local citizens in partnership with developers, entrepreneurs, and other decision-makers, we need to alter the fundamentals of tourism planning. We must move from seeing tourism as the *subject* and community as the *object* of development to a view that sees the community as the **subject** and tourism as only one of many vehicles for its development. The benefits of the CD approach are multitudinous. In embracing this approach, tourism develops from the inside out rather than from the outside in. This makes tourism development as much about local leisure as it is about tourism and economic development. The output of this focus is surely to provide a community that gives pleasure and satisfaction to both locals and visitors alike. It gives ownership of the 'plan' to the community rather than ownership residing outside, or to a small group of those inside the community. The process helps build community spirit and dialogue that is not only applied to the immediate project, but also to other community issues that arise from time to time.

Perhaps most importantly, the CD tourism planning process prevents or reduces tensions in communities where tourism development is taking place. It can go a long way in protecting community integrity and building solidarity.

Chapter 14

The Way Forward: Rethinking Rural Tourism Research and Practice

Introduction

The survival of many small and remote communities in Canada and around the world is being deeply tested. Environmental change, corporate globalization, economic restructuring, and adjustment programs embracing a neo-liberal approach have challenged their environmental, economic and social sustainability. This is especially true for communities whose economies are based upon the extraction of natural resources. Encouraging this corporate globalization has been the rapid increase and advancement of technology in the workplace, especially in primary industries, and the increasing sophistication of the communications process allowing for the instantaneous movement of capital, goods and services around the globe.

Underscoring these developments is a fundamental shift in power, from governments to corporations and business, giving governments less control to develop local economies and to protect the environment. Limited government control has led to the privatization of, and reduced access to, some long-standing public services and infrastructure developments. Today, transnational corporations, including those involved in the tourism industry, can place severe demands on countries to reduce regulations and legislation in the areas of performance requirements, labor regulations and environmental restrictions if they want to secure investment for their country. It would seem that competition, the backbone of the capitalist economy, is no longer only between corporations, but also among countries vying to attract these transnational firms to their jurisdiction. This is all done, particularly in the less developed world and in remote and marginalized communities in the more wealthy countries, in order to capture jobs and economic survival, including maintaining or developing a tax base. These changes present incredible challenges to the future of rural communities and it is within this context that tourism must be considered. This chapter wraps up our discussion of rural tourism by reinforcing the main arguments presented throughout the book and pointing towards what we think are very real opportunities for meaningful change through a new form of rural tourism planning.

Key Theoretical Concepts: Tourism Rural Development; Community Tourism Planning

Tourism has often been presented, particularly by the tourism industry and those concerned for economic development, as the savior for those communities that find themselves in economic transition. This has particularly been the case in resource-based communities that have found themselves in difficulty because of changes brought about by technological innovation, or by the exhaustion of resources on which they have relied. Additionally, tourism has often been presented as a benign industry that produces little negative impact on human communities or the environment in which it is situated. Of course, as we have demonstrated in this book, this is a problematic idea. Like any industry, tourism has produced unintended consequences and impacts for destination communities and their natural environments. So the question remains: Is tourism a savior or false hope for communities in crisis or experiencing economic downturn? As you might expect, the short answer is: both. However, given that tourism development can create such negative impacts for communities, a measured and thoughtful response to this dilemma is required.

At the micro level, tourism may provide income from new sources, thereby propping up a flagging economy that may otherwise collapse completely. However, small-scale tourism enterprises, like Bed & Breakfasts, for instance, are often merely temporary and unreliable 'stopgap' measures to help one family when their farm is in trouble or when opportunities for other work are not available.

Travel and tourism have increased greatly over the last 25 years, representing an opportunity for many entrepreneurs to enter the sector. However, the transition from a resource-based economy and job sector to a service-based industry like tourism is not an easy conversion. Not only are the skill requirements of the job different, but so is the product that is produced. For example, a fisher who becomes engaged in whale-watching tourism not only has to grapple with a wide range of human expectations and consumer demands but also a major alteration of equipment to accommodate different, service-related needs. The changes in attitudes required for service-based jobs and the hard infrastructure modifications needed to make the enterprise viable can also be vast. The issue of insurance and public safety both on and off the water is also a major condition that must be met. This is just one example among many that demonstrates the transition requirements when moving from a primary sector activity to the tertiary sector. Often, little thought is given to some of these new requirements because of the enthusiasm with which the project is approached.

The macro picture may be quite different from the micro sketch. While a single bed and breakfast operation may not have a major impact on the local community, tourism often builds incrementally in the community before severe impacts on the culture of the inhabitants become apparent (George, 2006). Indeed, the purpose of chapter 13 was to describe what we argue is a planning process that helps communities to anticipate and prepare for these issues before development is undertaken. As we have argued throughout this book, planning *a priori* can often help communities to construct a product that can avoid some of the thorniest issues and outcomes before they become damaging.

Additionally, our suggested approach for tourism development is to create an activity that is of interest to both the tourist and the local resident. In fact, our experience tells us that the most successful tourism events, particularly in rural communities, are those that begin as a local leisure event and are then expanded and eventually offered as a tourism product to a wider audience. Naturally, size is of concern. Any event, no matter how attractive to local people, will become burdensome if it becomes too large and disrupts all aspects of community life, and while this may seem like an easily controllable variable, experience would suggest that it is not easily resolved. Each of us has a tolerance level for crowds and intrusion. The only way to determine the carrying capacity for a local event is to determine that threshold prior to launching the event and then through continually monitoring the situation. This determination needs to be communitywide and not left to those who have a direct economic stake in the project.

Also, determining the type of patron that one is trying to attract is of concern as well. This is not always as easy as it sounds. Take for example the Friday the 13th event at Port Dover, near Lake Erie in Ontario, Canada. The attraction for this small community is the congregation of motorcycle owners in one place. On every Friday the 13th, bikers from all over Canada and the USA descend on this small community for a one-day congress. Upwards of 30,000 bikers have been known to attend this event. As we all know, this can include a wide array of people, including a criminal element as well as purely recreational bikers. While no one, to our knowledge, has studied the effect of this event on the community, it would appear that the impacts have been largely positive. This community has absorbed this event well with little incident, and while it has become a spectacle for those in attendance and the wider audience throughout the nation via the media, it appears to be absorbed by the community without major disruption. Of course, given that it is a day-long event it is easier to absorb than one that is constantly present, but even so, it seems to fit nicely with the everyday life of the community. Some businesses survive for the whole year on the activity of the few days that this event produces and then resumes normal conduct throughout the remaining part of the year. So, Port Dover demonstrates that communities can accommodate the most unusual tourism activity if it is well thought-out and planned.

That said, there are a number of issues that need the attention of any community that is considering the development of a tourism enterprise. As a way of concluding our discussion and pointing the way for future research, we present these issues below in the form of probing questions.

What constitutes development?

The first question to be dealt with is: what constitutes development? Growth has become synonymous with development, especially for governments and entrepreneurs. The problem is, however, that thinking about development in this way doesn't help us to consider the benefits and costs. Development has to be defined in the widest sense possible and those using this idea must ask hard questions and make in-depth assessments of the environmental, social and economic implications of development activities. This assessment needs to involve a large and representative section of the community as full partners in the discussion and the citizens of the community must not be viewed as unequal partners that simply need to be convinced of someone else's plan for development.

Planning for rural tourism development is an exploration of the potential of the community as a tourism destination that contains a spiritual, social and environmental dynamic and not simply an economic engine for growth. As part of this analysis, distribution of rewards is just as important to determine as is the size of the potential receipts of the proposed attraction. Often much of the receipts from tourism leave local areas and travel quickly to nonresident entrepreneurs or corporations, and in some cases out of the country in which they were generated altogether. Local citizens in rural tourism communities need to see the benefits of tourism-related development manifest in their community.

Often left out of this analysis is any focus on individual and collective human and social development. We argue, to different degrees in Chapters 10 through 12, that tourism development enterprises should provide a social learning component and be concerned with the total, ongoing education of the community. The outcomes in social learning gained through a well-conceived tourism development process may have greater value in terms of developing social cohesion, skills and expertise than a stand-alone attempt at economic development.

Given that tourism often depends upon a social and festive atmosphere, it can have great value as a leisure experience for locals in addition to its economic benefits. For this to be the case, however, a leisure orientation needs to be specifically embedded in the plan of development and not simply seen as a happy unanticipated consequence. Many of the cases cited here demonstrate the leisure value of locally initiated events. For instance, the art exhibition and show in Port Stanley presented the works of local artists and was clearly directed at local residents until over time, it became sufficiently sophisticated to become a tourism event.

What motivates development?

A second major question that needs to be addressed is: what motivates development? This question is often at the heart of tourism development in communities or rural communities that have faced economic crisis situations. Is it a reaction to some bad news like a plant closure or a moratorium on resource extraction, which puts into question the viability of the community? Or is it a well thought out strategy that develops organically within the community, perhaps as a leisure event for residents, as described above, that eventually gets shared with a wider audience?

Too often it is the reaction to some drastic event that drives the process. This appears to be the case in Lunenburg where the community was grappling with the collapse of the fishery. In Lunenburg's case this became more particularly accentuated after the UNESCO World Heritage site designation was received. The Canso case is also very much a response to the downturn in the economy because of the crisis in the Atlantic fishery. Reacting to this kind of pressure often results in giving up too much control of the project to outside and private interests and rushing through, perhaps even circumventing, the planning process. This process would, under normal circumstances, involve completing the necessary environmental and social impact assessments prior to development but the fear of economic downturn puts all these considerations on the back burner. A more thorough planning process would also consider the potential impacts of mass tourism on the culture and quality of life in the community. Numerous inaccuracies and oversights are often made when crisis, particularly economic crises, drives the planning and development of tourism. It is only after projects are underway, and perhaps on an exponential growth curve, that the impacts become obvious; it also becomes apparent that these could have been mitigated with a proper planning process.

In other cases like in Port Stanley, for example, it is difficult not to view the Port without tourism development that shares its rich beach and fresh water lake resources with outsiders. The resources on which Port Stanley's tourism is constructed are the heritage of South-western Ontario and not just the heritage of those few residents who inhabit the community. Tourism in a setting like this one is organic, and what matters is how that product is constructed and preserved and blended into the surroundings. Scale in such an enterprise counts. The motivation for development in such an instance as Port Stanley is in resource-sharing and preservation and not just economic development, although certainly that is an important outcome to those who are dependent on the long-term economic prospects of the Port. Port Stanley began as the playground and leisure site for the wider geographic area when such sites were scarce and travel to farther away sites was limited. While, no doubt, there was an economic motivation for tourism in Port Stanley, it was arguably a result of evolutionary development.

In the case of Canso, tourism was initially a deliberate, contrived undertaking that some would argue was an unconnected event staged purely for economic reasons. That said, it must also be reported that the Stan Rogers event, while beginning as purely an economic event, has now caught the leisure imagination of the local residents. They now see the event as a cultural and life-giving force in the community. Thus, what may start out as reactive one-shot, economically-driven development may become self-sustaining over the long term if it is well conceived and catches the imagination and support of the local inhabitants.

Who is in control of the development?

Perhaps the third major question to be addressed by those seeking development through tourism is: who is in control of this project? There have been too many instances where outside interests (including trans-national corporations and national governments) have stimulated and controlled the direction of growth and development. The result has often been a set of development criteria at odds with local values and needs.

For example, if the goal of the national government is to generate foreign currency to pay down foreign-held debt, then local or regional development goals are not likely to find their way into the planning of the development project. An extreme example includes cases in the developing world and marginalised areas, such as in some aboriginal communities, where locals have been relocated to make way for resort development owned by outsiders. These outsiders, often part of transnational corporations, may bring in their own staff in order to avoid training locals for the jobs in the new industry. In this sense, the control is very much out of the hands of community members.

Control can also be more subtle. In the case of Vulcan, for example, the members of the community may have given up psychological control as the pop culture appeal of *Star Trek* works to re-define the way the community feels to its members. While not giving over control of business, the community is at least partially subject to the whims of the *Star Trek* fans who visit and some locals feel that this is an unacceptable change to their community's image and reputation. The aesthetic of *Star Trek* brand, as well as *Star Trek* themed events, created and encouraged by few without the buy-in from the rest of the community, may continue to alienate locals and make them feel like they have no control over their town.

What is the appropriate development process?

Following on the above concern, the fourth question of interest is: What is the appropriate process for development? There are many types of planning processes that can be invoked depending on the environmental circumstances and what is to be achieved by the project. For the most part, tourism destination development needs to be highly participatory and predominantly the prerogative of local inhabitants. It must also have a long-term perspective. As explained earlier, there are too many instances where the citizen participation process has been a sham. This was clear in the case of Lunenburg, where public consultation about the community's future development did not occur until after processes had already been put in motion by town officials. In some cases, vital information about negative features or impacts may be withheld by proponents of a plan knowing that the proposal would not receive a favorable reception if those facts were widely know by the community and its officials.

Those engaged in the tourism planning process need to think about what the proposed development will look like 10 years hence. If a tourism project has some success, it will likely grow in size and become more intrusive into the everyday life of the community as time passes. These types of projects need to be assessed before a project is accepted. If this is not done and growth is too intensive, residents may choose to do their shopping and other normal daily activities outside their community. After tourism takes hold, congestion and rising prices may become unmanageable and may make the community unlivable. This may be too high a price to pay for development. In many instances, there is no evident management structure that is designed to monitor and evaluate tourism projects for growth over time and for the deteriorating conditions that lead to product decline, as outlined in Butler's model in Chapter 4. Meaningful participation by the locals is critical to the long-term stability of the area and the tourism businesses that establish themselves in it. Those engaged in the process must consider the proposal and its long-term implications with a rational eye.

What constitutes the knowledge base for development?

Finally, a major and often unasked question is: What constitutes the knowledge base for development? Decision-makers, including developers and those in government, often rely exclusively on data about rural areas that has been generated by outside experts. Additionally, a narrow range of data and particular types of knowledge are often preferred over other forms of information and this can restrict the focus of decision-making. As was noted in Chapter 13, there are many distinct yet complimentary types of knowledge that belong in the planning process, particularly in the tourism planning and development process. A discussion of what type of data and analysis is important to the tourism planning and decision process is critical to tourism development in rural communities, especially, and more generally, in all types of municipalities (see Figure 13.1 in Chapter 13 for more detail). While the rational choice model of data analysis has prevailed in tourism planning and decision-making, it is becoming more apparent that that approach is not sufficient. It is extremely important that data collection and analysis also focus on community issues and the relationships of people to their environment and community, however that may be defined.

The rational choice model depends on the fundamental principles of efficiency and effectiveness based on increasing and protecting individual self-interest through the concept of marginal utility. The rational choice model is based on the notion that decision-makers will collect, analyze and evaluate quantitative data. Based on their analysis, they act in the best interests of their constituents and most often those concerned with developing the tax base and increasing revenue flows into the community. Market analysis is often a major part of the rational choice model given that it is the demand for the product that will determine the entrepreneur's decision to act or not. Certainly, making some judgment about the likely financial success of a tourism project is an important component in the planning and decision-making process, but it need not be the only consideration.

The literature on 'sense of place', may add a necessary if little considered component to the tourism planning and decision-making process in rural communities. As Smale (2006: 3) suggests, 'only relatively recently has place, and to a lesser extent space, been considered in the leisure studies literature as an important contextual factor influencing behavior, shaping perceptions, and defining experiences'. Smale (2006: 370–372) suggests, there appears to be on the part of individuals in communities:

> a desire to reconnect with place as an integral part of the human experience ... place shifts attention to the subjective lived experience of location, to the profound meanings we ascribe to it, and to the wholly human experience of place. Place can possess meanings that are deeply personal and are typically expressed through emotional, aesthetic, and symbolic appeal of place ... So, while places might be associated with the physical locations defined by space, a space does not become a place until it achieves some deeper meaning ... *(S)ense of place* is the *awareness* of the spirit associated with place and the qualities it possesses, and therefore a faculty or feeling possessed by the individual rather than of the place itself. (italics are the authors)

Tourism planners and municipal decision-makers often forget the profound meaning that place has for their residents and treat development issues like tourism simply from the rational choice approach. As noted in Chapter 11, tourism has the potential to alter not only the physical space, but also the meaning of place and is influenced by more intangible factors like spirit and the relationships between people and physical spaces, built up over the years of living there. Psychological factors, such as one's sense of place, are much more difficult to identify and measure than the variables that are often used to calculate outcomes in the rational choice model. 'Sense of place' data are usually qualitative in nature whereas rational choice information is almost always quantitative. We traditionally rely and trust quantitative data and analysis, but are somewhat skeptical about the validity of qualitative data and their meaning. That said, there is beginning to exist a grudging acceptance of the usefulness of these types of measures as the techniques for their collection and analysis improve and their importance become understood. It is vital that tourism planners and decision-makers take a lead in supporting the use of new research tools and instruments to undertake and complete 'sense of place' analyses and to gather different kinds of data in non-traditional ways. Then, we can get a better sense of the real issues concerning development in communities and create a better understanding of the ways communities are created and experienced.

In addition to addressing the five important questions outlined above, those concerned with tourism within the context of community and environmental sustainability must also evaluate the impacts of decisions and manage the system over time. Returning now to the analytical framework for understanding tourism development introduced in Chapter 1 (see Figure 14.1), the next section examines how communities can determine where they fit' in the framework. Moreover, they might also consider how they might move to another position.

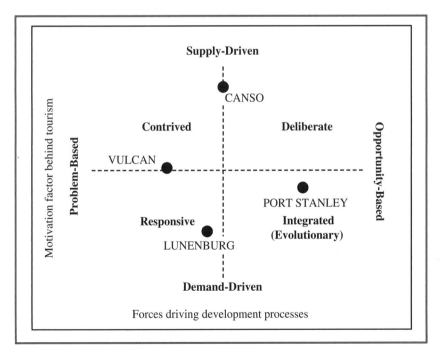

Figure 14.1 New analytical tourism development framework

Managing Rural Tourism Successfully

A tourism destination is not a stagnant entity, but is dynamic and ever-changing. Notwithstanding that reality, many communities manage their tourism product as if it were a particle suspended in time and space. As a result, the evolution of tourism products are not guided or managed, but left to drift into whatever state they will. At least two instruments can be used to avoid this type of drift.

The first is Butler's life-cycle model of development. While there may not be a sophisticated mathematical calculation on which to base judgments about placement on that scale at any given time, it can be used as a framework on which qualitative judgments about where a given community is located and what might be done to advance the product to the next stage or to avoid the eventual fall into decline. What is important in this discussion is to acknowledge that management is as much about determining the present and future state of the tourism system or product as it is in determining such micro issues as marketing or currency exchange rates. In addition to managing the product from a technical point of view that monitors issues of marketing and competitiveness, tourism management must also concern itself with managing the tourism system so that it avoids the stage of decline and embarks on the process of rejuvenation at the right time. Taking the macro view is difficult when one is immersed daily in the micro management of 'administrativia'.

A second framework that might also be employed to foster awareness and understanding about the present state of tourism product (in a community) and what might be done to manage its development appropriately was introduced as our analytical framework at the beginning of this book. We re-visit this framework in the next section.

A New Analytical Framework for Understanding Tourism Development

This framework can be considered a macro model, to help explain the foundation on which tourism destination areas are established and the basis on which they operate at any given time. Each of the four quadrants (Quadrant 1 – Contrived; Quadrant 2 – Deliberate; Quadrant 3 – Integrated/Evolutionary; and Quadrant 4 – Responsive) presupposes a fundamental starting point (motivation) for tourism development and factors driving the development process. It is important to bear in mind that we see this framework as a heuristic. Communities will take bits and pieces from each of the quadrants and will move through the framework as they work to determine new opportunities for (tourism) development over time.

For example, 'contrived' (Quadrant 1) tourism is usually a tourism product that has little or no relation to the history or environment on which the community is and has been based. For instance, the only reality that the community of Vulcan and the *Star Trek* television show have in common is the name Vulcan. This theme is not based on any legitimacy of the area in which Vulcan is located or the culture on which it has been established. The theme is purely opportunistic with little or no basis in social fact. It has, however, caught the imagination of some very devoted *Star Trek* fans whose activities in the community during conferences and festivals have caused some concern for locals. Whether or not this theme will provide lasting appeal to both tourist and local citizen remains to be seen.

Given that the *Star Trek* theme may wear a little thin over time and community buy-in, at least to date, is not sufficient for the theming to be complete, it may be advantageous for the community to consider strategies to move into Quadrant 3 (Integrated/Evolutionary) and look both at diversifying the tourism product and building upon some other aspects of community life. Many communities have developed successful tourism by beginning with a special event of some description, but subsequently move on to creating other festivals or events or other completely different types of tourism. Vulcan may want to continue with the *Star Trek* theme, but may also look into the future and plan more comprehensively for a diversified tourism development strategy. Relying on a single theme or event may not prove to be sustainable over the long term, so diversification of the product needs to be planned while the present approach is still in continued development. In our assessment, we predict the *Star Trek* theme in Vulcan will rapidly work its way through Butler's life cycle. Hence, the citizens of Vulcan can expect this theme to reach the stagnation and decline stage fairly swiftly and some new forms of products and development need to be on the horizon to meet the rejuvenation challenge.

Similarly, Lunenburg's UNESCO World Heritage designation has met the crisis of the downturn in the fishery, but it has also caused unanticipated side effects that now need to be dealt with. It has been reported that Lunenburg is dropping in population because of dramatically increased housing prices and the purchase of many of the historic homes by nonresidents who are seasonal. Lunenburg runs the risk of becoming a 'living museum', not unlike other places. It may be a nice place to visit, but becomes fairly hollow as a desirable place to live on a continuing basis. This situation presents some important challenges to Lunenburg and profound planning is needed to guide the community into a state of sustainability. Shifting into Quadrant 3 (Integration/Evolutionary), should now be its goal of its tourism planning strategy. While Lunenburg has commodified its culture (George, 2004) for tourism development, creating a new entrepreneurial climate in the community, it also needs to diversify into other ventures, both inside and outside the tourism sector. Allied industries, such as oceanography and marine services might be considered. Such activities would not only have scientific merit, but also have potential tourism capacity that could add diversification to the economic system.

Port Stanley, on the other hand, has integrated its community base in addition to rejuvenating its tourism system. Gentrification may, unlike prevailing thought, be a positive entity instead of a negative occurrence. Gentrification, in Port Stanley's case, is clearing out the old stock of cottages that have deteriorated and been part of the decline of the area; it is instituting a fresh and upscale permanent housing and cottage stock that will draw back the many visitors and part-time residents that have abandoned the Port for more pristine cottages and lake areas in Northern Ontario. Certainly, we need to be very careful with how far the processes of gentrification can go and safeguards need to be in place to protect the people already living there from being priced out of their own communities. Given that travel is now more time consuming and costly due to rising fuel costs, a rejuvenated Port Stanley will draw back many South-western Ontario residents for leisure and recreation experiences. Port Stanley, unlike the other case study sites in this text, will need to 'respond' to newly expressed needs as it diversifies its tourism product. There is also room for Port Stanley to actively 'contrive' tourism products as long as they are kept small and proportionate in scale to the better well-established tourism themes.

In Canso, the Stan Rogers Folk Festival, or StanFest, has a very tenuous connection relative to the evolution of the community itself; thus, it is positioned as a 'contrived' event. It so happens that Stan Rogers' mother calls Canso her hometown but, of course, has not lived there for many years. Stan Rogers was born and raised in Hamilton, Ontario. But, this circuitous connection was enough for one individual to conceive the idea of StanFest, which has become a very popular international event since its inception in 1996. Like Vulcan, Canso, because of its apparent success, should move quickly into Quadrant 3 (Integration/Evolutionary) and consider diversification strategies, both inside and extraneous to tourism. It might also move towards Quadrant 4

(Responsive), as it determines the range of needs, not only for economic development, but also strategies for leisure activities that may provide some fresh new ideas for other festivals or tourism events to augment the StanFest festival.

The brief discussion above provides some examples from the case studies presented earlier in this text on varying approaches to managing the community tourism product. It may seem to be advantageous for all tourism to be planned from an 'integrative' or even a 'deliberate' perspective where the process is not merely a reaction to an uncontrolled change. However, reality would suggest that, more often than not, tourism is planned from a 'contrived' or 'responsive' perspective and so we must take this into account and help communities manage their efforts in new ways. Planning is cyclical and ongoing and once an event or product is well underway, there will be continuous opportunity to refine or strategically alter the tourism product as problems arise or new ideas emerge that were not available at the time of invention. Reid *et al.* (1993) have provided a visual of a planning process that is cyclical and continuous in nature (Figure 14.2) that is discussed in the next section.

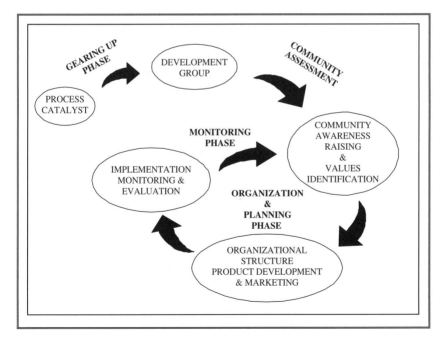

Figure 14.2 Community development tourism planning strategy

This process model may be useful for rural communities planning new tourism strategies.

Planning Tourism Development Strategies

Although a community may already have implemented a tourism development strategy, bypassing some of the stages outlined in Reid's model, it can still enter and benefit from the planning process. Often, and in many communities, those who form the development group are enthused with their ideas for tourism development and move directly to the marketing stage with those ideas, missing the community awareness and values clarification stage. If, however, the implementation of the event or product puts undue stress on the community (and in most cases this occurs), there will be a need to enter the planning process, as outlined above, and most likely at the monitoring and evaluation stage to assess what is wrong with the product. This may start with an evaluation or an assessment, then moving to the community awareness phase of the process where a communitywide discussion of community values would be important to consider; these become part of the next phase of product development and marketing plans for the revised product.

Consistent with the discussion in Chapter 13, the community tourism planning model outlined in Figure 14.2 is a highly community integrative model and participation by citizens in every phase of the planning process is imperative. If the original tourism event were planned and implemented by one person or a small select group of people without wide support from the community, it will be necessary to expand the process to include more voices in order to foster wider ownership of the product and strategy. The long-term success of the tourism product will depend on the engagement and support from all residents and not just depend on the resolve of a few.

This planning model can also integrate the resolution of the five questions presented earlier in this chapter. Ideally, the following questions will surface during the community awareness and values identification stage: (1) What is an appropriate product for our community? (2) What is our motivation for doing this? (3) Who is in control of what we are doing? (4) What is the right development process for us? and (5) What form of knowledge will we rely on as we build this product? These issues will permeate the informal discussion throughout the community regardless of whether or not they are formally raised in the ongoing planning process. We have found that it is in everyone's interest to promote this discussion in an organized manner as the planning process goes on.

The critical point to be made is that all community stakeholders must be involved in planning and decision-making if local tourism development is to be successful. As the tourism product evolves and grows, new forms of these issues will inevitably emerge. In the four case studies presented in this text, these issues have emerged in one form or another and in varying degrees of intensity. The key lesson learned is that a community needs to manage its relationship with the tourism development process as well as the product itself. It is often difficult for those who created and are emotionally attached to the product to understand that not everyone in the community has the same feeling towards it. Therefore, the underlying psychological and social anxiety that the tourism product creates will need to be identified and discussed as part of an ongoing values clarification process. It is conceivable that some of those values will have been intruded upon by the tourism product and steps need to be created and implemented to resolve these intrusions. Thus, the issues and questions raised here with regard to tourism product development and planning will *always* be part of the process.

Conclusion

It is indisputable that globalization is both a cause and an effect of tourism. These two phenomena are explicitly intertwined. Tourism in the 21st century is growing exponentially worldwide. In the last decade, we have seen the emergence of dozens of new destinations on the world scene, all competing for tourist dollars. Along with increasing tourist mobility and wealth, we are seeing global population shifts and dramatic restructuring. Most importantly for our purposes, there are big changes occurring in the rural and more remote regions of the globe and communities are feeling the impacts of all forms of migration and economic change. The restructuring of rural regions, once dominated by now nearly obsolete resource-based economies, has put immense pressures on many communities as they struggle to retain a viable economy and culture. Much of this effort has been directed to tourism development.

While the financial and physical ability of people to travel is at a level unsurpassed in history, we have become acutely aware of the changing needs and interests of a new cohort of tourists who seem to be searching for deeper and more meaningful experiences, many of whom are deeply concerned and sensitive to the environment and other issues affecting the world today. Paralleling this search for meaningful tourism is the huge shift from mass tourism activities to more specialized niche markets and customized products. This shift opens up a new world of opportunities for many rural communities that can provide culturally unique, one-of-a-kind experiences that cannot be replicated by larger tourism conglomerates or destinations anywhere in the world. Of course this is often at a high cost to both the tourism and the destination site. As these experiences become popular and sites are visited by more and more tourists, a destination can lose its appeal to both the tourist and the local resident. And, while the tourist can stop visiting, the resident is often left to pick up the pieces. The clamor for the receipts must not overtake the ability of the destination site to regenerate itself.

The goal of this book is to illustrate how four small communities in rural Canada have responded to the forces of change by undertaking tourism development as a mechanism to regain or establish and maintain a viable economy while preserving a desirable quality of life. To this end, several approaches to tourism development have been discussed.

While researchers continue to search for the ideal tourism development, it may be an impossible mission, for it may not exist. Tourism development is not static; it is dynamic and volatile. It can rejuvenate a community's economy and inspire a cultural renaissance. It can provide new 'places' and 'spaces' to foster sociability and nurture friendly relations between hosts and visitors, or, it can do the opposite. It is our belief that the outcome, positive or negative, depends on planning and management of the site. Research has shown that tourism, if it is to be truly successful and sustainable, has to have embedded within it certain key principles. Tourism has to be appropriately planned. As much as possible, tourism planning must involve all community stakeholders. Tourism development must be continually monitored and controlled; it must allow for adaptation and corrective action when needed. A host community and its residents provide the foundation for tourism development to evolve and flourish. The local people must have and maintain precedence in the planning and decision-making processes. Community involvement should not simply be seen as a hurdle the developer must clear to get the project going.

Challenging times initiated by forces of globalization and environmental change can provide exciting opportunities for rural communities if they can be innovative, creative, and inclusive in planning for their future. Being small, rural and unique gives many communities a competitive edge over other more established tourism destinations that are quickly becoming part of a homogenized and undifferentiated global economy. While tourism may not be an economic savior, neither can it be considered false hope. Through our research, four communities in rural Canada have emerged to illustrate the complexities involved in this global phenomenon as they attempt to pave the way to their future through tourism. While differences certainly exist, in many ways, the communities described here are just like others around the world as they try to adopt tourism as a means to viability. In these challenging and turbulent times, we hope that our discussion of these small places will help others find their path.

References

ACOA (2002) *Tourism Drives Economic Development in Antigonish, Guysborough and Eastern Halifax Counties. ACOA News Release* (February 2, 2002). On WWW at http://www.acoa-apeca.gc.ca/e/media/press/press.shtml?1714.

ACOA (2006) *ACOA Investment to Help Town of Canso and Surrounding Area. ACOA News Release* (June 27, 2006). On WWW at http://www.acoa.ca/e/media/press/press.shtml?3582.

Adams, W.M. (1995) Green development theory? Environmentalism and sustainable development. In J. Crush (ed.) *Power of Development* (pp. 87–99). London: Routledge.

Adorno, T.W. (1991) *The Culture Industry: Selected Essays on Mass Culture.* London: Routledge.

Aguiar, L.L.M., Tomic, P. and Trumper, R. (2005) Work hard, play hard: Selling Kelowna, BC as a year-round playground. *The Canadian Geographer* 29 (2), 123–139.

Allen, J., Massey, D. and Cochrane, A. (1998) *Rethinking the Region.* London: Routledge.

Andrews, C. (2003) Municipal restructuring, urban services, and the potential for the creation of transformative political spaces. In W. Clement and L. Vosko (eds) *Changing Canada: Political Economy as Transformation* (pp. 311–324). Montreal and Kingston: McGill-Queen's University Press.

Anonymous. (2006) Personal conversation. Canso, NS.

ARA/LORD (1997) *Nova Scotia Cultural Tourism Study.* Halifax, NS: Nova Scotia Economic Development and Tourism.

Ashworth, G.J. (1994) From history to heritage-from heritage to history: In search of concepts and models. In G.J. Ashworth and P.J. Larkham (eds) *Building a New Heritage: Tourism, Culture and Identity in the New Europe* (pp. 13–30). London: Routledge.

Asian Pacific Economic Co-operation (APEC) (2002) Declaration on tourism. *APEC meeting.* Korea.

Assmann, J. (1992) *Das kulturelle gedachtnis. Schrift, erinnerung und politische identitat in fruhen hochjulturen.* Munchen: Beck.

Ateljevic, I. (2001) Circuits of tourism: Stepping beyond the production/consumption dichotomy. *Tourism Geographies* 2 (4), 369–388.

Author unknown. (2003) *Cultural Capital.* On WWW at http://www.sociology.org.uk/tece1ef.htm. Accessed August 2003.

Ayad, C. (1999) Petra's new invaders. *The UNESCO Courier* (July/August).

Baron, C., Field, J. and Schuller, T. (2000) *Social Capital: Critical Perspectives.* New York: Oxford University Press.

Barthel-Bouchier, D. (2001) Authenticity and identity. *International Sociology* 16 (2), 221–239.

BBC (2001) World News. *BBC Radio Broadcast*. London.

Beauregard, R.A. (1986) The chaos and complexity of gentrification. In N. Smith and P. Williams (eds) *Gentrification of the City* (pp. 35–55). London: Allen and Unwin.

Benedetti, G. (1994) Adaptation des Communautés de Pêche en Atlantique. Research Study. Moncton: Université de Moncton.

Berry, B. (1980) Inner city features: An American dilemma revisited. *Transactions, Institute of British Geographers* 5 (1), 1–28.

Berry, W. (1990) *What are People for?* San Francisco, CA: North Point Press.

Betancur, J. (July, 2002) The politics of gentrification: The case of West Town in Chicago. *Urban Affairs Review* 37 (6), 780–814.

Birkland, T.A. (2001) *An Introduction to the Policy Process*. Armonk, NY: ME Sharpe.

Blake, J. (1996) Resolving conflict? The rural white paper, sustainability and countryside policy. *Local Environment* 1 (2), 211–218.

Blake, R. (2003) *Rural and Regional Development Strategies in Canada: The Search for Solutions*. Royal Commission on Renewing and Strengthening our Place in Canada. On WWW at www.gov.nf.ca/publicat/royalcomm/research/blake.pdf.

Bondi, L. (1991) Gender divisions and gentrification: A critique. *Transactions, Institute of British Geographers* 16, 190–198.

Bouquet, M. and Winter, M. (1987) *Who from Their Labours Rest? Conflict and Practice in Rural Tourism*. Aldershot: Avebury.

Bourdieu, P. (1973) Cultural reproduction and social reproduction. In R. Brown (ed.) *Contemporary Research in the Sociology of Education* (pp. 71–112). London: Tavistock.

Bourdieu, P. (1984) *Distinction: A Social Critique of the Judgment of Taste* (R. Nice, trans.). Cambridge, MA: Harvard University Press.

Bourdieu, P. (1986) The forms of capital. In J. Richardson (ed.) *Handbook of Theory and Research for the Sociology of Education* (pp. 241–258). New York: Greenwood Press.

Boyne, R. and Rattansi, A. (1990) *Postmodernism and Society*. London: Macmillan.

Bradford, N. (2004) Governing the Canadian economy: Ideas and politics. In M. Whittington and G. Williams (eds) *Canadian Politics in the 21st Century* (6th edn). Toronto: Thompson Nelson.

Bridge, G. (1994) The space for class? On class analysis in the study of gentrification. *Transactions, Institute of British Geographers* 26, 205–247.

Bryden, J. (1994) *Towards Sustainable Rural Communities*. Guelph, ON: University School of Rural Planning and Development.

Bund, P. (2003) *Co-operation and Partnerships in Tourism: A Global Perspective*. A report prepared KPMG Canada for the Canadian Tourism Commission, World Tourism Organization and World Tourism Organization Business Council.

Burns, P. (1999) *Tourism and Anthropology*. London: Routledge.

Burr, S.W. (1991) Review and evaluation of the theoretical approaches to community as employed in travel and tourism impact research on rural community organization and change. In A.J. Veal, P. Jonson and G. Cushman (eds) *Leisure and Tourism, Social and Environmental Changes* (pp. 540–553).

Papers from the World Leisure and Recreation Association Congress, Sydney, Australia.

Busby, G. and Klug, J. (2001) Movie-inducted tourism: The challenge of measurement and other issues. *Journal of Vacation Marketing* 7 (4), 316–332.

Butler, R., Hall, C.M. and Jenkins, J. (eds) (1998) *Tourism and Recreation in Rural Areas*. New York: John Wiley and Sons.

Butler, R. (ed.) (2006) *The Tourism Area Life Cycle (Vol. 1)*. Clevedon: Channel View Publications.

Cameron, S. (1992) Housing, gentrification and urban regeneration. *Urban Studies* 29, 3–14.

Campbell, C. and Kelly, M. (1999) *Social Capital and Health*. London: Health Education Authority.

Canadian Heritage Report (2005) *Arts and Culture – Music – Arts Presentation*. Canadian Heritage Canada. On WWW at http://www.pch.gc.ca/index_e.cfm.

Canadian Tourism Commission (CTC). *Corporate homepage*. On WWW at http://www.corporate.canada.travel/en/ca/index.html.

Canso Historical Society (2004) *Portrait of a Century*. Canso, NS: Town of Canso.

Chambers, E. (ed.) (1997) *Tourism and Culture: An Applied Perspective*. Albany, NY: State University Press of New York.

Chaney, D. (1994) *The Cultural Turn*. New York: Routledge.

Chang, T.C., Milne, S., Fallon, D. and Pohlmann, C. (1996) Urban heritage tourism: Exploring the global-local nexus. *Annals of Tourism Research* 23 (2), 284–305.

Church, A. (2004) Local and regional tourism. In A.M. Lew, C.M. Hall and A.M. Williams (eds) *A Companion to Tourism* (pp. 555–568). Oxford: Blackwell.

Clarke-Jones, M. (1987) *A Staple State: Canadian Industrial Resources in Cold War*. Toronto: University of Toronto Press.

Clay, P.L. (1979) *Neighborhood Renewal: Middle Class Settlement and Incumbent Upgrading in American Neighborhoods*. Lexington, MA: Lexington Books.

Clearwater [History] (2007) *Clearwater: History*. On WWW at http://www.clearwater.ca/inv-aboutus-e.asp?cmPageID=111.

Clearwater [What's New?] (2007) *Clearwater: What's new?* O WWW at http://www.clearwater.ca/inv-newsroom-e.asp?cmPageID=131.

Clement, W. and Vosko, L.F. (eds) (2003) *Changing Canada: Political Economy as Transformation* (pp. 109–134). Montreal/Kingston: McGill-Queen's University Press.

Cloke, P. (1993) The countryside as commodity: New spaces for rural leisure. In S. Glyptis (ed.) *Leisure and the Environment* (pp. 53–65). London: Belhaven.

Cloke, P. and Little, J. (1990) *The Rural State? Limits to Planning in Rural Society*. Oxford: Oxford University Press.

Cohen, D. and Prusak, L. (2001) *In Good Company: How Social Capital Makes Organizations Work*. Boston, MA: Harvard Business School.

Cohen, E. (1995) Contemporary tourism – trends and challenges: Sustainable authenticity or contrived post-modernity? In R. Butler and D. Pearce (eds) *Change in Tourism: People, Place and Processes* (pp. 12–30). New York: Routledge.

Cohen, J. (1989) *The Privileged Ape*. Lancashire: Parthenon.

Coleman, J. (1988) Social capital in the creation of human capital. *American Journal of Sociology* 94 (3), 95–120.

Coles, T. (2003) Urban tourism, place promotion and economic restructuring: The case of post-socialist Leipzig. *Tourism Geographies* 5 (2), 190–219.

Commission for Environment Cooperation (2000) *Promoting Sustainable Tourism in North America's Natural Areas: The Steps Forward.* Montreal, CA: Commission for Environment Cooperation.

Cooke, C. (2007) *Stanfest True UN of Music; Performers from Cape Breton to Scotland and Texas to China. The Chronicle-Herald* (July 2).

Cooper, C., Fletcher, J., Dilbert, D., Shepherd, R. and Wanhill, S. (1998) *Tourism: Principles and Practice* (2nd edn). Harlow: Addison Wesley Longman Limited.

Creswell, J. (1994) *Research Design: Qualitative & Quantitative Approaches.* Thousand Oaks, CA: Sage.

Cukier, J. (2002) Tourism employment issues in developing countries: Examples from Indonesia. In R. Sharpley and D. Telfer (eds) *Tourism and Development: Concepts and Issues* (pp. 165–201). Clevedon: Channel View Publications.

Dann, G. (1994) Tourism and nostalgia: Looking forward to going back. *Vrijetijd En Samenleving* 1 (2), 65–74.

Davidson, R. (1993) *Tourism.* Harlow: Addison Wesley Longman Limited.

Dayton-Johnson, J. and King, E. (2003) *Subsidizing Stan: Measuring the Social Benefits of Cultural Spending.* On WWW at http://economics.dal.ca/Files/wpstan.pdf.

DeGroot R. (1994) Environmental functions and the economic value of ecosystems. In A. Jansson, M. Hammer, C. Folke and R. Constanza (eds) *Investing In Natural Capital: The Ecological Economics Approach To Sustainability* (pp. 151–168). Washinton, DC: Island Press.

Dicken, P. (1998) *Global Shift: Transforming the World Economy* (3rd edn). London: Paul Chapman.

Dickens, D. (2007) Vulcan: The next generation in high-tech adventure. *A Media Release.* Vulcan Tourism Department.

Douglas, D.J.A. (2005) The restructuring of local government in rural regions: A rural development perspective. *Journal of Rural Studies* 21, 231–246.

Doxey, G.V. (1975) A causation theory of visitor-resident irritants: Methodology and research inferences. *Sixth Annual Conference Proceedings of the Travel Research Association* (pp. 195–198). UT: Travel and Tourism Research Association.

Doxey, G.V. (1976) When enough's enough: The natives are restless in Old Niagara. *Heritage Canada* 2 (2), 26–27.

Doxiadis, C.A. (1966) *Urban renewal and the future of the American city.* Chicago, IL: National Association of Housing and Redevelopment Officials.

Drache, D. and Gertler, M.S. (eds) (1991) *The New Era of Global Competition: State Policy and Market Power.* Montreal & Kingston: McGill-Queen's University Press.

Economic Planning Group (EPG) (2000) *The Business Case for Growing Tourism in Nova Scotia.* A Research Study. Halifax, NS: EPG.

Edensor, T. (2000) Staging tourism: Tourists as performers. *Annals of Tourism Research* 27 (2), 322–344.

Edgell, D. (1999) *Tourism Policy: The Next Millennium.* Champaign, IL: Sagamore.

Emery, M. and Purser, R.E. (1996) The *Search Conference: A Powerful Method for Planning Organizational Change and Community Action.* San Francisco: Jossey-Bass.

Etzioni, A. (1996) *The New Golden Rule.* New York: Basic Books.

European Geographic Information Systems (EGIS) (2000) *Conference Report.* Cambridge, MA: Harvard University Press.

Featherstone, M. (1991) *Consumer Culture and Postmodernism.* London: Sage.

Ferlenger, L. and Mandle, J. (2000) *Dimensions of Globalization.* Thousand Oaks, CA: Sage.

Fisher, I. (1906) *The Nature of Capital and Income.* New York: Macmillan.

Fisheries Museum of the Atlantic (2003) Documentation and Archives Centre. Lunenburg, NS.

Fjellman, S.J. (1992) *Vinyl Leaves: Walt Disney World and America.* Boulder, CO: Westview Press.

Flora, C. (2001) *Interactions Between Agroecosystems and Rural Communities.* Boca Raton, FL: CRC Press.

Flora, C.B. (1998) Sustainable production and consumption patterns: Community capitals. In G.B. Softing, G. Benneh, K. Hindar, L. Walloe and A. Wijkman (eds) *The Brundtland Commission's Report – Ten Years* (pp. 115–122). Oslo: Scandinavian University Press.

Forrester, S. and Singh, S. (2005) Contrived landscapes: Simulated environments as an emerging medium of tourism destinations. *Tourism Recreation Research* 30 (3), 69–76.

Fountain, J. and Hall, C.M. (2002) The impact of lifestyle migration on rural communities: A case study of Akaroa, New Zealand. In A.M. Williams and C.M. Hall (eds) *Tourism and Migration: New Relationship Between Production and Consumption* (pp. 153–168). Dordrecht: Kluwer Academic.

Francey, D. (2003) *David Francey Letters.* On WWW at http://www.davidfrancey. com/albertaletter.html.

Friedman, J. (2002) *Empowerment: The Politics of Alternative Development.* Cambridge, MA: Blackwell.

Friedman, M. (1975) *There's No Such Thing as a Free Lunch.* LaSalle, IL: Open Court.

Friedman, T.L. (2000) *The Lexus and the Olive Tree.* New York: First Anchor Books.

Friedmann, J. (1995) *Empowerment: The Politics of Alternative Development.* Cambridge, MA: Blackwell.

Fukuyama, F. (1995) *Trust: The Social Virtues and Creation of Prosperity.* New York: The Free Press.

Fuller, A.M. and Reid, D.G. (1998) Rural tourism planning: A community development approach. In S. Smith (ed.) *Rural Rehabilitation: A Modern Perspective* (pp. 260–274). Arnaudville, LA: Bow River.

Gallent, N., Mace, A. and Tewdwr-Jones, M. (2003) Dispelling a myth? Second homes in rural Wales. *Area* 35 (3), 271–284.

Gallent, N., Mace, A. and Tewdwr-Jones, M. (2005) *Second Homes: European Perspectives and UK Policies.* Aldershot: Ashgate.

Galston, W.A. and Baehler, K.J. (1995) *Rural Development in the United States: Connection Theory, Practice and Possibilities.* Washington, DC: Island Press.

Gannon, A. (1994) Rural tourism as a factor in rural community economic development for economies in transition. *Journal of Sustainable Tourism* 2 (1/2), 51–60.

George, E.W. (1995) Diversification strategies of one-industry towns. Unpublished Master's thesis. Saint Mary's University, Halifax.

George, E.W. (2002) Tourism and culture: A dichotomous affair. In D. Bélanger, S. Coupal, M. Ducharme, A. MacLeod and D. Phillips (eds) *Canada: Rupture and Continuity*. Montreal, QC: McGill Institute for the Study of Canada.

George, E.W. (2004) Commodifying local cultural for rural tourism development: The case of one rural community in Atlantic Canada. Unpublished dissertation, University of Guelph.

George, E.W. (2005) The power of tourism: A metamorphosis of community culture. *Journal of Tourism and Cultural Change* 3 (2), 88–107.

George, E.W. (2006) UNESCO World Heritage Site designation: Transforming tourism spaces: A site community's perspective. A paper presented at the *ATLAS Conference: The Transformation of Tourism Spaces*, Lotz, Poland, September 2006.

George, E.W. (2007) Against all odds: Though music and song, a new tourism destination is born. A paper presented at the *ATLAS Conference: Destinations Revisited: Perspectives on Developing and Managing Tourist Areas*, Viano do Castello, Portugal, September 2007.

Getz, D. (1986) Models in tourism planning toward integration of theory and practice. *Tourism Management* 7, 21–32.

Gibson, C. and Connell, J. (2003) *Music and Tourism: On the Road Again*. Clevedon: Channel View Publications.

Gilbert, N. (2002) *Dimensions of Social Welfare Policy*. Boston, MA: Allyn and Bacon.

Glass, R. (1964) Aspects of change. In Centre for Urban Studies (ed.) *London: Aspects of Change*. London: MacGibbon and Kee.

Gold, J.R. and Ward, S.V. (1994) Introduction. In J.R. Gold and S.V. Ward (eds) *Place Promotion: The Use of Publicity Marketing to Sell Towns and Regions* (pp. 1–18). Chichester, New York: John Wiley and Sons.

Gottdiener, M. (2001) *The Theming of America: American Dreams, Media Fantasies, and Themed Environments* (2nd edn). Boulder, CO: Westview.

Gouldner, A.W. (1979) *The Future of Intellectuals and the Rise of the New Class*. New York: Continuum.

Government of Newfoundland & Labrador (2001, February 2). 45 million in new funds for Newfoundland and Labrador's Comprehensive Economic Development Agreement. *A News Release*. On WWW at http://www.gov.nf.ca/releases/2001/exec/0202n01.htm.

Gramsci, A. (1971) *Selections from the Prison Notebooks of Antonio Gramsci*. New York: International Publishers.

Greencorn, T. (2006) *Interview with Troy Greencorn*. Radio PEI. Online audio recording. On WWW at: http://radio.upei.ca/stanfest/

Gruffudd, P. (1994) Selling the countryside: Representations of rural Britain. In J.R. Gold and S.V. Ward (eds) *Place Promotion: The Use of Publicity Marketing to Sell Towns and Regions* (pp. 247–264). Chichester, New York: John Wiley and Sons.

Guess, R. (1987) *The Idea of a Critical Theory: Habermas & the Frankfurt School*. London: Cambridge University Press.

Gunn, C. (1972) *Vacationscape: Designing Tourist Regions*. Austin, TX: Bureau of Business Research, University of Texas.

Gunn, C. (1988) *Tourism Planning* (3rd edn). New York: Taylor & Francis.

Gunn, C. (2002) *Tourism Planning* (4th edn). New York: Taylor & Francis.

Gunn, C. and Gunn, H.D. (1991) *Reclaiming Capital*. New York: Cornell University Press.

Halfacree, K.H. (1993) Locality and social representation: Space, discourse and alternative definitions of the rural. *Journal of Rural Studies* 9 (1), 23–37.

Hall, C.M. (1994) *Tourism and Politics: Policy, Power and Place*. London: Belhaven Press.

Hall, C.M. (1998) The politics of decision-making and top-down planning: Darling Harbour, Sydney. In D. Tyler, Y. Guerrier and M. Robertson (eds) *Managing Tourism in Cities* (pp. 9–24). Chichester, New York: Wiley.

Hall, C.M. and Jenkins, J. (1998) Rural tourism and recreation policy dimensions. In R. Butler, C.M. Hall and J. Jenkins (eds) *Tourism and Recreation in Rural Areas* (pp. 19–42). Chichester: John Wiley.

Hall, C.M. and Jenkins, J. (2004) Tourism and public policy. In A.M. Lew, C.M. Hall and A.M. Williams (eds) *A Companion to Tourism* (pp. 525–540). Oxford: Blackwell.

Hall, C.M. and Jenkins, J.M. (1995) *Tourism and Public Policy*. London: Routledge.

Hall, C.M. and Muller, D.K. (eds) (2004) *Tourism, Mobility and Second Homes: Between Elite Landscape and Common Ground*. Clevedon: Channel View Publications.

Hamnett, C. (1984) Gentrification and residential location theory: A review and assessment. In D. Herbert and R.J. Johnston (eds) *Geography and the Urban Environment: Progress in Research and Applications* (pp. 282 & 319). New York: Wiley and Sons.

Hamnett, C. (1991) The blind men and the elephant: The explanation of gentrification. *Transactions of the Institute of British Geographers* 16 (2), 173–189.

Hamnett, C. (1992) Gentrifiers or lemmings? A response to Neil Smith. *Transactions of the Institute of British Geographers* 17 (1), 116–119.

Hamnett, C. (2000) Gentrification, postindustrialism, and industrial and occupational restructuring in global cities. In G. Bridge and S. Watson (eds) *A Companion to the City* (pp. 331 & 341). Oxford: Basil Blackwell.

Hancock, T. (1999) People, partnerships and human progress: Building community capital. *Health Promotion International* 16 (3), 275–279.

Hannigan, J. (1998) *Fantasy City: Pleasure and Profit in the Postmodern Metropolis*. London: Routledge.

Hardy, A.L. and Beeton, R.J.S. (2001) Sustainable tourism or maintainable tourism: Managing resources for more than average outcomes. *Journal of Sustainable Tourism* 9 (3), 168–192.

Harp, J. (1994) Culture, the state and tourism: State policy initiatives in Canada, 1984–1992. *Culture and Policy* 6 (1), 17. On WWW at http://www.gu.edu.au.

Harvey, D. (1989) From managerialism to entrepreneurialism: The transformation in urban governance in late capitalism. *Geografiska Annaler B (Human Geography)* 17 (1), 3–17.

Harvey, D. (1990) *The Condition of Postmodernity: An Enquiry into the Origins of Cultural Change*. Cambridge, MA: Blackwell.

Harvey, D. (1996) Justice, nature and the geography of difference: Second-home domestic tourism. *Annals of Tourism Research* 13, 367–391.

Haywood, M. (1993) Sustainable development for tourism: A commentary with an organizational perspective. In J.G. Nelson, R. Butler and G. Wall (eds) *Tourism and Sustainable Development: Monitoring, Planning, Managing*. Waterloo, Ontario: University of Waterloo.

Henning, D.H. (1974) *Environmental Policy and Administration*. New York: Elsevier.
Hettne, B. (1995) *Development Theory and the Three Worlds* (2nd edn). Edinburgh Gate: Longman.
Hoelscher, S.D. (1998) *Heritage on Stage: The Invention of Ethnic Place in America's Little Switzerland*. Madison, WI: University of Wisconsin Press.
Hopkins, J. (1998) Signs of the post-rural: Marketing myths of a symbolic countryside. *Geografiska Annaler B* 80 (2), 65–81.
Hudman, L. and Hawkins, D. (1989) *Tourism in Contemporary Society*. Englewood Cliffs, NJ: Prentice-Hall.
Hunter, C. (1997) Sustainable tourism as an adaptive paradigm. *Annals of Tourism Research* 24 (4), 850–867.
Hunter, C. and Green, H. (1995) *Tourism and the Environment: A Sustainable Relationship?* New York: Routledge.
Industry Canada (2003) *The Quebec Declaration*. On WWW at http://strategis.ic.gc.ca/epic/site/dsib-tour.nsf/en/h_qq00101e.html.
Industry Canada (2004) *Building a National Tourism Strategy: A Framework for Federal/Provincial/Territorial Collaboration*. On WWW at http://strategis.ic.gc.ca/epic/site/dsib-tour.nsf/en/h_qq00000e.html.
Innis, H.A. (1954) *The Cod Fisheries: The History of an International Economy*. Toronto: University of Toronto Press.
Innis, H.A. (1956) *Essays in Canadian Economic History*. Toronto: University of Toronto Press.
Inskeep, E. (1991) *Tourism Planning: An integrated and Sustainable Development Approach*. New York: Van Nostrand Reinhold.
Jackson, J. (1970) Other-directed houses. In E. Zube (ed.) *Landscapes: Selected Writings of J.B. Jackson* (pp. 55–72). Amherst, MA: University of Massachusetts Press.
Jafari, J. (1996) Tourism and culture: An inquiry into paradoxes. *Proceedings of a Round Table: Culture, Tourism Development: Crucial Issues for the XXIst Century*. Paris
Jamieson, W. (1992) Women's role in rural cultural tourism in Western Canada. In W. Nuryanti (ed.) *Universal Tourism: Enriching or Degrading Culture*, pp. 91–99. Yogyakarta, Indonesia: Gadjah Mada University Press.
Jenkins, W.I. (1978) *Policy Analysis: A Political and Organizational Perspective*. London: M. Robertson.
Johnston, R.J., Gregory, D., Pratt, G. and Watts, M. (2000) *The Dictionary of Human Geography*. Oxford: Blackwell.
Kasarda, J.D. (1982) Symposium: The state of the nation's cities. *Urban Affairs Quarterly* 18, 163 & 186.
Keen, D. and Hall, C.M. (2004) Second homes in New Zealand. In C.M. Hall and D.K. Muller (eds) *Tourism, Mobility and Second Homes: Between Elite Landscape and Common Ground* (pp. 174–195). Clevedon: Channel View Publications.
Keesing, R. and Keesing, F. (1971) *New Perspectives in Cultural Anthropology*. New York: Hold, Rinehart and Winston.
Kennedy, M. and Leonard, P. (2001) *Dealing with Neighborhood Change: A Primer on Gentrification and Policy Choices*. A Discussion Paper. Washington, DC: The Brookings Institute Centre on Urban and Metropolitan Policy.

Keohane, N.O., Van Roy, B. and Zeckhauser, R. (1999) *Controlling Stocks and Flows to Promote Quality: The Environment, with Applications to Physical and Human Capital.* Cambridge, MA: National Bureau of Economic Research.

Kerans, P. and Kearney, J. (2006) *Turning the World Right-side Up: Science, Community and Democracy.* Halifax: Fernwood Press.

Kovac, B. (2001) Rethinking postmodern culture tourism in small states: The role of cultural heritage and economic development. *Informatologia* 34, 1–165.

Kreutzwiser, R. (1993) Desirable attributes of sustainability indicators for tourism development. In J.G. Nelson, R. Butler and G. Wall (eds) *Tourism and Sustainable Development: Monitoring, Planning, Managing* (pp. 243–248). Waterloo, Ontario: University of Waterloo.

Kroeber, A. (1948) *Anthropology: Race, Language, Culture, Psychology, Prehistory.* New York: Harcourt Brace.

Kroeber, A. and Kluckholn, C. (1952) Culture: A critical review of concepts and definitions. *Peabody Museums Papers* 47 (1). Cambridge, MA: Harvard University Press.

Lavalette, M. and Pratt, A. (2001) *Social Policy: Theories, Concepts and Issues.* Thousand Oaks, CA: Sage.

Law, A. (2001) Industry of last resort: Negotiating admissible identities in leisurescape. *Society and leisure/Loisir et société* 24 (1). On WWW at http://www.erudit.org/revue/ls/2001/v24/n1/000171ar.html.

Leach, B. and Winson, A. (1995) Bringing "globalization" down to earth: Restructuring and labour in rural communities. *The Canadian Review of Sociology and Anthropology* 32 (3), 341–64.

Lees, L. (1996) In the pursuit of difference: Representations of gentrification. *Environment and Planning* 28, 453–470.

Lees, L. (1999) The weaving of gentrification discourse and the boundaries of the gentrification community. *Environment and Planning D: Society and Space* 17, 127–132.

Lees, L. (2000) A Re-appraisal of gentrification: Towards a geography of gentrification. *Progress in Human Geography* 24 (3), 389–408.

Ley, D. (1978) Inner city resurgence and its social context. Paper presented at the *Annual Conference of the Association of American Geographers*, New Orleans, LA.

Ley, D. (1981) Inner-city revitalization in Canada: A Vancouver case study. *Canadian Geographer* 25, 124–148.

Lin, N., Cook, K. and Burt, R. (2001) *Social Capital: Theory and Research.* New York: Aldine de Gruyter.

Lipton, S.G. (1977) Evidence of central city revival. *Journal of the American Institute of Planner* 43, 136–147.

Littig, B. and Griessler, E. (2005) Social sustainability: A catchword between political pragmatism and social theory. *International Journal of Sustainable Development* 8 (1/2) pp. 65–79.

MacCannell, D. (1976) *The Tourist: A New Theory of the Leisure Class.* New York: Schocken Books Inc.

MacCannell, D. (1999) *The Tourist: A New Theory of the Leisure Class.* Berkeley, CA: University of California Press.

Mair, H. (2006) Global restructuring and local responses: Investigating rural tourism policy in two Canadian communities. *Current Issues in Tourism* 9 (1), 1–45.

Mankiew, N.G., Romer, D. and Weil, D.N. (1992) A contribution to the empirics of economic growth. *The Quarterly Journal of Economics* 107, 407–437.

Marchak, M.P. (1991) *The Integrated Circus: The New Right and the Restructuring of Global Markets*. Montreal and Kingston: McGill-Queen's University Press.

Marcouiller, D.W. (1997) Toward integrative tourism planning in rural America. *Journal of Planning Literature* 11 (3), 337–357.

Marjavaara, R. (2007) Route to destruction? Second home tourism in small island communities. *Island Studies Journal* 2 (1), 27–46.

Mason, T. (SOCAN) (2006) *Troy Greencorn and Stan Rogers Festival put Canso on the map*. On WWW at http://www.socan.ca/jsp/en/news_events/feature_stories/Rogers.jsp.

Matarasso, F. (1997) *Use or Ornament? The Social Impact of Participation in the Arts*. Stroud: Comedia.

Matheson, D. (2000) *Music to Their Ears*. Coastal Communities News Magazine. On WWW at http://www.coastalcommunities.ns.ca/magazine/backissues/v6_i3.html#cs.

Mathieson, A. and Wall, G. (1982) *Tourism: Economic, Physical and Social Impacts*. Essex: Longman Scientific & Technical.

Mayor of Lunenburg (2003) Interview. Lunenburg, NS.

McIntosh, A.J., Hinch, T. and Ingram, T. (2002) Cultural identity and tourism. *International Journal of Arts Management* 4 (2), 39–49.

McKay, I. (1994) *The Quest of the Folk: Antimodernism and Cultural Selection in Twentieth Century Nova Scotia*. Montreal, Kingston: McGill-Queen's University Press.

McKeen, W. and Porter, A. (2003) Politics and transformation: Welfare state restructuring in Canada. In W. Clement and L. Vosko (eds) *Changing Canada: Political Economy as Transformation* (pp. 109–134). Montreal, Kingston: McGill-Queen's University Press.

McKercher, B. and du Cros, H. (2002) *Cultural Tourism: The Partnership Between Tourism and Cultural Heritage Management*. New York: The Haworth Hospitality Press.

McPherson, C.B. (1977) *The Life and Times of Liberal Democracy*. Toronto: Oxford University Press.

Meek, J. (2007) Mood upbeat but songs so sad. *The Chronicle-Herald* (July 1).

Meek, J. (1994) Canso relief effort will just go on and on. *The Halifax Chronicle Herald* (August).

Meethan, K. (2001) *Tourism in Global Society: Place, Culture, Consumption*. Hampshire: Palgrave.

Mills, C. (1993) Myths and meanings of gentrification. In J. Duncan and D. Ley (eds) *Place/Culture/Representation* (pp. 149–170). London: Routledge.

Mill, R.C. and Morrison, A.M. (1984) *The Tourism System*. Englewood Cliffs, NJ: Prentice-Hall.

Mills, RadioPEI (2006) *Interview with Paul Mills*. Online audio recording: http://radio.upei.ca/stanfest/

Milne, S. and Ateljevic, I. (2001) Tourism, economic development and the global-local nexus: Theory embracing complexity. *Tourism Geographies* 3 (4), 369–393.

Mincer, J. (1993) *Studies in Human Capital*. Brookfield, VT: E. Elgar.

Mitchell, C.J.A. (1998) Entrepreneurialism, commodification and creative destruction: A model of post-modern community development. *Journal of Rural Studies* 14 (3), 73–286.

Mitchell, C.J.A. and Coghill, C. (2000) The creation of a cultural heritage landscape: Elora, Ontario, Canada. *The Great Lakes Geographer* 7 (2), 88–105.

Moore, B. (1997) Tracing settlers' lives through a hauntingly beautiful landscape. *The Sophisticated Traveller: New York Times Magazine* (March 2).

Mordue, T. (2001) Performing and directing resident/tourist cultures in Heartbeat country. *Tourist Studies* 1 (3), 233–252.

Morgan, N. (2004) Problematizing place promotion. In A.M. Lew, C.M. Hall and A.M. Williams (eds) *A Companion to Tourism* (pp. 173–183). Oxford: Blackwell.

Morgan, N. and Pritchard, A. (1998) *Tourism Promotion and Power: Creating Images, Creating Identities*. Chichester, New York: Wiley.

Morgan, N. and Pritchard, A. (1999) *Power and Politics at the Seaside*. Exeter: University of Exeter Press.

Morgan, N. and Pritchard, A. (2004) Meeting the destination branding challenge. In N. Morgan, A. Pritchard and R. Pride (eds) *Destination Branding: Creating the Unique Destination Proposition* (2nd edn, pp. 59–78). Oxford: Elsevier Butterworth-Heinemann.

Mormont, M. (1987) Rural nature and urban natures. *Sociologia Ruralis* 27, 3–20.

Mowford, M. and Munt, I. (1998) *Tourism and Sustainability: New Tourism in the Third World*. London: Routledge.

Mubarak, H. (2002) *President Mubarak's Concept of Tourism*. On WWW at http://www.touregypt.net/mubarak.htm.

Müller, D.K., Hall, C.M. and Keen, D. (2004) Second home tourism impact, planning and management. In C.M. Hall and D.K. Müller (eds) *Tourism, Mobility and Second Homes: Between Elite Landscape and Common Ground* (pp. 15–33), Clevedon: Channel View Publications.

Munt, I. (1994) The "other" postmodern tourism: Culture, travel and the new middle classes. *Theory, Culture and Society* 11, 101–123.

Murdoch, J. and Marsden, T. (1991) Reconstituting the rural in an urban region: New villages for old? *ESRC Countryside Change Initiative Working Paper 26*. Newcastle: University of Newcastle.

Murphy, P.E. (1985) *Tourism: A Community Approach*. New York: Methuen.

Murphy, P.E. (1998) Tourism and sustainable development. In W.F. Theobald (ed.) *Global Tourism: The Next Decade* (pp. 79–102). Boston, MA: Butterworth and Heinemann.

Nelson, J.G., Butler, R. and Wall, G. (1993) *Tourism and Sustainable Development: Monitoring, Planning, Managing*. University of Waterloo, Ontario: Department of Geography.

Nickerso, N.P. and Kerr, P. (2001) *Snapshots: An Introduction to Tourism*. Scarborough, ON: Prentice Hall Canada.

Nova Scotia Department of Tourism, Culture and Heritage (2007) *2006 Visitation to Nova Scotia, by Origin*. On WWW at http://www.gov.ns.ca/dtc/pubs/insights/AbsPage.aspx?siteid=1&lang=1&id=6.

Nuryanti, W. (1996) Heritage and postmodern tourism. *Annals of Tourism Research*, 23 (2), 249–260

Olins, W. (2004) Branding the nation: The historical context. In N. Morgan, A. Pritchard and R. Pride (eds) *Destination Branding: Creating the Unique*

Destination Proposition (2nd edn, pp. 17–25). Oxford: Elsevier Butterworth-Heinemann.

Organization for Economic Cooperation and Development (OECD) (1994) *Tourism Strategies and Rural Development.* On WWW at http://www.oecd.org/dataoecd/31/27/2755218.pdf.

Organization for Economic Cooperation and Development (OECD) (2007) *Tourism.* On WWW at http://www.oecd.org/searchResult/0,3400,en_2649_201185_1_1_1_1_1,00.html.

Overton, J. (1996) *Making a World of Difference: Essays on Tourism, Culture and Development in Newfoundland.* St. John's, Newfoundland: Institute of Social and Economic Research. Memorial University of Newfoundland.

Overton, J. and Scheyvens, R. (1999) *Strategies for Sustainable Development.* New York: Zed Books.

Paddison, R. (1993) City marketing, image reconstruction and urban regeneration. *Urban Studies* 30 (2), 339–350.

Padilla, F. (1987) *Puerto Rican Chicago.* South Bend, IN: University of Notre Dame Press.

Page, S. and Getz, D. (1997) The business of rural tourism: International perspectives. In S. Page and D. Getz (eds) *The Business of Rural Tourism* (pp. 3–37). London: International Thomson Business Press.

Panelli, R. (2001) Narratives of community and change in a contemporary rural setting: The case of Duaringa, Queensland. *Australian Geographical Studies* 39 (2), 156–166.

Paradis, T.W. (2002) The political economy of theme development in small urban places: The case of Roswell, New Mexico. *Tourism Geographies* 4 (1), 22–43.

Paradis, T.W. (2004) Theming, tourism, and fantasy city. In A.M. Lew, C.M. Hall and A.M. Williams (eds) *A Companion to Tourism* (pp. 195–209). Oxford: Blackwell.

Parrinello, G.L. (2001) The technological body in tourism research and praxis. *International Sociology* 16 (2), 205–219.

Patin, V. (1999) Heritage and tourism: Will market forces rule? *UNESCO Courier* (July/August).

Pearce, D. (1987) *Tourism Today: A Geographical Analysis.* Essex: Longman Scientific & Technical.

Pearce, D.G. (1981) *Tourist Development.* London: Longman.

Pearce, P.L., Moscardo, G. and Ross, G.F. (1996) *Tourism Community Relationships.* Queensland, AU: Pergamon: Elsevier Science Ltd.

Pedlar, A. (1996) Community development: What does it mean for recreation and leisure. *Journal of Applied Recreation Research* 21 (1), 5–23.

Pedlar, A. (2006) Practicing community development and third way politics. *Journal of Applied Recreation Research* 30 (2), 427–436.

Perdue, R., Long, P. and Allen, L. (1987) Rural resident tourism perceptions and attitudes. *Annals of Tourism Research* 17, 337–352.

Phillips, M. (2002) The production, symbolization and socialization of gentrification: Impressions from two Berkshire villages. *Transactions, Institute of British Geographers* 27, 282–308.

Plaskett, B. (2001) *Heritage Conservation District Plan and By-Law and Design Guidelines.* Lunenburg, NS: Town of Lunenburg.

Port Stanley (2001) *Mandate: Section 204 (1), Municipal Act 2001*. On WWW at http://portstanley.net/index.php/PortStanley/Index.

Porter, J. (2004) *Star Trek* conventions as pilgrimage. In E. Badone and S.R. Roseman (eds) *Intersecting Journeys: The Anthropology of Pilgrimage and Tourism* (pp. 160–179). Urbana and Chicago, IL: University of Illinois Press.

Pretes, M. (1995) Postmodern tourism: The santa claus industry. *Annals of Tourism Research* 22, 1–24.

Pretty, J. (1998) *The Living Land: Agriculture, Food and Community Regeneration in Rural Europe*. London: Earthscan Publications.

Pretty, J. and Hine, R. (2001) *Reducing Food Poverty with Sustainable Agriculture: A Summary of New Evidence*. Essex: University of Essex.

Pritchard, A. and Morgan, N. (2000) Privileging the male gaze: Gendered tourism landscapes. *Annals of Tourism Research* 27 (3), 884–905.

Proshansky, H.M. (1978) The city and self-identity. *Environment and Behavior* 10 (2), 147–169.

Proshansky, H.M., Fabian, A.K. and Kaminoff, R. (1983) Place-identity: Physical world socialization of the self. *Journal of Environmental Psychology* 3, 57–83.

Prothero, F. (1980) *Port Stanley: Musings & Memories*. Port Stanley, ON: Nan-Sea Publications.

Prugh, T.R., Costanza, R. and Daly, H. (2000) *The Local Politics of Global Sustainability*. Washington, DC: Island Press.

Prugh, T.R., Costanza, R., Cumberland, J., Daly, H., Goodland, R. and Norgaard, R.B. (1995) *Natural Capital and Human Economic Survival*. Maryland: ISEE.

Putnam, R. (1993) *Making Democracy Work*. Princeton, NJ: Princeton University Press.

Ray, C. (1998) Culture, intellectual property and territorial rural development. *Sociologia Ruralis* 38 (1), 1–20.

Ray, C. (2001) Further ideas about local rural development: Trade, production and cultural capital. *Working Paper No. 49*. Newcastle upon Tyne: Centre for Rural Economy University of Newcastle upon Tyne.

Redclift, M. (1984) *Sustainable Development: Exploring the Contradictions*. London: Routledge.

Rees, W.E. (1996) Revisiting carrying capacity: Area-based indicators of sustainability. *Population and Environment: A Journal of Interdisciplinary Studies* 17 (3), 195–215.

Rees, W.E. (2000) The dark side of the force (of globalization). A paper presented at the *Parklands Institute Conference*. (November 2005). Edmonton, AB.

Reid, D. and van Dreunen, E. (1996) Leisure as a social transformation mechanism in community development practice. *Journal of Applied Recreation Research* 21 (1), 45–65.

Reid, D.G. (2003) *Tourism, Globalization and Development: Responsible Tourism Planning*. London: Pluto Press.

Reid, D.G., Mair, H. and Taylor, J. (2000) *Rural Tourism Development: Research Report*. Guelph, ON: Ontario Agriculture Training Institute.

Reid, D.G., Mair, H. and Taylor, J. (2000) Community participation in rural tourism development. *World Leisure* 42 (2), 20–27.

Reid, D.G., Mair, H., George, W. and Taylor, J. (2001) *Visiting Your Future: A Community Guide to Planning Rural Tourism*. Guelph, ON: Ontario Agriculture Training Institute.

Reid, D.G., Mair, H. and George, E.W. (2004) Community tourism planning: A self-assessment instrument. *Annals of Tourism Research* 31 (3), 623–639.

Relph, E. (1976) *Place and Placelessness*. London: Pion.

Renshaw, P. (2002) *Globalisation, Music and Identity*. On WWW at http://www.creativecommunities.org.uk/pdf/2.3GlobMusicIden.pdf.

Riley, R., Baker, D. and Van Doren, C.S. (1998) Movie-induced tourism. *Annals of Tourism Research* 25 (4), 919–935.

Ritchie, J.R. and Crouch, G.I. (2003) *The Competitive Destination: A Sustainable Tourism Perspective*. Wallingford: CABI Publishing.

Robinson, M. (1999) Is cultural tourism on the right track? *UNESCO Courier* (July/August).

Rogers, RadioPEI. (2006) *Interview with Ariel Rogers*. Online audio recording: http://radio.upei.ca/stanfest/

Roppel, C., Desmarais, A.A. and Martz, D. (2006) *Farm Women and Canadian Agricultural Policy*. Ottawa: Status of Women Canada. On WWW at http://www.swc-cfc.gc.ca.

Rose, D. (1984) Rethinking gentrification: Beyond the uneven development of Marxist urban theory. *Environment and Planning D: Society and Space* 2, 47–74.

Ross, M.G. (1967) *Community Organization: Theory, Principles, and Practice* (2nd edn). New York: Harper & Rowe.

Russo, A.P. (1999) Venice: Coping with culture vultures. *The UNESCO Courier* (July/August).

Sanders, I.T. (1970) The concept of community development. In L.J. Cary (ed.) *Community Development as a Process* (pp. 9–31). Columbia, MO: University of Missouri.

Schackley, M. (1999) The Himalayas: Masked dances and mixed blessings. *The UNESCO Courier* (July/August).

Schein, E.H. (1985) *Organizational cultural and leadership*. New York: McGraw-Hill.

Schouten, F. (1996) Tourism and cultural change. *Proceedings of a Round Table: Culture, Tourism Development: Crucial Issues for the XXIst Century*. Paris.

Schugurensky, D. (2002) *Pierre Bourdieu's the Forms of Capital is Published in English*. On WWW at http://fcis.oise.utoronto.ca/~ daniel_schugurensky/assignment1/1986bourdieu.html.

Seligman. M.E.P. (1995) *Helplessness*. San Francisco, CA: W.H. Freeman.

Seltzer, K. (1999) *The Creative Age: Knowledge and Skills for the New Economy*. London: Demos.

Selwood, J. and Tonts, M. (2004) Recreational second homes in the south west of Western Australia. In C.M. Hall and D.K. Muller (eds) *Tourism, Mobility and Second Homes: Between Elite Landscape and Common Ground* (pp. 149–161). Clevedon: Channel View.

Sharpley, R. (2004) Tourism and the countryside. In A.M. Lew, C.M. Hall and A.M. Williams (eds) *A Companion to Tourism* (pp. 374–386). Oxford: Blackwell.

Sharpley, R. and Telfer, D. (2002) *Tourism and Development: Concepts and Issues*. Clevedon: Channel View Publications.

Sharpley, R. and Sharpley, J. (1997) *Rural Tourism: An Introduction*. London: International Thomson Business Press.

Shaw, G. and Williams, A.M. (2004) *Tourism and tourism spaces*. London: Sage.

Shaw, K. (2003) Local limits to gentrification: Implications for a new urban policy. A presentation. *Gentrification forum: Tracking the Changes*. Port Phillips, AU.

Shilling, D. (2006) *Civic Tourism*. On WWW at http://www.civictourism.org.

Shucksmith, M. (1991) Still no homes for local? Affordable housing and planning controls in rural areas. In T. Champion and C. Watkins (eds) *People in the Countryside: Studies of Social Change in Rural Britain* (pp. 53–66). London: Paul Chapman.

Slater, T. (2002) *What is Gentrification?* On WWW at http://members.lycos.co.uk/gentrification/whatisgent.html.

Slater, T. (2002) Looking at the 'North American City' through the lens of gentrification discourse. *Urban Geograph* 23 (2), 131–153.

Smale, B. (2006) Critical perspectives in place in leisure research. *Leisure/Loisir, Journal of the Canadian Association of Leisure Studies* 30 (2), 370–372.

Smith, N. (1979a) Gentrification and capital: Practice and ideology in Society Hill. *Antipode* (11) 24–35.

Smith, N. (1979b) Toward a theory of gentrification: A back to the city movement by capital not people. *Journal of the American Planners Association* 35, 538–548.

Smith, N. (1996) *The New Urban Frontier: Gentrification and the Revanchist City.* London and New York: Routledge.

Smith, N. (2002) New globalism, new urbanism: Gentrification as global urban strategy. *Antipode* 34 (3), 427–450.

Smith, N. and Williams, P. (1986) *Gentrification of the City.* Boston: Allen & Unwin.

Smith, V. (1989) *Hosts and Guests: The Anthropology of Tourism* (2nd edn). Philadelphia, PA: University of Pennsylvania Press.

Sorkin, M. (1992) See you in Disneyland. In M. Sorkin (ed.) *Variations on a Theme Park* (pp. 205–232). New York: Hill and Wang.

Statistics Canada (2000) *Definitions of Rural. A Study.* Ottawa: CA.

Statistics Canada (2001) *2001 Census.* On WWW at http://www12.statcan.ca/english/census01/home/index.cfm.

Statistics Canada (2002) *Study: Demographic Changes Across an Urban-to-rural Gradient.* On WWW at http://www.statcan.ca/Daily/English/070426/d070426a.htm.

Statistics Canada (2006) *2006 Census.* On WWW at *http://www12.statcan.ca/english/census06/release/index.cfm.*

Stokowski, M. (2002) Languages of place and discourses of power: Constructing new senses of place. *Journal of Leisure Research* 34 (4), 368–382.

Sumner, J. (2005) *Sustainability and the Civil Commons: Rural Communities in the Age of Globalization.* Toronto: University of Toronto Press.

Sveiby, K. (1998) *Intellectual Capital and Knowledge Management.* On WWW at http://www.sveiby.com.au/IntellectualCapital.html.

Task Force (1993) *Task Force Report on the Incomes and Adjustment in the Atlantic Fishery.* Ottawa: Government of Canada.

Taylor, J. (2001) Authenticity and sincerity in tourism. *Annals of Tourism Research* 28 (1), 7–26.

Teeple, G. (2000) *Globalization and the Decline of Social Reform.* Aurora, Ontario: Garamond Press.

The Chronicle Herald (2007) Stanfest true UN of music; Performers from Cape Breton to Scotland and Texas to China. *The Chronicle Herald* (July 2).

The Collins Concise Dictionary (2001). Glasgow: Harper Collins.

The Lunenburg Waterfront Association Inc. (2007) *Backgrounder.* On WWW at http://www.lunenburgwaterfront.ca/Waterfront%20Background.html.

Theobald, T. (1998) *Global tourism* (2nd edn). Boston, MA: Butterworth Heinemann.

Thompson, G.D. (1999) Cultural capital and accounting. *Accounting Auditing & Accountability Journal* 12 (4), 394–442.

TIAC (2007) *Welcome to the Tourism Industry Association of Canada.* On WWW at http://www.tiac-aitc.ca/english/welcome.asp.

Titmuss, R. (1974) *Social Policy: An Introduction.* London: George Allen and Unwin.

Town of Lunenburg (2004) *Explore Lunenburg.* On WWW at http://www.explorelunenburg.ca.

Town of Vulcan (2007) On WWW at http://www.town.vulcan.ab.ca/town/index.html.

Tradewinds (2005) *Historic Waterfront Property Purchased by Nova Scotia.* Nova Scotia Real Estate Blog. On WWW at http://tradewindsrealty.com/blog/2005/08/.

Tylor, E. (1871) *Primitive Culture: Researches into the Development of Mythology, Philosophy, Religion, Art and Customs.* London: Gordon Press (1974).

United Nations (1948) *Universal Declaration of Human Rights.* On WWW at http://www.un.org/Overview/rights.html.

United Nations Education, Scientific and Cultural Organization (UNESCO) (1996) *Round Table: Culture, Tourism Development: Crucial Issues for the XXIst Century.* Paris

United Nations Environment Program (2003) *Tourism and Local Agenda 21: The Role of Local Authorities in Sustainable Tourism.* Paris, France: United Nations Publication.

United Nations Environment Program (2007) On WWW at http://www.uneptie.org/pc/tourism/sust-tourism/home.htm.

United Nations World Tourism Organization (2001) *Global Code of Ethic for Tourism.* On WWW at http://www.unwto.org/code_ethics.

United Nations World Tourism Organization (UNWTO). (2006). *Tourism Highlights 2006.* Madrid, Spain: United Nations World Tourism Organization.

Urry, J. (1990) *The Tourist Gaze: Leisure and Travel in Contemporary Societies.* London: Sage.

Urry, J. (1995) *Consuming Places.* London: Routledge.

Var, T. and Ap, J. (1998) Tourism and world peace. In W. Theobald (ed.) *Global Tourism* (2nd edn, pp. 44–57). Boston, MA: Butterworth Heinemann.

Veblen, T. (1896) *Theory of the Leisure Class.* New York: New America Library.

Visitor Information Center (2003) *Map of Lunenburg.* Lunenburg, NS: Lunenburg Board of Trade.

Visser, G. (2004) Second homes: Reflections on and unexplored phenomenon in South Africa. In C.M. Hall and D.K. Müller (eds) *Tourism, Mobility and Second Homes: Between Elite Landscape and Common Ground* (pp. 196–214). Clevedon: Channel View Publications.

Vitek, W. and Jackson, W. (1996) *Rooted in the Land.* New Haven, NY: Yale University Press.

Voisey, P. (1988) *Vulcan: The Making of a Prairie Community.* Toronto: University of Toronto Press.

Waite, M. (ed.) (1998) *The Oxford Colour Dictionary.* Oxford University Press.

Wall, E. (1996) *Using Social Capital for Measuring Rural Community Health in Southern Ontario.* A paper presented at the Annual Meetings for the Rural Sociological Society, August 13–15, Des Moines, Iowa.

Warde, A. (1991) Gentrification as consumption: Issues of class and gender. _Environment and Planning D: Society and Space_ 9, 223–232.

Warren, R.L. (1978) _The Community in America_. Chicago, IL: Rand McNally.

Weaver, D. and Fennell, D. (1997) Rural tourism in Canada: The Saskatchewan vacation farm operator as entrepreneur. In S. Page and D. Getz (eds) _The Business of Rural Tourism_ (pp. 77–92). London: International Thompson Business Press.

Wetzel, T. (2004) _What is Gentrification?_ On WWW at http://www.uncanny.net/ ~ wetzel/gentry.htm.

White, S. (ed.) (1995) _The Cambridge Companion to Habermas_. New York: Cambridge University Press.

Whitson, D. (2001) Nature as playground. Recreation and gentrification in the mountain west. In R. Epp and D.Whitson (eds) _Writing off the Rural West: Globalization, Governments and the Transformation of Rural Communities_ (pp. 141–164). Edmonton: University of Alberta Press and Parkland Institute.

Whittington, M. and Williams, G. (eds) (2004) _Canadian Politics in the 21st Century_. (6th edn, pp. 231–253). Toronto: Nelson.

Williams, A.M. and Montanari, A. (1999) Sustainability and self-regulation: Critical perspectives. _Tourism Geographies_ 1 (1) (February), 26–40.

Williams, A.M. (2004) Toward a political economy of tourism. In A.M. Lew, C.M. Hall and A.M. Williams (eds) _A Companion to Tourism_ (pp. 61–73). Oxford: Blackwell.

Williams, D.R. (2002) Leisure identities, globalization, and the politics of place. _Journal of Leisure Research_ 34 (4), 351–367.

Williams, G. (1994) _Not for Export: The International Competitiveness of Canadian Manufacturing_ (3rd edn). Toronto: McClelland & Stewart.

Winson, A. and Leach, B. (2002) _Contingent Work, Disrupted Lives: Labour and Community in the New Rural Economy_. Toronto: University of Toronto Press.

Wolf, E. (1975) _Philadelphia: Portrait of an American city_. Harrisburg, PA: Stackpole.

Woolcock, M. (2001) The place of social capital in understanding social and economic outcomes. _ISUMA_ 2 (1), 11–17.

World Commission on Environment and Development (WCED) (1987) _The Bruntland Report: Our Common Future_. Oxford: Oxford University Press.

World Summit on Sustainable Development (2002) _Tourism Sector Report: Industry as a Partner for Sustainable Development_. On WWW at http://www.uneptie.org/ outreach/wssd/docs/sectors/final/tourism.pdf.

World Travel and Tourism Council (2007) _Welcome_. On WWW at http://www. wttc.org.

Wyly, E. and Hammel, D. (2001) Gentrification, housing policy, and the new context of urban redevelopment. In K.F. Gotham (ed.) _Critical Perspectives on Urban Redevelopment_ (pp. 211–276). London: Elsevier Science.

Yin, R.K. (1989) _Case Study Research: Design and Methods_. Newbury Park, CA: Sage.

Yu, L. and Chung, M.H. (2001) Tourism as a catalytic force for low-politics activities between politically divided countries: The cases of South/North Korea and Taiwan/China. _New Political Science_ 23 (4) 537–545.

Ziff, B. and Rao, P.V. (1997) _Borrowed Power: Essays on Cultural Appropriation_. New Brunswick, NJ: Rutgers University Press.

Subject Index

Note: an Author Index follows this index.

Author Index

Note: a Subject Index precedes this index.